I0092651

Healing Together

Trauma-Informed Care, Recovery, and the Authentic Self

A Practical Book for Spiritually Informed Communities

Aemina Razzano

TEHOM CENTER

TEHOM
CENTER

Copyright © 2024 by Aemina Razzano

All rights reserved.

No part of this book may be reproduced in any form or by any electronic or mechanical means, including information storage and retrieval systems, without written permission from the author, except for the use of brief quotations in a book review.

Tehom Center Publishing is a 501(c)3 nonprofit publishing feminist and queer authors, with a commitment to elevate BIPOC writers. Its face and voice is Rev. Dr. Angela Yarber.

Paperback ISBN: 978-1-966655-09-1

eBook ISBN: 978-1-966655-10-7

To Ruth who witnessed it all
and to traumatized people — may you feel seen, heard, empowered,
and loved in these pages

Contents

Preface

This book is a paradigm for spiritually based and/or spiritually aware organizations to engage in the process of trauma recovery by providing trauma-informed care through direct care, programming, awareness, and education. Intended to be accessible to all persons' leaders, faith communities, and spiritually aware, this book is structured to provide education regarding trauma, traumatic injury, and the neurobiological, spiritual, and psychological responses thereof, and to generate intentional engagement with traumatized persons to provide spiritually integrated trauma-informed care as an aspect of trauma recovery.

My research, education, and experience of trauma centers on the neurobiological protection of the Authentic Self. Often, this protection is interpreted (or experienced) as brokenness, but if individuals, faith communities, and spiritual leaders understand the neurobiological underpinnings of trauma and the protection of the Authentic Self, their capacity to witness the resiliency of the Authentic Self allows them to better offer themselves as a source of healing and support to traumatized people. This requires endeavoring to understand the power of the brain in protecting the soul, addressing the historical and current abuses within spirituality, and witnessing the overwhelming effects of trauma on the mind and body while affirming the beauty and resiliency of the soul.

While this is not an exhaustive resource, it provides the framework for understanding trauma and developing appropriate responses. Additionally, I hope that all who have experienced traumatic injury will find themselves and their bravery reflected in these pages and they will feel seen, comforted, and empowered. Finally, this book serves as a testament to the power of change and the culpability to do so should we endeavor to experience a world in which each person's Authentic Self is visible, honored, and embraced.

Glossary

Authentic Self (AS) - is the unique and protected part of every individual that no one else may claim and is the vital connection to life.[1] It is a truth in which all humanity exists; each person is unique, irreplaceable, with ineffable worth, and longs to give and receive love. The Authentic Self may mourn, grieve, and even rage for the pain and injustice it witnesses and endures but it cannot be destroyed or broken.

Internal Family Systems (IFS) – A psychotherapeutic approach

---

1. Throughout this book, the language of Authentic Self and soul will be used interchangeably as soul is often used in trauma literature as well as conversations from a Christian and/or Jewish faith tradition. However, in my practice and work with traumatized persons, I use the term Authentic Self. This is in consideration of the implied understanding and societal connotations of soul often linked to a specific interpretation of a divinity which may then be an impediment to relationship, idea, and self-exploration. I have found that the term 'Authentic Self' more effectively captures the concept and removes any preconceived ideas and/or emotional or spiritual baggage attached thereof. As recovery is the purpose, anything which causes or creates impediments to recovery should be removed if at all possible.

that identifies and addresses the subpersonalities (denoted as 'parts') of a person which constitutes the painful emotions and wounded parts. These 'parts' work together to protect the Self. This concept was developed by Richard Schwartz in the 1980's. For more information, see ifs-institute.com.

Post Traumatic Stress Disorder (PTSD) – A clinical diagnosis for persons for whom the psychological, emotional, and physiological effects of trauma are causing "significant distress or impairment in social, occupational, or other important areas of functioning."[2] One must have been experiencing symptoms for more than one month.

Spiritual Care Provider – Anyone who, with or without ecclesiastical endorsement, provides spiritual care to individuals by honoring the Authentic Self and providing encouragement and guidance in spiritual matters as defined by those for whom they are caring.

Spirituality – The ability to experience awe and wonder and seek meaning in life while recognizing the interconnectedness and interdependence between humans as well as humans and the natural environment.

Spiritually Aware Person – A person, regardless of religious affiliation, who recognizes the inherent worth of all persons and honors and seeks to engage, support, and encourage the Authentic Self.

Spiritually Integrated Community – A group of people, regardless

---

2. Center for Substance Abuse Treatment (US), "Exhibit 1.3-4, DSM-5 Diagnostic Criteria for PTSD," Text (Substance Abuse and Mental Health Services Administration (US), 2014), https://www.ncbi.nlm.nih.gov/books/NBK207191/.

of religious affiliation which constitute a community that recognizes the inherent worth of all persons and honors and seeks to engage, support, and encourage the Authentic Self.

Trauma – A generalized term for the event(s) that precipitate a physiological response and may lead to PTSD.

Traumatic Injury – The pain that results from the traumatic event.

Traumatized Person (TP) – an individual who has experienced trauma and the effects thereof.

Witness/Journeyer – One who intentionally engages, supports, and is attentive to the needs of a traumatized person.

Prologue

THIS BOOK BEGAN as the work of my dissertation. Within an academic writing, one would not disclose of their personal history or experiences. So, when a colleague and friend read the manuscript, she encouraged me to add a little more of myself into the work. To be vulnerable and share to allow others to connect with me

In telling you a little bit about myself before we work together to try and bring positive change through education and caring for those who have been traumatized, I'm inviting you into my story as you build trust in me as a survivor and a trained expert.

I have an issue with perfection. I have tried to be perfect my whole life. Which means I've spent most of my life internally miserable because I wasn't perfect. Blaming and shaming myself for my inability to do it all, to know it all, to be it all. Convinced I was worthless. Yet, I am perfect at one thing – the ACE score. It's not really something on which anyone wants to have a perfect score. I mean ideally, a perfect score is zero, right? But I have a 10. A 10 out of 10. My childhood was filled with chronic abuse, torture, and violence - annihilated by monsters - and much of my adult life has been filled with the effects of PTSD and great emotional harm. In the midst of that, I have fought hard for recovery, have developed life-sustaining relationships, and have worked constantly to have a job I love. After decades of intentional effort, I embrace my worth more each day and have learned that my narrative is one of hope and healing not of terror and harm.

Introduction

My theology of trauma recovery is rooted in the presumption that each person has an Authentic Self that contains their unique attributes and believes it is loveable and worthy. This Authentic Self cannot be broken or permanently damaged by trauma and is also the dwelling of the spirit/soul. As the brain and body absorb the trauma, the Authentic Self can and will experience grief, rage, agony, loss, and distrust, yet those emotions reflect an intrinsic truth of caring and of worth. If this were not so, harm to one's body, mind, emotions, and spirit would not hurt.[1] Thus, the journey of recovery is one of reclaiming and/or uncovering the Authentic Self and allowing and empowering it to cultivate healing of the brain and body while also encouraging it to engage in safe and healthy relationships. This requires practical and

---

1. Additionally, Bowlby (1982) and Kirkpatrick (2005) addressing attachment issues present an internal working model that, as Jana Pressley explain, is the "primary evaluation of the self as worthy of love and protection. That it is inextricably linked with secure attachment experience." Hence, this is why many TP struggle with the concept and embodiment of worth; they did not experience secure attachment.

ethical guidance, education, and utmost compassion as well as preparation on the part of the journeyer to ensure the traumatized person receives the care they deserve for body, mind, and spirit.

The concept of a soul is recognized in almost every spiritual tradition and/or practice as a part of a person which is intrinsic, unduplicatable, and sacred. For purposes of trauma recovery, the concept of the soul is not concerned with nor connected to any supposition of eternal life, reincarnation, or any existence after death. It is confined to the understanding that there is an intrinsic part of oneself which is the vital, animating connection to life and relationships and is unique and of worth in every person. While my theological education is broad, my locus is the Christian faith2[2] and I will be intentionally discussing trauma within that context. Nevertheless, spiritually integrated communities and persons will be able to relate to and extrapolate from the data and information provided.

Finally, regarding the use of language: When individuals place words/labels on people, they can inadvertently cause harm. For instance, using the word survivor, one may believe that they are empowering the person who has experienced trauma, yet the 'survivor' may feel that it is a mantle being placed upon their neck. Suddenly, they have 'survived' which can create connotations of 'being over it' or that they *should* be over it; this labeling may then be experienced as invalidation. Individuals who have endured traumatic injury may call themselves survivors for they have earned it. Likewise, describing someone as a victim can mitigate their experience and the challenging work of survival; disempowering and infantilizing them. Yet, there are times when one needs to and should be supported in using the term victim to address the

2. I will be using the term "the church" to refer to Christians and their respective communities. When appropriate, I will use the exact denominational designation. For purposes of extrapolation, spiritually integrated communities should consider their tradition/religion/practice within the confines of the word, church.

atrocity they have endured. However, what is crucial in language is ensuring people feel supported, seen, and empowered. Utilizing the term 'Traumatized Person' (TP) provides legitimacy to the totality of one's experience and allows the individual who has withstood the trauma to choose how they want to be identified.

A Model for Recovery

THE RECOVERY MODEL that I espouse is threefold: Meeting in the Middle, Healing & Recovery, and Justice & Reconciliation. Each of these phases are painful, and exhausting, and will require a resilience and tenacity unparalleled in life. The work of recovery is an undoing; it is like that of an electrician working on a home that had been wired by a sadist. There are wires everywhere, some dangling live and some from decades ago that are defunct. Fuse boxes connect to other fuse boxes seemingly without being connected to the main breaker. The work of saving the home from a complete short circuit and catastrophic event requires dismantling all the faulty wiring, testing each wire for life, reactivity, and necessity, and then snipping away that which shorts the circuit, is dead, or is so hot they will cause others to catch fire. Then carefully, painstakingly removing them, putting them in an ice bath before sending the faulty wiring to be melted down somewhere far away. Yet, for the wires that are live and necessary, the work is to ground them and connect and integrate them safely into the breaker.

The first phase, Meeting in the Middle, attends to the prima

facia requirement that to care for those who have been traumatized, they must be met and accompanied in and from whatever
emotional or psychological space they inhabit. Often, this 'middle'
is the liminal space between death and life in which the traumatic
event has ended but the interminable pain and hypervigilance of
trauma is undiminished. This work requires witness in all its
forms; mental health provider, spiritual care provider, friend,
mentor, and family. However, one must undergo preparation and
education before the introduction and subsequent journeying.
Understanding and identifying trauma, trauma responses, and
examining oneself is imperative.[1]

The second phase, Healing & Recovery, is the time in which
all skills, support, and methodologies are engaged and provided to
the TP so that they may have the tools to undertake the grueling
work of sorting through the mental, physiological, and emotional
"wiring". Reconnecting to that which is healthy and dismantling
that which is not. Implementing and embodying new patterns and
concepts. The work of the witness has not ended but transitions
from one of solely accompanying abject pain to supporting new
ways of being and embodying the self as TP journey through the
world. Though the recovery of trauma is provided in a linear
context, it does not occur in a perfect trajectory. At times, it may
feel as if there are 4 steps 'backward' for every 2 steps 'forward'.
This judgment of momentum may occur in the observer as they
may not understand the mental and psychological demands
required of the TP to engage and undertake the work of healing.

Traumatized persons may also experience disjointed momentum, finding themselves enacting previously learned behavior and
utilizing unhealthy or harmful coping tools. TP may experience
being 'stuck'; focused on the same memory or feeling associated

---

1. Self-awareness of biases, personal experience and/or history with/of trauma,
and identification of boundaries is crucial to the work.

with it. This is expected as there is not an exact formula for recovery. New concepts must be learned, revisited, ingrained, tested, and embodied. Old habits, thoughts, patterns, and concepts need to be discussed and challenged consistently. It is imperative that feelings be acknowledged, pain held, anger expelled, and sadness met with compassion. All work is good and necessary work regardless of how often it needs to be repeated. Moreover, that which may seem counterintuitive (self-inflicting pain - emotional or physical for example) is yet another opportunity for the TP to hear their worth affirmed, be (re)invited into a new way of self-engagement, validated in their experiences and emotions, and encouraged to share their pain with others instead of singly embodying it.

Finally, the last phase is Justice & Reconciliation. While this will be different for each person, what is required is that the TP experiences the acts, words, and embodiments of justice and reconciliation specific to their needs and recovery. For some, this will be public and for others, it will be the personal acknowledgment of their pain. Not all TP will want to engage in formal legal action, nor will all TP have the privilege of that option (statute of limitations may prevent that as well as issues of safety and/or risking reprisal for speaking out). However, justice is accomplished not only in formal legal action but in the ability to own one's story, to choose to engage with organizations addressing trauma, to be recognized for one's resilience, and to be supported in the community. Reconciliation is the work of individuals, organizations, and the community in reconnecting to the traumatized person, supporting them by speaking out, implementing policies of protection, engaging in acts of justice, and admitting mistakes that were made which allowed the trauma to be tolerated, covered, or unaddressed.

Before delving into education and trauma-informed care and practice, it is vital to understand the spiritual and theological implications of the work as situated in a spiritually aware setting.

Aemina Razzano

One cannot claim that the Authentic Self (AS) matters in trauma recovery without recognizing why, how, and any barriers that may need to be addressed or overcome. To do so in entirety would be to write a series of books on trauma-informed spiritual care from every dimension. This book will provide you with education, ideas, and questions to examine to provide trauma-informed care. However, there will be much unaddressed (what to do when an accusation is brought forward – that is a separate program I address in my consulting) and there are always opportunities to seek further education, collaboration, and consultation.

The Authentic Self

"The soul, like quicksilver, slips away as soon as we try to grasp it with language."[2]

Traumatized persons often self-describe or disclose feeling "broken" or "shattered". In my research, 90% of respondents who identify themselves as experiencing a traumatic event report feeling broken, and 62% believe that the self can be damaged.[3,4] Contained in the scientific research and writing compiled on the effects of trauma, many witnesses, therapists, and others confirm such identifications and they, too, speak of a 'broken soul' or generalized brokenness.[5] These presumptions for spiritual persons and

2. Donald Kalsched, *Trauma and the Soul* (London and New York: Routledge, 2013), 10.
3. The self is a generic term for the soul, spirit, and/or Authentic Self. This was clearly identified to participants in the research.
4. See appendix for additional details.
5. Judith L. Herman, "Recovery from Psychological Trauma," *Psychiatry and Clinical Neurosciences* 52, no. S1 (1998): 61, https://doi.org/10.1046/j.1440-1819.1998.0520s5S145.x; Danielle McGraw et al., "Consequences of Abuse by Religious Authorities: A Review," in *124th APA Convention* (Denver, Colorado: California School of Professional Psychology, 2016), 250; S. J. Sandage et al., *Rela-*

particularly for Christians require a difficult question to be asked. If God indwells or the image of God is located within the soul (the Authentic Self), is not God or that image then capable of being broken? "However, these concerns, suspicions, fears, and/or emotions of being fundamentally broken are just one dimension of the experience of processing trauma. They matter and honoring the concerns and fears is important; however, it is not the whole, existential, ontological truth."[6]

For thousands of years theologians, philosophers, and others have hypothesized and attempted to parse out the substance of the soul. The ancient Greek philosopher, Plato, believed that the soul was an "immortal, immaterial, and a spiritual form."[7] He claimed it was distinct from the body and the basis of knowledge. Many people and cultures view the soul as a spiritual entity or aspect of oneself. In Christianity, the soul is identified in several different modes depending upon one's theology, denomination, and personal belief.[8] However, Christianity maintains that humans are created in the image of God and carry the living spirit within one's soul (the *imago Dei*). Thomas Aquinas, a theologian in the Middle Ages who was incredibly influential in Christian doctrine, identified the soul as both being in the body and "an incorporeal and subsistent principle" that is incorruptible.[9] He argued that the body decays and can be adulterated but that the soul is a

tional Spirituality in Psychotherapy: Healing Suffering and Promoting Growth (American Psychological Association, 2020), 98.

6. Jennifer Baldwin, *Trauma-Sensitive Theology: Thinking Theologically in the Era of Trauma* (Eugene, Oregon: Cascade Books, 2018), 10.

7. Joseph Nietlong and Gideon Kato, "Aquinas on the Soul," *Pinisi Journal of Art, Humanity and Social Studies* 1, no. 3 (2021): 6–10.

8. One of the issues in identifying the soul is its modality; whether one is a monist or holds dichotomous or trichotomous theories/understandings. Thus, are the soul and the body one being, separate but interdependent, or is there a body, soul, and spirit.

9. Robert Pasnau, "Thomas Aquinas," in *The Stanford Encyclopedia of Philosophy*, ed. Edward N. Zalta and Uri Nodelman, Spring 2023 (Metaphysics

"subsistent entity" and thus has no reason to cease existing.[10] For better or worse, Aquinas's philosophy is the theological foundation of the understanding of the soul in Christianity.

Yet, in trauma the soul may *feel* corruptible, one may feel that their soul, very essence, spirit, or Authentic Self has been broken and may even cease to exist. Therefore, a multitude of questions arise. Can the soul be broken? If the soul can be broken, does that then imply God's spirit - the Holy Mystery - living within one can be broken?[11] Would or could the Holy Mystery be reflected in a fractured soul? If God is indwelling, are they harmed as well by the perpetrator of violence? How much power is given to the perpetrator of violence, harm, and torture if the soul and subsequently the *imago Dei* can be broken, fractured, or harmed? These are questions that require consideration if one affirms the soul can be broken. I posit that believing the soul could be broken, fractured, or separated from us places far too much power in the hands of hateful, harmful, and abusive people, disregards science, and obfuscates hope. Moreover, as Christians believe God is immortal and incorruptible, I posit that the Holy Mystery cannot be fractured (neither indwelling nor the image thereof) nor can the Authentic Self.

Regardless of religion or spirituality, TP long for their being, their soul, and their Authentic Self to feel strong, intact, and connected. Especially as the pain is so immense as to feel completely crushed, overpowered, and left helpless. Jennifer Baldwin, theologian and clinical therapist writes, "It is vital to clearly state and understand that traumatic wounding is an *injury*; it is

---

Research Lab, Stanford University, 2023), https://plato.stanford.edu/archives/spr2023/entries/aquinas/.

10. Pasnau.

11. I personally use the term, Holy Mystery, to refer to God, the Divine, universal energy.

NOT ontology."[12] This statement, accompanied by the following quote regarding the Self from Schwartz, defines the foundational function and existence of the soul being addressed in the thesis of this work. "Everyone does indeed have an undamaged Self. ...Our parts are organized to protect the Self and remove it from danger in the face of trauma at all costs...Nevertheless, the Self remains whole."[13] Therefore, the authentic Self (AS) is neurobiologically protected in trauma and cannot be broken and is deserving, loveable, and has ineffable worth.

This concept of an undamaged self may seem confusing; if the self cannot be damaged, why would it need protecting? Yet the question assumes that it is invincible which I am not affirming. The Authentic Self is undamaged *because* it is protected. I posit the question to which TP deserve an answer is not whether hypothetically the AS *could* be damaged but rather functionally *is* it damaged by traumatic events. In theory or theology, there are countless arguments that augment one's persuasion. Engaging in endless discussion of the substance of the soul does not provide comfort to the traumatized as theories of theology, eschatology, and pneumatology can obscure praxis instead of informing it. Few people can agree on the exact substance of the soul, but many can agree that there is a spirituality present in all people; an animating presence inhabited solely by the individual. Likewise, people may not agree on issues of theology and organized religion while also accepting that spirituality is separate from such doctrine. Though academic rigor is important and theological, ontological, and psychological questions and studies regarding the AS and trauma should be engaged and further debated, we must act on what is

---

12. Baldwin, *Trauma-Sensitive Theology*, 2018, 27.
13. Richard C. Schwartz and Robert R. Falconer, *Many Minds, One Self: Evidence for a Radical Shift in Paradigm* (Oak Park, Illinois: Trailheads Publications, 2017), 155.

known currently in the spring of 2024 which is how the brain behaves in trauma is as a survivalist protecting oneself.

Returning to the concept of the Authentic Self, though Schwartz and Baldwin acknowledge it is intact and undamaged, neither delves into the concept of the self as inherently worthy and loveable separate from its productivity. This is incredibly critical to the recovery of TP as for many, especially in cases of interpersonal violence and neglect, their worth has been defined by their actions in service to another person. For Schwartz and Baldwin, the self remains defined as the expression of the best attributes of an individual. The emphasis on these extrinsic expressions obscures the foundation of those attributes: that one is capable and deserving of being loved and has ineffable worth. As humans were created for and function best in relationships, extrinsic actions are important, and appropriate attention-seeking behavior is desired and deserves to be returned. This then creates a symbiotic relationship which is required for the continuation of humanity, the fostering of ideas, and the development of community. The vitality of relationships is unequivocal as all trauma experts and therapies emphasize that healing cannot take place outside of them and that the fracturing thereof is one of the most damaging effects of trauma. Yet, the actions of an individual reflect the AS but do not create worth.[14]

As a result of traumatic injury, not only are TP unable to recognize, embody, or embrace their worth, but humans often define their worth and capacity to be loved by extrinsic factors

---

14. There is a concept in Christianity of 'original sin' which espouses that all beings are sinners and incapable of being 'saved' outside of divine intervention. Moreover, this concept has permeated all of culture in that it has shaped the idea of worth and productivity. For those in theological/spiritual leadership, this is an important moment to examine one's understanding of and/or belief in the concept of original sin and consider how the concept affects those who have experienced trauma. I commend the book, "Original Blessing" by Danielle Shroyer for further exploration.

including the validation of others. For many TP, those validations and factors they have received were cultivated by information that completely defies any such belief of their intrinsic worth and value as perpetrators have ingrained destructive information and narratives, attempting to maliciously define the individual in order to control, manipulate, and inflict pain. In healing, one must witness themselves and be witnessed by others. In so doing, TP are invited to reclaim their inherently worthy and lovable Authentic Self as safe from and uncontrolled by another.

If traumatized persons are also able (to begin) to consider their Authentic Self as not only defined by the extrinsic attributes and actions of curiosity, compassion, calm, confidence, courage, clarity, creativity, connectedness, and kindness (as defined by Schwartz) but simply by their very existence as worthy and loveable, the Authentic Self is therefore able to espouse and embody what it believes and the healing is transformational as it is then intrinsically owned and not solely reliant upon extrinsic validation.[15] This conception is critical to my interpretation and contribution to trauma recovery.

Therefore, with neurobiological, theological, and psychological understanding, the operational definition of the Authentic Self (AS) which I espouse is the unique and protected part of every individual of which no one else may claim and is the vital connection to life. It is a truth in which all humanity exists; each person is unique, irreplaceable, with ineffable worth, and longs to give and receive love. The Authentic Self may mourn, grieve, and even rage for the pain and injustice it witnesses and endures but it cannot be destroyed or broken.

The AS experiences emotions on *behalf* of the wounded parts – the brain and the body. The wounds do not settle nor reside in

---

15. Richard C. Schwartz and Martha Sweezy, *Internal Family Systems Therapy*, Second edition (New York: The Guilford Press, 2019), 45.

the soul rather it is the root of empathy and compassion. This concept is challenging for many as it may be received as a diminishment of the tragedy and the overwhelming pain of trauma. It is not intended to be a depreciation or abbreviation of the pain. What is experienced in traumatic injury is so substantial that the brain literally reorganizes itself for survival. There are no adequate English words to capture the kind of overwhelm, horror, and revulsion for those who inflict such acts onto another person as to cause this unspeakable pain. Rather, the protection of the soul in neurobiology and the discussion thereof is to (hopefully) empower and encourage traumatized persons that there is a part of them that no one has ever touched. In that place, there are no fingerprints other than their own. There are no bruises. There are no hateful words. There is no death. There are no rapists, abusers, perpetrators, or terrorists who can break the Authentic Self. There is simply an ineffable, undefinable, unexplainable, beautiful, powerful, connected AS that no one can duplicate or capture. That no one can own. There is only the Authentic Self, and it is enough.

Returning to Schwartz's declaration of the self in Internal Family Systems,

> IFS takes as a given that *all* persons have a Self and that the Self remains even in the midst of life's most horrific experiences. It is always available as a resource for resilient recovery and wisdom. In cases of chronic traumatization, parts "take the hits" of traumatic wounding in protection of the Self. Rather than being "shattered," "broken," or "annihilated," the Self is covered over and protected by the parts who then take on roles of increasing leadership of the person, sometimes in problematic and unhealthy ways.[16]

---

16. Baldwin, *Trauma-Sensitive Theology*, 2018, 42.

Schwartz furthers his philosophy of the protection of the self in his explanation and theoretical development of 'parts'. According to IFS, parts are those that make up one's emotional and intellectual engagement with the world and constitute the whole regardless of their behavior, functioning, or ability thereof.

These parts are known as the manager, exile, and firefighter and they navigate the traumatic injury and work to supervise the outcome. Managers are the parts of oneself that endeavor to control the environment by establishing safety through being "highly protective and strategic."[17] The exile is the part(s) of oneself that bear the pain of being injured, rejected, and/or abandoned. Within IFS, the exiles are often "banished for their own protection and the good of the system."[18] Firefighters strive to distract from or suppress the pain of the exiles by "reacting powerfully and automatically, without concern for consequences, to their distress as well as to the overinhibition of managers...they fight the flames of exiled emotion."[19] The parts work together for survival and in so doing, the Self remains protected - the undertaking of parts sealing the Authentic Self away until it is safe for it to emerge. "When we can understand the challenges issued by post-traumatic psychological response as a prolonged resource of survival rather than as a sign of brokenness that indicates future potential, we can more clearly see the processes at work in the psychological impact of traumatization."[20] Another benefit of parts work is that they conceptually provide tools for therapeutic conversation.

As the brain rewires itself for survival it adapts; creating pathways and responses (such as the utilization of parts) that allow one to endure and experience unimaginable physical and emotional

17. Schwartz and Sweezy, *Internal Family Systems Therapy*, 31.
18. Schwartz and Sweezy, 31
19. Schwartz and Sweezy, 31.
20. Baldwin, *Trauma-Sensitive Theology*, 2018, 50.

pain, shame, and complete heartbreak.[21] Additionally, I posit that brain functionality is not merely acting to protect the physical requirements of living; breathing and circulation. For what purpose would be served in keeping the body alive if the soul is destroyed? The simple functioning of breathing and circulation only qualifies one to be in a vegetative state. The ability to cognate is not living; a calculator can do math. A computer can provide analysis. It is through meaningful emotional engagement with others and the world that one lives. It is the work of the brain's endurance of pain through functional adaptations (such as dissociation) that further solidifies the theory of the protected self. For instance, when working with those who have been traumatized as children, they are (usually) unable to recall all the details or emotions of the traumatic events concurrently, if ever. If they could recall the totality of a given moment, their hearts would break at the cruelty. It is why for most adults pieces of the trauma return a bit at a time to create a whole picture. Through the work of the brain in doing so, the Authentic Self is protected.[22]

Judith Herman, a psychiatrist who wrote the groundbreaking and foundational work on trauma, eloquently explains this phenomenon of protection:

---

21. Benjamin Suarez-Jimenez, "Researchers Reveal How Trauma Changes the Brain," URMC Newsroom, accessed June 19, 2023, https://www.urmc.rochester.edu/news/publications/neuroscience/researchers-reveal-how-trauma-changes-the-brain.

22. "IFS takes as a given that *all* persons have a Self and that the Self remains even in the midst of life's most horrific experiences. It is always available as a resource for resilient recovery and wisdom. In cases of chronic traumatization, parts "take the hits" of traumatic wounding in protection of the Self. Rather than being "shattered," "broken," or "annihilated," the Self is covered over and protected by the parts who then take on roles of increasing leadership of the person, sometimes in problematic and unhealthy ways." Baldwin, *Trauma Sensitive Theology*, p. 42

Time sense may be altered, often with a sense of slow motion, and the experience may lose its quality of ordinary reality. The person may feel as though the event is not happening to her, as though she is observing from outside her body, or as though the whole experience is a bad dream from which she will shortly awaken. These perceptual changes combine with a feeling of indifference, emotional detachment, and profound passivity in which the person relinquishes all initiative and struggle. *This altered state of consciousness might be regarded as one of nature's small mercies, a protection against unbearable pain.*[23] (italics are mine)

Traumatized persons may *feel* broken or even shattered. In no way should this feeling be minimized or disregarded. As a TP, I have felt broken. In hindsight, I was in excruciating pain emotionally, mentally, physically, and spiritually. My brain wasn't functioning the way I wanted, anticipated that it would, or believed that it should. I was expecting cognitive knowledge to alleviate the agony of suffering and heartache and stop the intrusive thoughts, flashbacks, and memories. The depth of devastating, unimaginable emotional pain, which was unable to be alleviated solely through psychoeducation, or quickly reduced through either trauma recovery therapy or my own gritty determination caused me to believe that I, my Authentic Self, was indeed broken. Nevertheless, I was not broken.

In working with TP, I have witnessed repeatedly that their inability to stop the neurobiological effects creates a confirmation bias that they are broken, and their Authentic Self is shattered despite the fact that their brain is functioning correctly. Feelings

---

23. Judith Herman, M. D., *Trauma and Recovery* (New York, New York: Basic Books, 1997), 43.

frequently translate into belief and when one embodies a belief of brokenness, it becomes an intolerable burden that must be escaped. For some, that is through the use of food, alcohol, drugs, and misuse of medication. For others, it is the fracturing of relationships, believing themselves to be too broken for and/or unworthy of love. TP often experience their brokenness as too enormous, too shameful to allow others to witness. Issues of suicidality may arise out of these beliefs and must be immediately addressed. If one's narrative and emotional and cognitive experience recounts and declares to them that they are broken, they may be unable to conceive and/or believe that anyone – from family and friends to spiritual care providers and therapists – are able to see them as anything else.

Another question arises in the concept of a broken soul, that of worth. Does brokenness (the perception and experience of feeling broken) affect the worth of the individual? Many TP experience feelings of worthlessness. Affecting the Authentic Self and/or its engagement and relationship to others is whether one believes in their inherent worthiness and capability to be loved. If people do not believe themselves to have worth, this hampers recovery as it is difficult to put the excruciating work into something/someone deemed worthless. One's inability to conceive of their worth and/or being loved or lovable is epistemologically explained by situating it in the harm rendered by trauma.

In the Christian tradition, within the Gospels, it is noted that Jesus consistently healed people; no one was ever turned away nor was anyone asked to justify their worthiness of being healed or to explain why they mattered to their community. Their "brokenness" – self or community identified – did not cause Jesus to inquire as to their worthiness. They were not asked to provide a resumé or bank statement to rationalize their seeking healing. If one is seeking an answer of worth from the Christian faith tradition, the consistent interaction between Jesus and his disciples as well as strangers would ostensibly speak to the inherent worth of all people. Furthermore, Jesus is recorded in all three of the synoptic gospels as announcing that he was willing, θέλω, to heal.[24] This verb is in present indicative active tense which denotes a relationship of the verb to the actuality of the action as opposed to a probability of a hope.[25] θέλω (willing) wasn't simply a wish to do something but an imperative of Jesus' ethic and his desire to heal which in so doing, affirmed the *imago Dei* in all persons and their intrinsic worth.

The concepts of worth and being loveable are not meant to infer that everything will be fine if they are embraced and understood or that they therefore will nullify feelings of brokenness. The soul mourns at unfathomable depths. Non-traumatized persons cannot imagine the crushing devastation of what was once known and has now been eradicated and effaced. The soul can ache - so deeply that words are absurdly useless and meaningless and yet it is nevertheless intact. However, when one is rooted in the truth of worthiness and that one is loveable, pushback is immediate to the harmful narratives usually experienced - or even developed - by traumatized persons. "Healing cannot occur if we do not accept our worthiness – that we are worth healing, even if doing so might shake up our view of the world and how we interact with others."[26]

A traumatized person has experienced their lives unimaginably disrupted and they may have endured the fracturing of relationships including within themselves. The loss of years of health and well-being can make one feel less than whole. Yet, to claim brokenness or that a traumatized person is not whole dismisses the power of the brain to survive and diminishes the phenomenal

---

24. Matthew 8:1-3, Mark 1:40-41, Luke 5:12-13
25. Gknt.org
26. Gabor Maté and Daniel Maté, *The Myth of Normal: Trauma, Illness & Healing in a Toxic Culture*, First Edition (New York, NY: Avery, 2022), 422.

resilience of the Authentic Self. Unsurprisingly, the concept of brokenness also ties to the idea of being 'whole'. Often, people refer to returning to wholeness when discussing trauma recovery. Yet, if the soul is not shattered or broken, how is wholeness defined? Gloria Anzaldúa, a Chicana feminist scholar, wrote "The process of making yourself whole requires all your parts – you can't define yourself by any single genetic or cultural slice."[27] Wholeness isn't about the mending of a soul, but rather the incorporation of one's soul and brain and body and accepting all those parts, compiling them into one whole person. The soul is still intact, rather, it is the integration of parts that is the issue.

To feel whole "isn't something we acquire by stacking achievements, checking boxes. or acquiring products or consumer goods," says Dr. Vivek Murthy, U.S. Surgeon General, but "to truly feel is about remembering who we fundamentally are."[28] Culturally, Americans equate wholeness with not having an injury and with everything – physically, cognitively, and emotionally – being 'okay'. A quick Google search produces multiple threads and memes articulating that being whole is about feeling unbroken, in harmony with the self, and feeling aligned. For TP, their Authentic Self is often inaccessible as the effects of trauma – dysregulation, flashbacks, fear, anxiety, intrusive thoughts, harmful narrative, etc. keep one separated from it. When that inaccessibility is associated with an assumption of brokenness and rendered as truth of a broken soul, TP do not feel whole. I posit that wholeness is not the absence of pain or struggle but the recognition that dissociation, fracturing, and compartmentalization are tools utilized to remain whole and protect the Authentic Self. A puzzle in a box is a whole puzzle regardless of whether the pieces are

---

27. Gloria Anzaldúa, *Light in the Dark* (Durham, North Carolina: Duke University Press, 2015), 89.
28. "Vivek Murthy — To Be a Healer," The On Being Project, accessed January 9, 2024, https://onbeing.org/programs/vivek-murthy-to-be-a-healer/.

connected. One can be whole while they are sick or wounded. These are not exclusionary concepts, and when society approaches and engages another human as a *whole* person in evolution, compassion, hope, and understanding are engendered.

Defining wholeness by one's emotional state – especially when one has been traumatized – does not present a complete picture. Wholeness cannot be determined by the intensity of one's suffering, or one's approval or tolerance of their behavior. Recall that a traumatized person neurobiologically exists in a state of heightened, or constant, survival mode. Therefore, the idea of *returning* to wholeness continues to perpetuate the concept of brokenness and fracturing. Traumatized persons *are* whole. They are a whole person who is surviving unspeakable things. A serious detriment is done to them by implying or stating outright, anything otherwise.

When used as a measure, wholeness becomes something one is ever chasing or working toward, and it becomes an object. Additionally, the concept and experience of healing are also elusive as the two are often conflated. There is not a line of demarcation for being healed. While markers of healing include how one handles an activating event or thought, they pertain to that explicit moment. If a TP, regardless of how they handled the activating moment, does not recognize that the moment is fleeting rather than believing it is the permanency of one's being, TP may experience the infuriating and demoralizing vacillation between feeling whole and broken. This is not to say that healing doesn't exist - rather the insidiousness of trauma is that there is evermore a scar which can become tender and/or irritated by life events in which the traumatic injury may cause pain. The body remembers and it can be activated again. If the measure of being whole, of being healed permanently is evidenced by never having to deal with the traumatic injury again, then TP would forever be fractured, and this is untrue.

For instance, someone who undergoes knee replacement

surgery may identify the mark of their healing as being when they're able to walk again without pain. If one were to inquire six months after their surgery regarding their healing, they may say they are healed. However, if one were to inquire at a year, I hypothesize/suspect they would respond that they feel more healed than they did 6 months ago. Healing is an evolution.

Furthermore, if a person believes they are broken, often accompanying that is a hopelessness and a desperation to be fixed. Yet, to regard one as whole **and** in pain leaves space for self-acceptance, compassion, and a reclaiming of power from the perpetrator and/or event that caused the traumatic injury. The concept of wholeness doesn't cease the pain, terminate the effects of traumatic injury such as flashbacks, night terrors, and intrusive thoughts, nor does it negate the need for therapy. The TP remains in the pain of recovery. However, affirming the wholeness of the Authentic Self may allow for introjections and plant concepts that come to fruition later. Believing the concept of wholeness may momentarily disrupt the feelings of worthlessness and/or broken-ness engendering a faint sense of hope and perhaps even wonder to enter the TP's consciousness. These small introjections prove to be critical in the arduous work of recovery.

"To be clear, traumatic wounding when not supported, processed, and cared for can undermine a person's stability, daily function, and even survival; however, traumatic wounding is not a final word."[29] TP are beautiful people terribly wounded with capacities and abilities within them that are simply covered over and inaccessible due to the pain. To equate the pain and behaviors thereof with the intrinsic being of a person is false. The brain is operating and the body responds as it is programmed to do for survival.

A critical issue for TP is the awareness that others are not able

---

29. Baldwin, *Trauma-Sensitive Theology*, 2018, 27.

to know their Authentic Self. Between the pain of recovery and the emotional and bodily activation of trauma which causes dysregulation, TP are not able to interact with people as they want. Often, they are judged on their behavior in survival mode. It is assumed that the actions and interactions one has with a trauma-tized person are of the Authentic Self and therefore, behaviors witnessed are deemed as personality traits and/or character faults. "What we call personality traits, in addition to reflecting genuine inborn temperaments and qualities, also express the ways that people, as children, had to accommodate their emotional environment. They reflect much that is neither inherent nor immutable about a person, no matter how closely identified he or she is with them. Nor are they character faults; though they may cause us difficulty now, they began as modes of survival."[30] Recovery must include a community that understands survival behavior and seeks to witness and affirm the AS, loving and caring for the whole person, all the parts.

While I espouse that the soul is protected, there is consider-able struggle and undertaking to uncover it from the rubble of trau-matic injury. The brain has done its job; the soul is intact. Yet accessing it is the issue, for it has been hidden beneath the layers of fear, horror, grief, rage, guilt, sadness, hopelessness, and distrust that make up the jawbreaker of traumatic injury.[31] This is not an easy or quick process. Just as the traumatic injury took time to manifest, so, too, does the uncovering of the soul. Therapeutic engagement is critically important to the accessing of the AS and

---

30. Maté and Maté, *The Myth of Normal: Trauma, Illness & Healing in a Toxic Culture,* 77.

31. Imagine a jawbreaker cut in half. One would see many layers surrounding the center. The center stands for the Authentic Self. In trauma, those layers are not only the emotional pains but also correlate to the length of time the trauma was endured. Complex trauma is more difficult to access, having more layers to treat than acute trauma. This is not to say that some trauma hurts more but rather the tools needed to attain the center are different and may require more time.

healing. Additionally, the work of a trained spiritual provider can be incredibly helpful. Each person with whom a traumatized person shares their story has the ability to assist in the re-emergence of the Self.

The journey of recovery begins with compassion - for the person who has been traumatized – and their brain and body. Compassion for the parts of the self that protect and work to control the external world to save the internal world. Compassion for the parts of self that over function, estranging and exiling the Self for its protection. Compassion for the parts that have had to be courageous when that courage appears to the outside world as "crazy" or dysregulated, angry, broken. Compassion for the Self. What is needed is empathy for the parts and the bodies holding the trauma and the grace of accepting traumatized persons as they are and loving them as they are – not what they will become.

This is the work of spiritually informed communities (SIC) and spiritually aware persons (SAP). As those caring for traumatized persons, SIC, SAP, and other providers acknowledge that they are the walking wounded - still whole, if wobbly. Seeking the Authentic Self and reflecting it to the traumatized person, engenders belief in an undamaged soul and their wholeness which also begins to diminish the power of the perpetrator and allow TP to undertake the restoration of their power. These are not moments that fix traumatic injury. These are the tiny seeds required to be planted again and again until the TP may harvest them.

Finally, it is clear to me, having worked with so many traumatized persons, that when the brain is healed - recovered - the Authentic Self becomes clearly visible again. During trauma, it is hidden in a veil of grief, torment, anger, shame, and anguish. It is hidden to protect itself from the pernicious pain of trauma. In recovery, the soul does not have to hide. The Authentic Self emerges and can claim that it is loveable, deserving of love, and has ineffable worth.

History of Trauma in Christianity

It would be unethical to write a book on how spiritually integrated communities can participate in the work of trauma recovery without acknowledging the trauma that has been directly inflicted by them, as well as their participation in systems of oppression and violence that perpetuate and/or cause traumatic injury.

The church cannot meaningfully, effectively, and ethically engage in trauma-informed care until it confesses the harm it has done and its complicity in systems of oppression and violence and recognizes its impact on the current understanding and collective experience. It is only in naming and unmasking the trauma that it is possible to address it and the prevalence of harm within religious and spiritual institutions. Yet this should be more than a concession or acknowledgment in a book, a pamphlet produced, or a sermon delivered. Education and awareness are to be a fire that once ignited continues to burn in the hearts and minds of all impelling action towards justice, reconciliation, and reparation. It is not enough to simply acknowledge the harm done; the church must work to provide care and support for trauma recovery.

Since the beginning of time, humans have sought a connection to the divine – through gods, myths, creation, and religion as it has evolved. Historically, the development of religion has generally provided structure and emotional/moral support which has enveloped humans in a sense of community and has often been the source of a variety of services and charities including healthcare, food, and shelter. Despite the myriad of ways that religious institutions have been communities of stability and care, they have also been places of secrets, shame, and harm as, specifically within the Christian tradition, physical and emotional violence have been a perpetual issue for thousands of years.

Much of the current philosophy and justification of harm began in the 5th century when Augustine espoused a just war

27

theory that laid a foundation for the Crusades of the 11th century. He had no qualms regarding the Christian empire and imperial power as the central theme of his work "remained the justification of the right of Christendom to use violent means."[32] Other prominent Catholic leaders continued to carry the rhetoric and particular theology of European power as can be seen in Thomas Aquinas' work *Summa Theologica* when he advocated that just war was a "means to address injustice, wrong-doing, and heresy."[33] Though initially, the concept of just war may invoke images of heroics as demonstrated in WWII, Aquinas' inclusion of heresy was not simply a means for protection of vulnerable, marginalized, or targeted. Aquinas wrote, "They [heretics] deserve not only to be separated from the church by excommunication, but also to be severed from the world by death...Wherefore if forgers of money and other evil-doers are forthwith condemned to death by the secular authority, much more reason is there for heretics, as soon as they are convicted of heresy, to be not only excommunicated but even put to death."[34] While the notion of 'just war' may imply a morally substantive and ethical determination for assisting others, the basis is the subjugation of persons who are deemed "evil-doers" by the arbitrary decision making of white persons in power.

While one could construe that Aquinas was addressing only those within the church, heretics are anyone who differs in opinion from the dogma of established religion. Anyone not adhering to papal decree, who does not affirm Christianity as it is presented to them, is a heretic. Aquinas merged the church and secular powers by elevating heresy to a death sentence carried out

---

32. Mark Charles and Soong-Chan Rah, *Unsettling Truths: The Ongoing, Dehumanizing Legacy of the Doctrine of Discovery* (Downers Grove, Illinois: InterVarsity Press, 2019), 62.

33. Charles and Rah, 63.

34. Charles and Rah, 63.

by secular authorities. Such agreements only cemented the church as an arbiter of white supremacist justice.[35]

For almost 700 years, from 380 when Catholicism became the official religion of the Roman Empire until 1054 and the formal split between Roman Catholicism and the Eastern Orthodox churches, Catholicism was the only recognized form of Christianity. After which Roman Catholicism remained the only recognized Christian religion in the Western world until the Protestant Reformation in 1517. By then, Catholic indoctrination had not only shaped religion, but was also rooted in literature, music, art, and science and provided funding thereof. The influence of the Catholic church on culture, societal norms, and politics cannot be underscored enough. Thus, on June 18, 1452, when Pope Nicholas V issued the papal bull, *Dum Diversas,* which

---

35. "Beginning in the 12th century, Church Councils required secular rulers to prosecute heretics. In 1231, Pope Gregory IX published a decree which called for life imprisonment with salutary penance for the heretic who had confessed and repented and capital punishment for those who persisted. The secular authorities were to carry out the execution. Pope Gregory relieved the bishops and archbishops of this obligation, and made it the duty of the Dominican Order, though many inquisitors were members of other orders or of the secular clergy. By the end of the decade the Inquisition had become a general institution in all lands under the purview of the Pope. By the end of the 13th centuries the Inquisition in each region had a bureaucracy to help in its function. The judge, or inquisitor, could bring suit against anyone.. The accused was given a summary of the charges and had to take an oath to tell the truth. Various means were used to get the cooperation of the accused. Although there was no tradition of torture in Christian canon law, this method came into use by the middle of the 13th century. The findings of the Inquisition were read before a large audience; the penitents abjured on their knees with one hand on a bible held by the inquisitor. Penalties went from visits to churches, pilgrimages, and wearing the cross of infamy to imprisonment (usually for life but the sentences were often commuted) and (if the accused would not abjure) death. Death was by burning at the stake, and it was carried out by the secular authorities. Death or life imprisonment was always accompanied by the confiscation of all the accused's property." http://galileo.rice.edu/chr/inquisition.html

"initiated the first set of documents that would compose the Doctrine of Discovery", the world listened.[36,37]

In their book on the Doctrine of Discovery (DOD), Mark Charles and Soong-Chan Rah write, "In the thirteenth century, the writings of the church begin referring to a subhuman class known as the infidel. The theological problem of the other would undergird the dysfunctional theological narrative needed for the European powers to justify violent conquest of the entire world."[38] By the time the Doctrine of Discovery was written in the 15th century, the foundation of hatred, violence, and oppression was well documented and understood as a tenet of many Western nations. The 'other' had been identified and no energy was left unexpended attempting to eradicate them. While there are numerous examples over the millennia of the institution of religion inflicting trauma, within the Christian church, the DOD should be considered one of the most egregious acts against humanity that the church has engaged.

Read in its exact language, it states:

> The official decree of the pope granted permission to King
> Alfonso V of Portugal "to invade, search out, capture,
> vanquish, and subdue all Saracens (Muslims) and pagans
> whatsoever, and other enemies of Christ wheresoever
> placed, and the kingdoms, dukedoms, principalities,
> dominions, possessions, and all movable and immovable
> goods whatsoever held and possessed by them and to
> reduce their persons to perpetual slavery and to apply and
> appropriate to himself and his successors the kingdoms,

---

36. Papal Bulls are official documents in the Catholic church issued by the Pope including charters, patents, or public decree.
37. Charles and Rah, *Unsettling Truths: The Ongoing, Dehumanizing Legacy of the Doctrine of Discovery*, 15.
38. Charles and Rah, 63.

dukedoms, counties, principalities, dominions, possession, and goods, and to convert them to his and their use and profit.[39]

Via this doctrine, "there would be an unashamed elevation of the European rulers with a subsequent diminishing and demonizing of non-Europeans who would be rightly vanquished."[40] Though it has been used continually against Native peoples in the United States and Canada, it also empowered Prince Henry, "the very person verified by the pope as an agent of God", to establish (further) the African slave trade.[41] The Doctrine encouraged white-controlled nations to enslave others by providing theological justification and blessing their actions.

However, it was not only the papal bull *Dum Diversas* that contributed to the Doctrine of Discovery but rather a total of 3 papal bulls.[42] On May 4, 1493, Pope Alexander VI issued the papal bull, *Inter Caetera*, offering "a spiritual validation for European conquest, that in our times especially the Catholic faith and the Christian religion be exalted and be everywhere increased and spread, that the health of souls is cared for and that barbarous nations be overthrown and brought to the faith itself."[43] This bull was issued to King Ferdinand and Queen Isabella as "ecclesial affirmation of the state-sanctioned expedition and work of

---

39. Charles and Rah, 15.
40. Charles and Rah, 17.
41. ibid
42. This also included the bull Romanus Pontifex which provided access and conquest rights to the Portuguese Crown and Infante Dom Henrique (Henry the Navigator) as a reward for their service to the church.webfeller, "Romanus Pontifex," *Papal Encyclicals* (blog), June 16, 2017, https://www.papalencyclicals.net/nicholo5/romanus-pontifex.htm; Ivana Elbl, "The Bull Romanus Pontifex (1455) and the early European trading in sub-Saharan Atlantic Africa.," *Portuguese Studies Review* 17, no. 1 (January 1, 2009): 59–82.
43. Charles and Rah, *Unsettling Truths: The Ongoing, Dehumanizing Legacy of the Doctrine of Discovery*, 19.

conquest by Christopher Columbus."[44] Not merely enough to overthrow 'barbarous nations' and enslave people 'in perpetuity', Pope Alexander VI asserted that "anyone opposing this doctrine would be considered opposing the will of God. Let no one, therefore, infringe, or with rash boldness contravene, this our recommendation, exhortation, requisition, gift, grant, assignment, constitution, deputation, decree, mandate, prohibition, and will. Should anyone presume to attempt this, be it known to him that he will incur the wrath of Almighty God."[45]

These papal bulls, known as the DOD, not only created 'other' and insider/outsider status in a profound, brash, unrestrained document lasting for perpetuity but constructed identities still espoused for non-Europeans specifically "African bodies as inferior and only worthy of subjugation" and Indigenous people as disposable land dwellers.[46] This revulsive and egregious document is an inconceivable standout among religiously inflicted trauma in its reduction of "persons to perpetual slavery" with its litany of horrors and must be acknowledged and addressed for the historical, collective, and transgenerational trauma it has enacted for more than 570 years. It contains the formal establishment of white supremacy, empowering and instructing whites to rule, dominate, and subjugate, and clearly defines those who should be oppressed. By targeting Muslims and pagans, anyone non-European, it created the "other" and perpetrated harm that is still unresolved in the world. It has systematically empowered whites and decimated entire communities.

In 1823, the United States Supreme Court used the Doctrine of Discovery as a basis for its decision-making in *Johnson v. McIntosh*. Chief Justice John Marshall's opinion in the unanimous

---

44. Charles and Rah, 19.
45. Charles and Rah, 20.
46. Charles and Rah, 21

decision held "that the principle of discovery gave European nations an absolute right to New World lands." In essence, American Indians had only a right of occupancy, which could be abolished."[47] Yet, as recently as 2005, The United States Supreme Court used the Doctrine in its decision to deny the right of the Oneida Indian Nation of New York to regain its territory.[48] Joseph Heath, General Counsel for the Onondaga Nation, summarized the repeated use of the Doctrine of Discovery to oppress and disenfranchise Native peoples of their liberty, freedom, and land in his Statement on the Historic Use of the Doctrine of Christian Discovery by the United States Supreme Court since 1823. Not only does he provide a history of relevant court cases, but he also calls for action by saying, "We must face the realities of the racism of these rulings against our sovereignty and human rights and work collectively to reverse them. To be successful in these efforts, we must always denounce the doctrine of Christian discovery and its use against us by the US courts."[49]

Using the words of Prof. Robert A. Williams, Jr. to further advocate for engagement and action, he quotes him saying, "strategy that focuses on identifying and bringing to the fore the nineteenth-century racist judicial language on Indian savagery used by the present-day Court in its major Indian rights decision does not entail one axiom of belief and Native knowledge: Indian rights will never be justly protected by any legal system or any civil society that continues to talk about Indians as if they are

47. "The Doctrine of Discovery, 1493 | Gilder Lehrman Institute of American History," accessed November 7, 2023, https://www.gilderlehrman.org/history-resources/spotlight-primary-source/doctrine-discovery-1493.

48. "Doctrine of Discovery," American Indian Law Alliance, accessed February 12, 2024, https://aila.ngo/issues/doctrine-of-discovery/.

49. Joseph J. Heath, Esq., "Statement on the Historic Use of the Doctrine of Christian Discovery by the United States" (Onondaga Nation General Counsel, May 24, 2014), 30.

uncivilized, unsophisticated, and lawless savages."[50] Despite the obvious, unequivocal harm and trauma caused by this doctrine including the enslavement of Africans, the marginalization and oppression of people of color, and the forced conversion and Christian indoctrination upon Native Americans, the Catholic Church did not repudiate these doctrines until March 30, 2023.[51]

It is undeniable that these doctrines and foundational tenets have caused extreme historical, intergenerational, and religious trauma. Separating humans from one another, breaking relationships, enslaving (literally and symbolically) BIPOC[52] to 'other' status – including as 'savages', shunning, and inflicting shame and indescribable pain, it becomes clear that for those espousing such narratives, the image of God is not reflected in anyone other than white Anglo-Saxon Christians. For if it were, there would be no terra nullius. There would be no colonization. The idea of American exceptionalism continues to marginalize and remove access from the imago Dei to anyone not white. "Racism in the United States is rooted in the theological distortion that elevates white bodies and minds to a privileged position over others. This sinful expression racializes the image of God and links God's image to whiteness. Whiteness becomes the embodiment of all that is good, true, and honorable, including the positive godly attribute of self-governance and the desire to spread this form of godliness to savages."[53]

By understanding the conditioning of the current societal

---

50. Heath, Esq., 30.

51. Bill Chappell, "The Vatican Repudiates 'Doctrine of Discovery,' Which Was Used to Justify Colonialism," NPR, March 30, 2023, sec. Religion, https://www. npr.org/2023/03/30/1167056438/vatican-doctrine-of-discovery-colonialism-indigenous.

52. Black, Indigenous, and People of Color

53. Charles and Rah, Unsettling Truths: The Ongoing, Dehumanizing Legacy of the Doctrine of Discovery, 85.

philosophy and beliefs through the historical and current indoctrination of supreme Christian whiteness as the absolute truth and measure of one's worth, there is hope for change. Spiritually integrated communities may begin to dismantle the systems and dogmas that cause traumatic harm by recognizing the history of how information has been ingrained and assimilated. Moreover, not only is there the possibility of healing and reparations to BIPOC/TP, but non-traumatized persons might begin to find compassion and understanding of the functioning of a traumatized person's brain and how it assimilates information.

The reality of one's worldview being constructed and dominated by another, entrenching an inability to see anything beyond what has been indoctrinated, is something that traumatized people also experience. Just as many white people are only now beginning to explore racism and its traumatic effect as they are provided new information and additional perspectives, for TP their worldview and understanding may also have been completely constituted by another. This is especially true in child abuse and chronic interpersonal violence. Traumatized persons cannot see or comprehend any different way of being in the world, who they are, or the construct of their world and believe that they have an accurate perspective about themselves, their environment, and those within their community. Yet, they are framing that understanding in a narrative unwritten by them and imposed upon them. Anytime a person is unable to see outside of their worldview and open themselves to other information, there is harm. Returning to the Doctrine of Discovery and its impact, the difference is that for TP, their worldview originates or has been developed because harm has been heaped upon them, and for the Christians espousing "common sense" or the Doctrine of Discovery, it is because *they* are the ones causing harm.

In working from the philosophy and conviction that humans are created for relationships and function best within them, anything that hinders relationships has the potential of inflicting traumatic injury. At the very least, causing pain and fracturing. It is obvious within American society that the Doctrine of Discovery still looms large in our psyche. Take for instance the comments made regarding Vice-President Kamala Harris on her announcement to seek the presidency of the United States. J.D. Vance, Vice-President Harris' opponent stated that she "should be grateful" for the opportunity to lead this country.[54] A white man telling a woman of color that she needs to be grateful is 'logic' direct from the DOD. Thus, the continued racism inherent in the public vernacular and understanding as well as policies of governments against BIPOC, refugees, migrants, etc., and the systematic oppression and perpetuation of poverty renders traumatic injury an almost inescapable experience for many. This impacts the spiritually integrated, specifically Christians, as they benefit most from the millennia of doctrines of oppression and white supremacy. "It is noble for the exceptional white American church to go help those "over there," but not for them to come over here to a nation reserved for exceptional white Americans. This assumption of exceptionalism hinders the work of reconciliation as a dysfunctional imagination of white supremacy and exceptionalism continues unabated in the US church and US society."[55]

However, the idea of conquest and absolute ownership and entitlement of land and humans is not a new concept. Throughout the Bible, people were owned and dominated. This brings the next traumas of the church to light - the abuse of women and the sexual abuse of children, cloaked in secrecy and hidden from view.

One such Christian community that has inflicted harm in their

---

54. Thom Hartmann, "J.D. Vance Wants Kamala Harris to Be 'Grateful' for White Male Power," *The New Republic*, accessed July 25, 2024, https://newrepublic.com/article/184142/jd-vance-attacks-kamala-harris-grateful-white-male-power.
55. Charles and Rah, *Unsettling Truths: The Ongoing, Dehumanizing Legacy of the Doctrine of Discovery*, 81.

treatment of women and coercion of silence is those who identify as part of the Evangelical church. (Often, these are non-denominational without any ecclesiastical management or accountability.) Not only are the communities harmful to women, but these churches believe in literal Bible translations as the written authority to which they adhere, adopting thereby a creationist understanding of science, male-only leadership, and the condemnation of LGBTQ persons. Daphne Marsden has researched the phenomena regarding Christian women abused within evangelical churches and the response of the church leadership and community. She states, "Violence against women within Christian families are not given proper attention."[56] Her study encompasses first-person interviews and examines not only the relevant literature but also the use and application of Scripture in evangelical churches as it pertains to women's opinions and choices. In so doing, she notes the role of patriarchy, issues of forced forgiveness, doctrine of submission, and the concept of original sin. Marsden concludes, "Responses by evangelical communities to women suffering domestic abuse are for the most part limited and inadequate, often as a result of a theological bias in favor of hierarchy and patriarchy."[57]

Natalie Collins writes of her experience in the evangelical church as a woman who remained in a relationship with an abusive partner for years due to the teachings and manipulations of the evangelical culture in which she was raised.[58] She writes, "Even as trauma theory gives hope for Christianity's capacity to

---

56. Daphne Marsden, "Okay, Now You Can Turn It Off," *Stimulus* 21, no. 3 (November 2014): 5.
57. Marsden, 13.
58. This understanding is traditionally based upon the biblical text, Ephesians 5:22-24, "Wives, submit yourselves unto your own husbands, as unto the Lord. For the husband is the head of the wife, even as Christ is the head of the church: and he is the saviour of the body. Therefore, as the church is subject unto Christ, so let the wives be to their own husbands in everything." (KJV)

care for traumatized people, certain Christian cultures, theologies, and practices raise concerns. Can this capacity be realized, and can the evangelical church ever truly be a safe place for traumatized people, particularly those traumatized by intimate partner violence?"[59] This experience is spotlit by the response given by Paige Patterson, then President of the Southern Baptist Convention, at a convention in 2002; when asked whether women should leave their abusive husbands his reply was, "No woman should ever divorce an abusive husband."[60]

When I worked as a chaplain at a hospital in upstate New York, I'll never forget the woman who was brought to the ED who had lacerations and bruises on her face as well as on her arms and two broken ribs. Her husband had beaten her for insubordination. "He is the head of the house as God has instructed and I should not have talked back. I should have just had dinner ready as he needed." This is not an isolated incident nor an unheard-of interpretation of "wives submit to your husbands".[61] In my conversation with this woman, I asked about her need for safety and her right to not be hit. She said that God planned marriage and made her husband the head of the house and she was determined to return to her husband as soon as possible.

It is not only the evangelical branch of Christianity that has harmed and marginalized women. For example, examining current statistics released in 2022 of women in church leadership in Protestant churches, they account for about 13% of pastors holding the title of senior pastor or as solo pastors.[62] This is despite most

---

59. Karen O'Donnell and Katie Cross, eds., *Feminist Trauma Theologies* (London, UK: SCM Press, 2020), 205.

60. O'Donnell and Cross, 207.

61. Ephesians 5:22

62. Young-joo Lee, "Women in the Pulpit: Characteristics of Protestant Churches Led by a Female Pastor," *Nonprofit Management and Leadership* n/a, no. n/a, accessed February 24, 2024, https://doi.org/10.1002/nml.21612.

Protestant denominations endorsing women to ordination as well as the fact that women account for approximately 36% of the total enrollment of Association of Theological Schools member institutions.[63] Women are not only marginalized in leadership. The continued role of patriarchy within American culture continues to contribute to the oppression of women across all theological (and secular) spectrums. The trauma embodied by women - especially women of color - as a result of Christian communities must be acknowledged and reckoned with. Patriarchal power has led to the final subject I include in this chapter which the Christian church must address and confess before engaging in the work of trauma-informed care: the sexual abuse of children.

It is extremely difficult to procure accurate and complete statistics on the rate of sexual abuse within Christian churches as well as the age of victims. Not only is the subject often deemed too distressing for persons to discuss but the victims are often unable to inform their family, friends, or community due to, among many factors, fear of reprisal or disbelief.

Advisen is an insurance data provider and reports that religious organizations account for 30% of all child sexual abuse losses in Advisen's database.[64,65] "This is the second greatest frequency for all industries, behind only elementary and secondary schools at 39%. All other industries account for less than 10% of the total child sexual abuse losses."[66] Yet, the true number of abuse cases is unknown. In 2002, the Boston Globe released a series of reports

63. The Association of Theological Schools, "Annual Data Tables: 2022-2023" (Pittsburgh, PA: The Commission on Accrediting, 2023).

64. Charlene Farside, "Insurance Program Benchmarking Methodology," Advisen Ltd., July 6, 2015, https://www.advisenltd.com/data/insurance-program-benchmarking-methodology/.

65. Advisen's database "contains nearly 4 million insurance programs which represent over 650,000 insureds, 7200 brokerages, 4,400 carrier, and 140 LOBs."

66. Bitner Henry, "Child Sexual Abuse Is the Second Most Frequent Loss at Religious Institutions," *Bitner Henry Insurance Group* (blog), October 19, 2022,

on sexual abuse in the Catholic Church which began to challenge the status quo of silence, concealment, and complicity. This investigation revealed a massive cover-up of abuse by Cardinal Bernard Francis Law going back decades and between 2002 and 2003, the Catholic Church paid $95 million to 638 victims within the Boston Archdiocese.[67] However, there are thousands more.

In only two news reports covering one state (Illinois) and 6 dioceses in Pennsylvania between the years of 1950 to 2018 and 1947 to 2019 respectively, there were more than 3,000 victims of clergy sexual abuse in the Catholic church.[68] Regarding the Pennsylvania report which includes information from the grand jury indictment, it is noted, "We believe that the real number of children whose records were lost or who were afraid ever to come forward is in the thousands."[69] According to Bishop Accountability (a database website for public information on Catholic clergy abuse), the total amount thus far that the Catholic church has paid out is over $4 billion in lawsuits for more than 8,600 cases of abuse by clergy going back to the 1950s.[70] The Catholic church, while being the most recognized regarding sexual abuse, is not the

---

https://bitnerhenry.com/child-sexual-abuse-is-the-second-most-frequent-loss-at-religious-institutions/.

67. "Sexual Abuse Scandal in the Roman Catholic Archdiocese of Boston," in *Wikipedia*, January 28, 2024, https://en.wikipedia.org/w/index.php?title=Sexual_abuse_scandal_in_the_Roman_Catholic_Archdiocese_of_Boston&oldid=1200177852#cite_note-Bruni336-5.

68. "Catholic Clergy Sexually Abused Nearly 2,000 Kids in Illinois, State Finds," NBC News, May 23, 2023, https://www.nbcnews.com/news/us-news/catholic-clergy-sexually-abused-nearly-2000-kids-illinois-state-finds-rcna85856; Daniel Burke Cullinane Susannah, "Report Details Sexual Abuse by More than 300 Priests in Pennsylvania's Catholic Church," CNN, August 14, 2018, https://www.cnn.com/2018/08/14/us/pennsylvania-catholic-church-grand-jury/index.html.

69. Cullinane, "Report Details Sexual Abuse by More than 300 Priests in Pennsylvania's Catholic Church."

70. "Home - BishopAccountability.Org," January 1, 2023, https://www.bishop-accountability.org/.

only denomination to have abused children and covered the actions, protected the perpetrators, and silenced victims.

The Southern Baptist Church, officially called the Southern Baptist Convention (SBC), is the world's largest Christian Protestant denomination with more than 13 million members in the United States.[71] In February of 2019, reports of sexual abuse in the SBC churches were reported by the Houston Chronicle which was followed by a resolution at their annual denominational meeting to create a special committee to investigate the abuse of which the findings were reported in May 2022.[72] Not only was it reported that the SBC had knowingly covered up sexual abuse and ignored and "even vilified" victims, but there was a secret database of abusers and some of them had been allowed to retain their positions within the church.[73]

Yet, these crimes against children are not exclusive to the Catholic or Southern Baptist church. The Presbyterian Church (U.S.A.), Evangelical Lutheran Church in America, Jesus Christ of Latter Day Saints (Mormon), Presbyterian Church in America, and Methodist Church all have had lawsuits brought against them by survivors of clergy sexual abuse.[74] While there are numerous

---

71. "Southern Baptist Convention," in *Wikipedia*, February 23, 2024, https://en.wikipedia.org/w/index.php?title=Southern_Baptist_Convention&oldid=1209798707.

72. Sarah Pulliam Bailey, "Southern Baptist Leaders Covered up Sex Abuse, Kept Secret Database, Report Says," *Washington Post*, May 26, 2022, https://www.washingtonpost.com/religion/2022/05/22/southern-baptist-sex-abuse-report/.

73. ibid

74. James Evinger, Carolyn Whitfield, and Judith Wiley, "Final Report of the Independent Abuse Review Panel Presbyterian Church (U.S.A.)" (Louisville, KY: Presbyterian Church (U.S.A.), October 2010); Jamie Satterfield, Tennessee Lookout June 7, and 2022, "Court Allows John Does to Sue Presbyterian Church over Decades-Old Sexual Abuse," *Tennessee Lookout* (blog), June 7, 2022, https://tennesseelookout.com/2022/06/07/court-allows-john-does-to-sue-presbyterian-church-over-decades-old-sexual-abuse/; "The Presbyterian Church in America Has an Abuse Crisis Too...... | News & Reporting | Christianity Today," accessed February 24, 2024, https://www.christianitytoday.com/news/2023/june/pres

news reports of abuse and harm, as there is no clearinghouse of data, the total number of people sexually abused and/or assaulted by church leaders remains unknown. Obtaining reports from denominations is difficult and many victims do not report their abuse, or the issue is handled within the individual church without information sent to any governing body. Furthermore, there are thousands of non-denominational congregations who do not have any ecclesiastical oversight. Therefore, reports would need to be obtained by each individual church which has no compulsory requirement to disclose such information as many of the accusations are dealt with "in-house". This means that members of the church agree to be bound by the rules of discipline for that specific church/congregation and therefore outside of the church, there are no authorities who are aware of the situation.

Moreover, in many denominations, if a pastor, priest, or other church leader chooses to permanently leave the church and/or renounce their ordination, the investigation ceases – even if the investigation is incomplete, as the governing bodies of the church say that they "no longer have authority to monitor them."[75] Some

byterian-church-in-america-abuse-response.html; Jim Yardley, "Abuse by Clergy Is Not Just a Catholic Problem," *The New York Times*, April 13, 2002, sec. U.S., https://www.nytimes.com/2002/04/13/us/abuse-by-clergy-is-not-just-a-catholic-problem.html; Andrea Smardon, "For Mormon Women, Saying #MeToo Presents a Particular Challenge," *The Guardian*, November 29, 2017, sec. World news, https://www.theguardian.com/world/2017/nov/29/mormon-women-metoo-partic ular-challenge-sexual-abuse; "Clergyman Accused of Sexual Misconduct, Abuse," United Methodist News Service, accessed February 24, 2024, https://www. umnews.org/en/news/clergyman-accused-of-sexual-misconduct-abuse; "Methodist Church Apologises for Abuse Spanning Decades," *BBC News*, May 28, 2015, sec. UK, https://www.bbc.com/news/uk-32909444; Peter Janci, "Church Sexual Abuse Statistics: Understanding the Prevalence Abuse," *Crew Janci LLP: Sexual Abuse Attorneys* (blog), May 24, 2023, https://www.crewjanci.com/church-sexual-abuse-statistics/.

75. "Almost 1,700 Priests and Clergy Accused of Sex Abuse Are Unsupervised," NBC News, October 4, 2019, 17, https://www.nbcnews.com/news/religion/nearly-1-700-priests-clergy-accused-sex-abuse-are-unsupervised-n1062396.

church leaders have been defrocked which is the removal of their rights to practice within that denomination. However, as there may not be legal action outside of the denomination, they are free to be employed without future employers having knowledge of their crime.

In the book, *Resurrecting Wounds: Living in the Afterlife of Trauma* by Shelly Rambo, she discusses the issue of historical trauma in terms of racism. Drawing upon works of Michael Rothberg, Willie James Jennings, Judith Butler, and others, she discusses the "imperial matrix" which "insists on keeping histories from touching one another" as related to the competition model which pits one trauma against another, therefore, leaving no room for there to be simultaneous traumas as they are "jockeying for space in the marketplace of memory".[76] This concept is vitally important to employ in the understanding of sexual abuse within the Christian church. For the separation of these events not only competes for space but allows the history to seem singular in nature as opposed to a collective issue affecting multiple generations out of the white, patriarchal structure of privilege, power, and spiritual intimidation inherent in ministerial roles.

> The hidden wound images the effects of living under those conditions and how harms, left unaddressed, become part of the architecture. He [Wendell Berry] says that registering and bringing the wounds to the surface will not be easy, especially given that the logic is smooth, facilitating a certain way of life for some. The logic constructed over time is protective for some, and when the collective wound is exposed, fear can take over, and occupants can react in

---

76. Shelly Rambo, *Resurrecting Wounds: Living in the Afterlife of Trauma*, Illustrated edition (Baylor University Press, 2018), 95–96.

often-surprising ways. Those most powerful can perceive themselves as under attack.[77]

Though sexual assault is not limited to religious organizations or the Christian denomination, it is anathema to the teachings of Jesus to engage in any activity that harms another person. Jesus, in the synoptic Gospels, instructs humans to "Love your neighbor as you love yourself."[78] In the Gospel of John, Jesus is quoted as saying, "Love others as I have loved you."[79] This is not an issue of interpretation or ecclesiastical dogma; there is nothing contained in the Gospels recording of Jesus' life that allows for any behavior that would harm another. Especially the egregious, disgusting, destructive, and sinful sexual acts committed against a minor. These heinous acts perpetrated against children cause untold emotional, physical, psychological, and spiritual damage as both victims, their families, and friends are left wondering why didn't the church/spiritual community protect them and/or come to their defense? Why were they abandoned by both their community and God? What is wrong with them?

Returning to authors Charles and Rah from their book, *Unsettling Truths*, they write, "The difference is in who writes the history."[80] The writer of the history controls the narrative. History has not been written by the masses but by a few. Speaking from within the Christian church, the persons who have written the history have obscured facts about the marginalization and abuse of children and women. Therefore, truth-telling of the history of harm, abuse, oppression, and marginalization within the Christian church is imperative to work towards healing, repair, and justice;

---

77. Rambo, 86.

78. Matthew 19:19, 22:39; Mark 12:31; Luke 10:27

79. John 13:34

80. Charles and Rah, *Unsettling Truths: The Ongoing, Dehumanizing Legacy of the Doctrine of Discovery*, 137.

empowering those who have been harmed to be bold and tell their story as an act of accountability. History needs to be told not only by those who have inflicted the damage but by those who have survived it; voices of those who identify as women, LGBTQIA+, TP, and other marginalized individuals and groups.

Finally, it should be noted that narrative is an extremely important concept in trauma and trauma recovery, especially in dealing with chronic or complex trauma. Is the narrative internalized by the traumatized person their own, one imposed upon them by those who have committed harm, or the part of themselves that so desperately needs to have an explanation that it will create one regardless of the truth or whole picture. The words that TP use about themselves and the stories they tell of themselves are often narratives given to them by the person/persons who inflicted the traumatic injury. Even in cases of acute trauma, the narrative fueled by 'what if' often is so pervasive that it becomes a reality. Importantly, the church has a voice/role in creating the narrative that either heals or continues to harm. When spiritually integrated communities are allowed to journey alongside traumatized persons and provide support, they have an opportunity to offer a narrative that TP may hold until they can write their own: they did not deserve this, they are loved, they are worthy of love.

Case Study

Marie was a 35-year-old woman with twin 9-year-old boys who were, what church member Mrs. Abernathy termed, a 'handful'. They were inquisitive, boundary-pushing, attention-seeking, and at times physical with other children and adults. Within the tight-knit Midwestern community church, the children's behavior stood out. However, the larger issue was Marie's parenting style and skills or perceived lack thereof. When her child hit another child across the face, she did not engage other than to say to her child,

'Don't do that'. She then told those nearby and the pastor that the other child had instigated such a response. Throughout worship, there would be screams and arguments from and between her children. Even though the church had created a warm and welcoming space in a classroom for children to play and be outside of worship if needed (with speakers so that all could still hear what was happening within worship), Marie never took her children out to allow them a space to find calm, play, or simply express themselves. When she would leave worship, it was to leave the building completely with much attention drawn to her as she loudly narrated her reasons for leaving – embarrassment, frustration, and/or loneliness (she brought her children to church without her spouse).

The community responded with love and nonjudgment at first, assuming that coming into a new space was challenging and she needed to find her way. Marie and her children were welcome at events and engaged in activities as her children continued to engage in hitting and screaming, other parents began to have concerns for their children and the interactions they were having and they chose to limit their exposure. Weekly attendance at evening activities by multiple families declined. Marie noticed this and, upset at being only one of two families or the only family in attendance, reached out to the pastor to find out why stating, "I am not included in this community." The pastor, with full knowledge of the choices other families were making and why, having witnessed her children's behavior, chose to focus on Marie's feelings of exclusion and invited her to share her feelings.

They subsequently had a meeting and at that time, Marie disclosed that her twins had been born prematurely at 28 weeks in a harrowing birth ordeal and she had worried every minute of every day of their lives that they would die. Her sons had spent a few months each in the NICU with multiple complications and had been critically ill multiple times during their stay. She said that since she brought them home from the hospital, she had never been away from them for more than a few hours outside of the days when the children were in school. Marie had never been away from them for the evening routine of tucking them in at night for fear that they would die during the night. She discussed her need to give them everything because "they almost didn't make it."

Additionally, Marie had experienced infertility for years before conceiving her sons, enduring numerous medical treatments as well as the heartbreak of multiple miscarriages. During this time, her parents, particularly her mother, were quite vocal about needing grandchildren saying that they felt like they were being "denied what everyone else has." Marie shared that she came from an incredibly close, large Italian family and despite numerous siblings, aunts, uncles, and extended family, she has always felt responsible for her mother's happiness since she was little. Her mother was an exacting person who expected perfection, complete loyalty, and full attention. In the years that she and her husband didn't have children, Marie stated that it was made clear to her the "harm" being done to the family without grandchildren and a "full line of cousins" both in her family's actions and direct comments to her. Finally, she noted that she had felt "worthless" in her family until they had children and even then, she has always questioned her worth.

As the pastor listened, it became clear that Marie was dealing with trauma related to her infertility and son's birth and that she may benefit from professional mental health support. Trying to affirm Marie's experience, the pastor told her that "it sounds like such an intense weight – to have such never-ending worry and fear. That seems like it would make parenting difficult." Marie took this as an indictment of her parenting. The pastor tried to explain that they were affirming the incredible strength it took to deal with such fear while also parenting twins. Noting that parenting is extremely hard work (the pastor had two children as well.) Marie heard the pastor's attempt and continued attending church. However, at Marie's reaction, the pastor did not explore direct conversation regarding the boys' behavior, and relationships within the community did not improve as no action was taken to change and/or correct her son's behavior.

Though the pastor could not reveal Marie's story for confidentiality reasons, they did attempt to facilitate conversation between Marie and others, specifically with others who had experienced traumatic events (and were well into their recovery) and/or with persons who could listen and provide compassion and in which relationships could develop and subsequently help Marie feel safe and perhaps allow her to share her story. However, as her children continued to be physical with other children and Marie continued to not intervene, the pastor and community were left to provide interventions for safety telling her children, "In our community, we do not hit. We treat others how we want to be treated. Please do not hit (other child's name)". Marie found that to be intolerable and was convinced that everyone hated her, judged her parenting, hated her children, and shamed them for their behavior and chose to leave the community church.

This story highlights how what many in the congregation perceived as a lack of care, laziness, or bad parenting is rather a TP stuck in the never-ending experience of traumatic wounding. For Marie, she lived in a constant state of fear as her infertility looms (I'll never have the chance to have more children) and within her, she experiences her sons as remaining in critical care with their very lives threatened, fighting for every breath. The traumatic injury that months in the NICU had left upon her, as well as the emotional challenges within her family of origin, caused Marie to be unable to imagine a different way of being. Moreover, Marie's marriage had suffered during this time as her husband was experiencing this traumatic injury as well and to cope, began running marathons, training daily for hours at a time, leaving her physically and emotionally alone in the experience. Marie could not control what happened to her children at birth, recalling that "they must have been miserable" and felt the overwhelming need to control her son's happiness as much as possible; ensuring that nothing threatened it.[81]

Her internal narrative of believing that anything good or bad in her children's life was a direct 'fault' of hers led her to an inability to cope with the existential threat that all parents face – life is not certain for one's children. This left Marie completely vulnerable. These real experiences and struggles are not excuses for the inability to participate in ensuring a safe space for all – including other children – but rather understanding her responses and actions as ones rooted in trauma allow for different conversations and interventions that may be better received and less harmful.

Marie's actions, or lack thereof, make sense in the context. Her seeming unwillingness or inability to intervene and set boundaries for her children is rooted in the fear that they may have a short life and she must make every moment one without pain – even the discomfort of learning appropriate boundaries. When placed in context, compassion is easily extended, and subsequent conversations may begin that provide care for Marie and her children.

What is Trauma?

To support traumatized persons in their recovery, one must have a basic understanding of trauma, its types, and its effects. Otherwise, unintentional harm may be inflicted and thereby further complicate an arduous journey of recovery.

Trauma is the bodily response to an event of a perceived threat

---

81. Sandage et al., *Relational Spirituality in Psychotherapy: Healing Suffering and Promoting Growth*, 95.

to self. It is a line of demarcation between feeling fundamentally safe in one's existence, (as much as is possible for anyone), and experiencing people and the world as constant threats. Structurally, trauma biochemically changes a person and therefore anything previously assumed may be/is displaced, marginalized, and/or rendered null. Physiologically, the body responds by producing epinephrine, decreasing the production of cortisol, and increasing blood flow to muscles for survival by overriding normal bodily and psychological responses, including the short-circuiting of critical thinking in the frontal cortex via the "fight, flight, and freeze" response.

Due to the shock and severity of a traumatic event(s), the brain is incapable of situating the occurrence (s) in linear time and consequently, TP are unable to integrate the experience into their memory as a historical, concluded event. Subsequently, feelings and sensations associated with the trauma continue, and "a simple and unrelated sensory experience in the present can evoke the past events, rendering the present surroundings indistinguishable from the past. These "invasions" are often coupled with an inability to cognitively access the facts of the original event. ...The body directly experiences in the *present* what the mind could not grasp in the past."[82] Time does not heal traumatic injury. While the event is experienced as interminable, further complicating the effect of traumatic injury and healing is that not all trauma is known. One can have PTSD and suffer greatly without being able to know and/or articulate the action/event that led to the suffering.

Most people think of trauma and PTSD as interchangeable terms. However, PTSD is the *reaction* to a traumatic event. Research at the University of Oxford suggests that "there may be a

---

82. Shelly Rambo, "Trauma and Faith: Reading the Narrative of the Hemorrhaging Woman," *International Journal of Practical Theology* 13, no. 2 (2009): 237, https://doi.org/10.1515/IJPT.2009.15.

spectrum of traumatic effect on the brain, where people who have experienced trauma may not meet the threshold for a diagnosis of PTSD but may have similar changes within the brain."[83] For purposes of this work, it is not necessary to diagnose PTSD according to the DSM, but instead to recognize how PTSD presents in affected persons and understand the effects of trauma.

Approximately 6 out of every 100 people (or 6% of the U.S. population) will have PTSD at some point in their lives.[84] In any given year, approximately 5 out of every 100 adults (or 5%) in the U.S. have PTSD, translating to about 13 million Americans experiencing PTSD in 2020.[85] Women are more likely to develop PTSD than men, in part due to the types of traumatic events that women are more likely to experience—such as sexual assault. About 5 of every 10 women (or 50%) and 6 of every 10 men (or 60%) will experience a trauma at some point in their life.[86] Terrifyingly, more and more of the population is exposed to trauma with 70% of the world having been exposed to a traumatic event.[87] Though this does not mean that all persons are experiencing PTSD and/or the effects of trauma, the exposure remains.

There is no simple or straightforward explanation as to why some individuals develop PTSD and others do not. A multitude of

---

83. "Traumatic Experiences Change the Brain Even in Those without PTSD | University of Oxford," accessed December 16, 2023, https://www.ox.ac.uk/news/2015-08-04-traumatic-experiences-change-brain-even-those-without-ptsd.

84. "PTSD Statistics And Facts: How Common Is It?," Forbes Health, September 14, 2023, https://www.forbes.com/health/mind/ptsd-statistics/.

85. "How Common Is PTSD?," General Information, accessed October 3, 2023, https://www.ptsd.va.gov/understand/common/common_adults.asp.

86. "Post-Traumatic Stress Disorder (PTSD) 2023," Text, National Institutes of Health, June 2, 2021, https://hr.nih.gov/working-nih/civil/post-traumatic-stress-disorder-ptsd-2023.

87. C. Benjet et al., "The Epidemiology of Traumatic Event Exposure Worldwide: Results from the World Mental Health Survey Consortium," *Psychological Medicine* 46, no. 2 (January 2016): 327–43, https://doi.org/10.1017/S0033291715001981.

factors including the vulnerability of the person or community prior to the event(s), the resources available before, during, and after the event, and the degree of support and empathy accessible to the individual and/or community all facilitate or hinder the processing of the experience. These myriad factors also include socioeconomics, education and access to education, history of mental illness, heart rate variability, age, gender, family of origin, environmental impacts, etc.[88] Yet, there is not one specific factor that determines the effects of trauma and resiliency. Resiliency should not be conflated with the appearance of health and/or functioning as it is not determined by the ability to conform to societal expectations. Rather, it is the ability to survive the unthinkable and unfathomable. When examining factors and why some develop PTSD, equating PTSD with resiliency is an incommensurate explanation. Current culture tends to assign resiliency to those who emote, behave, and endure in expressive attitudes and conduct that is comfortable for or deemed appropriate by the observer. However, resiliency cannot be categorized strictly by external or perceptible behavior. Trauma is a physiological response that occurs within neural pathways and at a cellular level. Resiliency must include that which is unseen as well.

A traumatic injury (PTSD) is not a bad day, a bad week, or a bad month. It is not a strenuous challenge of emotional strife. If one still can think and feel and can experience suffering without having intrusive thoughts, utilizing avoidance, or engaging in dangerous, destructive, harmful, and/or addictive self-soothing behaviors (*e.g.* overconsumption of alcohol, food, drugs, cutting, overworking), they are not traumatized. **This does not mean a person isn't having a difficult time and is**

88. Joshua Feriante and Naveen P. Sharma, "Acute and Chronic Mental Health Trauma," in *StatPearls* (Treasure Island (FL): StatPearls Publishing, 2024), http://www.ncbi.nlm.nih.gov/books/NBK594231/.

undeserving of emotional, spiritual, and physical care. There are horrible things that are experienced by humans that require deep care and consistent professional and supportive help which are not traumatic. Trauma is a physiological response that debilitates the capacity for awe, wonder, love, and curiosity.

History of Trauma

Despite humans experiencing trauma since the dawn of time, it was seemingly not until the late 19th century that it began to be recognized as a factual marker of psychological distress. Priorly, what was described as trauma, and is now known as Post Traumatic Stress Disorder (PTSD), was regarded as an issue of religiosity, possession, witchcraft, hysteria, or simply a matter about "unmanageable" persons.[89] Moreover, the effects of what we now call trauma were professedly only "a disease proper to women and originating in the uterus. Hence, the name, hysteria."[90] Prior to the late 19th century, women were thought of as malingerers and paid little credence until Jean-Martin Charcot focused on the issue of hysteria and was followed by students Pierre Janet and Sigmund Freud.[91]

Jean-Martin Charcot, considered the father of neurology, began the explorations into the effects of trauma at the Salpêtrière in Paris which served as a "prison, hospital, and asylum" for "prostitutes, the mentally ill and criminally insane, alongside the unwell destitute of Parisian society."[92] It was there that he became

---

89. Herman, M. D., *Trauma and Recovery*, 1997, 10.
90. ibid
91. Herman, M. D., 12.
92. Manni Waraich and Shailesh Shah, "The Life and Work of Jean-Martin Charcot (1825–1893): 'The Napoleon of Neuroses,'" *Journal of the Intensive Care Society* 19, no. 1 (February 2018): 48–49, https://doi.org/10.1177/1751143717709420.

fascinated with the postures and body movements affecting his patients as Charcot witnessed "paralyses, jerky movements, swooning, sudden collapse, frenzied laughter, and dramatic weeping" which he came to know as the "physical imprints of trauma".[93] He educated his students by offering live demonstrations, putting his young female patients on display who had found refuge in the Salpêtrière from lives of unremitting violence, exploitation, and rape.[94] Charcot worked with them, as his students witnessed, to attend to the depth of pain – physical, emotional, and psychological – that these women were experiencing. Deeply committed to changing their care and increasing their status and educating society, Charcot "restored the dignity" of women who were suffering from hysteria by utilizing his power and privilege, indeed the "weight of his authority", advocating that the hysterical phenomenon was, in fact, genuine and deserving of objectivity and compassion.[95] Despite the evidence he presented, it would be another 155 years before the 'Me Too' movement in which women collectively had their voices heard.[96]

Yet, it was Charcot's student, Pierre Janet, who wrote the first scientific book detailing traumatic stress; *L'automatisme psychologique.*[97] Janet is credited with positioning the issue of memory as it relates to trauma in the center of the conversation of treatment and reactivity. "Trauma is held in procedural memory – in automatic actions and reactions, sensations and attitudes, and that trauma is replayed and reenacted as visceral sensations (anxiety and panic), body movements, or visual images (nightmares and

---

93. Peter A. Levine Ph.D., *Trauma and Memory* (Berkeley, California: North Atlantic Books, 2015). xi

94. Judith Herman, M. D., *Trauma and Recovery* (New York, New York: Basic Books, 1997), 10.

95. Herman, M. D., 11.

96. "MeToo Movement," in *Wikipedia*, October 5, 2023, https://en.wikipedia.org/w/index.php?title=MeToo_movement&oldid=1178664664.

97. Levine Ph.D., *Trauma and Memory*.

flashbacks)."[98] Thus, TP are "attached to an insurmountable obstacle" as when they experience reminders of their trauma, they react in ways that are the manifestations of their body and soul as it is attuned for survival.[99] Though their reactions and behavior may be at odds with or seemingly out of place in the context and with their peers, within their body and understanding, their behavior makes sense. For instance, someone who jumps and hides when a door is slammed or shuts down completely when they hear a baby crying. Janet noted that "as long as people are unable to integrate the memories of the trauma, fragments of the experience keep returning as intense emotions, images, bodily sensations, and as irrelevant behaviors."[100]

While Charcot and Janet documented the effects and characteristic symptoms, Freud sought the etiology of 'hysteria' which led him to uncover traumatic events. Through his patients, Freud uncovered major traumatic events of childhood that were concealed beneath the more recent, often deemed relatively trivial, experiences that had triggered the onset of hysterical symptoms. In 1893 Freud wrote *The Etiology of Hysteria* and noted,

> The memory of the trauma acts like a foreign body which long after its entry must be regarded as an agent that is still at work. The memories which have become the determinants of hysterical phenomena persist for a long time with astonishing freshness and with the whole of their affective coloring. At first sight it seems extraordinary that events experienced so long ago should continue to operate so intensely – that their recollection should not be liable to

---

98. Levine Ph.D.
99. Janet 1919, VDK lecture 8/8/2022
100. L'automatisme psychologique, 1889, VDK lecture 8/8/22)

the wearing away process to which, after all, we see all our memories succumb.[101]

Working with his colleague, Josef Breuer, *The Mechanisms of Hysterical Phenomena* was also written in 1893 regarding traumatic memories. "We must, however, mention another remarkable fact, namely... that these memories, unlike the memories of the rest of their lives, are not at the patient's disposal. On the contrary, these experiences are completely absent from the patient's memory when they are in a normal psychical state or are only present in a highly summary form." These observations were foundational to the continued seeking and understanding of what we now know as the neurobiology of the brain. Yet, however crucial, significant, and fundamental these examinations and studies were, they were only explaining and/or addressing the effects and issues that women were experiencing but not examining the underlying etiology.

By 1896 Freud believed he had found the source. In a report on eighteen case studies, entitled *The Aetiology of Hysteria*, he made a dramatic claim: "I therefore put forward the thesis that at the bottom of every case of hysteria there are *one or more occurrences of premature sexual experience*, occurrences which belong to the earliest years of childhood, but which can be reproduced through the work of psycho-analysis in spite of the intervening decades. I believe that this is an important finding, the discovery of a caput Nili in neuropathology.[102]

This discovery/analysis, which would prove true in the coming centuries, was rejected by Freud's colleagues and contemporaries. To accept it would be to admit that there was widespread harm, "perverted acts against children", and that it was endemic. Freud

---

101. VDK Lecture 8/8/22
102. Herman, M. D., *Trauma and Recovery*, 1997, 13.

became "troubled by the radical social implications of his hypothesis" which, if true, would expediently erase lines of class and create an equality of dysfunction among all families; including the proletariat and those in power.[103] Despite the factuality of his work, "Freud's discovery could not gain acceptance in the absence of a political and social context that would support the investigation of hysteria, wherever it might lead."[104] Subsequently, Freud was shunned and recanted his work. For a traumatized person, this may be yet another abandonment. Freud had identified the issues of pain within them and there had suddenly come to be a tiny window of hope in telling the stories that had caused such mental and emotional pain only to be informed that this couldn't be the case because people didn't want their dirty laundry aired.

Turning from his research and analysis which pointed to sexual abuse as the traumatic event, Freud proposed the Oedipal complex to then explain the issues of psychosexual development. It remains critical to an understanding of trauma to acknowledge the depth of influence that Freud's Oedipal complex theory had and continues to impact the understanding of sexual abuse and the treatment of those socialized as women. The concept is that the development of "children's psyche is shaped as they grow to sexually desire a parent of different sex and competitively revile a parent of the same sex."[105] Yet, as this is culturally taboo, children then obscure their desire and replace it with fantasy which then, in Freud's theory, becomes more harmful to one's psyche than actual abuse. Thus, the fantasy influences the relationship to history; was it fantasy or actuality? Freud believed that the reality of history (abuse, incest, rape) was "not as likely to be the cause of trauma as

---

103. Herman, M. D., *Trauma and Recovery*, 1997, 14.
104. Herman, M. D., 18.
105. O'Donnell and Cross, *Feminist Trauma Theologies*, 51.

one's intrapsychic conflict. The child's simultaneous desire for her father and disgust with herself for desiring her father is taken to be the root of hysterical symptoms. A hysterical patient's suffering, in other words, is no longer conceived as a response to external, inter-subjective experience. It is taken to be self-inflicted."[106] This new theory stands in stark opposition to his previous ones. Recognizing Freud's theories as the prevalent historical basis of current psychotherapy, regardless of whether one continues to ascribe to such thought, it is strikingly apparent that women's experiences were to be questioned, not believed, and to be dismissed as 'all in one's head'.

After Freud's recantation, it was decades before psychology moved forward and truly invested in the research, care, and under-standing of trauma outside of the trauma experienced in war. It was in the early 20th century that the First World War brought psychological trauma to public awareness as something beyond hysteria and/or a women's issue. However, as with the contention of hysteria, the 'moral character of the patient' was once again a central question.[107] Herman shares this window into the under-standing of trauma at that time, "The soldier who developed a traumatic neurosis was at best a constitutionally inferior human being, at worst a malingerer and a coward. Medical writers of the period described these patients as "moral invalids."[108] There were those who advocated on behalf of the soldiers, "progressive medical authorities", that asserted "combat neurosis was a bona fide psychiatric condition that could occur in soldiers of high moral character."[109] However, as we see even today, it is easier to blame the victim than change the circumstances that create conditions for abuse, terror, and violence including, for instance, the trauma

---

106. O'Donnell and Cross, 51.
107. Herman, M. D., *Trauma and Recovery*, 1997, 21.
108. ibid
109. ibid

of natural disasters and the unwillingness of much of the population to acknowledge climate change.

As World War II once again brought trauma to the forefront, a handful of psychiatrists and psychologists sought to understand, identify, and treat those experiencing trauma. Abram Kardiner published *The Traumatic Neuroses of War* in 1941, "a comprehensive clinical and theoretical study" from which he then went on to develop the outline of what we know as Post Traumatic Stress Disorder (PTSD) today. Despite this groundbreaking work, the focus was not on recovery or healing but on returning soldiers to duty. "Little attention was paid to the fate of these men once they returned to active duty, let alone after they returned home from the war. As long as they could function on a minimal level, they were thought to have recovered...The lasting effects of war trauma were once again forgotten."[110]

It was not until the height of the Vietnam War that the treatment of trauma began to take hold. "The moral legitimacy of the antiwar movement and the national experience of defeat in a discredited war had made it possible to recognize psychological trauma as a lasting and inevitable legacy of war."[111] Yet, as the effects of trauma were being discussed and addressed in military context, more than 75 years later the issue most affecting women, sexual violence, had not only continued to be ignored but, by some, were maligned and even considered beneficial. In 1974 Freedman and Kaplan's Comprehensive Textbook of Psychiatry stated that "incest is extremely rare and does not occur in more than 1 out of 1.1 million people." This authoritative textbook extolled the possible benefits of incest: "Such incestuous activity diminishes the subject's chance of psychosis and allows for a better

---

110. Herman, M. D., 26.
111. Herman, M. D., *Trauma and Recovery*, 1997, 28.

adjustment to the external world. The vast majority of them were none the worse for the experience."[112]

They continued, persisting, "There is little agreement about the role of father-daughter incest as a source of serious subsequent psychopathology. The father-daughter liaison satisfies instinctual drives in a setting where mutual alliance with an omnipotent adult condones the transgression... The act offers an opportunity to test in reality an infantile fantasy whose consequences are found to be gratifying and pleasurable.... such incestuous activity diminishes the subject's chance of psychosis and allows for a better adjustment to the external world. The vast majority were none the worse for the experience."[113] Clearly, the field of psychology was not in agreement regarding trauma and its impact. Not only were girls and young women at the mercy of those educated in this way but there were little protections for adult women regarding sexual assault. Consider that it was not until July 5, 1993, that "marital rape became a crime in all 50 states."[114]

As the women's movement gathered stamina, the stories of women and their experiences became increasingly at the forefront of discussion, acknowledgment, and research. The National Institute of Mental Health created a center for the research on rape in 1975. Unsurprisingly, "sexual assaults against women and children were shown to be pervasive and endemic in our culture."[115] Despite a new legitimacy, the work of establishing trauma recovery as necessary continues to this day. In the early

112. Bessell Van Der Kolk, M.D., *The Body Keeps the Score: Brain, Mind, and Body in the Healing of Trauma*, Reprint edition (New York, NY: Penguin Publishing Group, 2015), 190–91.
113. Bessell Van Der Kolk Lecture 8/8/22. Freedman, Kaplan, & Sadock's Comprehensive Textbook of Psychiatry, II. 1975
114. "Marital Rape: New Research and Directions," VAWnet.org, accessed August 7, 2024, https://vawnet.org/material/marital-rape-new-research-and-directions.
115. Herman, M. D., *Trauma and Recovery*, 1997, 30.

1980s, Diana Russell conducted an epidemiological survey which revealed that "one in four women had been raped and one in three women had been sexually abused in childhood."[116] Yet, in 2022, the numbers remain closely the same according to the CDC (Center for Disease Control and Prevention): "1 in 4 girls and 1 in 13 boys in the United States experience child sexual abuse."[117]

As will be discussed later, trauma isn't something that simply affects the traumatized person. Their behavior and experience impact all around them. The toll on first responders, clinicians, trauma specialists, and spiritual care providers as well as friends and family become evident in the rates of burnout and increasing need for pharmaceutical intervention. Simply noting the wait time to see a therapist or establish care with a psychiatric provider in your area speaks to the great need.[118] Moreover, the matter of epigenetics and the patterns of illness that are exposed in generational trauma will also be explored, bringing to light the need for traumatized persons to receive the care they deserve to recover.

Though the early research into trauma centered on the lives of women, it seems plausible that it didn't rise to the level of global consciousness within the psychiatric community because it was initially believed to *only* affect women who were already marginalized and were deemed as the weaker sex. Is it any wonder with textbooks espousing this information that the church would be

---

116. Herman, M. D., *Trauma and Recovery*, 1997, 37.

117. "Fast Facts: Preventing Child Sexual Abuse |Violence Prevention|Injury Center|CDC," June 9, 2022, https://www.cdc.gov/violenceprevention/childsexualabuse/fastfact.html.

118. "Lack of Access to Evidence-Based Mental Health Care Poses Grave Threat," American Medical Association, November 3, 2022, https://www.ama-assn.org/about/leadership/lack-access-evidence-based-mental-health-care-poses-grave-threat; "Study Reveals Lack of Access as Root Cause for Mental Health Crisis in America," National Council for Mental Wellbeing, accessed January 19, 2024, https://www.thenationalcouncil.org/news/lack-of-access-root-cause-mental-health-crisis-in-america/.

slow to engage, respond, and/or acknowledge the issue of child sex abuse or incest? Or that it would try to cover up the incidents? Men were basically given a pass for their behavior, especially if the victims were, 'no worse for the experience.'

Even in 2024, as a trauma survivor and expert with vast experience and knowledge in advocating for TP and explaining their experiences and needs, I still am often dismissed, ignored, or shamed for needing accommodations as it relates to my past trauma. Recently I required an MRI which included a weight bag being placed on my pelvis. Thus, lying flat, unable to move, in a small –basically enclosed space – was very activating of my body's memory and I could not endure the MRI without sedation. However, I was told, "But it's over. You are fine now." "You just need to remember you are okay or just tell your mind you'll be fine." "If you meditate, you will be able to move on." These statements were communicated to me by medical professionals (in 2024) assumedly with training in trauma-informed care. The idea that trauma is a bad day/experience and something that we can simply turn off or "get over" by controlling one's mind is pervasive. Not to mention the subtext often accompanying such positions, weak people can't move forward; strong ones can. My trauma history doesn't control me or stop me from living a full, healthy life. It does mean there are things I do (and need to do) differently to protect and respect my body, mind, and spirit.

Despite repeated documentation of the effects of trauma, we are only beginning to reach a critical mass of understanding the phenomenon/reality of the neurobiological effects. In 1980, for the first time, the characteristic syndrome of psychological trauma became a "real" diagnosis. In that year, the American Psychiatric Association included in its official manual of mental disorders a new category, called "post-traumatic stress disorder identified as an anxiety disorder resulting from an overwhelming and fragmenting experience, or multiple experiences, of violence."[119]

There are 'progressive medical authorities', who advocate for traumatized persons and the legitimacy of their experience, pain, and need for recovery. However, it remains today that it is easier to blame the victim and/or the abuser as a singular instance than to change the circumstances that created the conditions that allowed, instigated, and/or condoned abuse, terror, and violence. An example of this in terms of collective and, one could argue, chronic trauma, is the issue of climate change and the consistency of '100 year' floods, fires, hurricanes, tornados, etc. In the United States, we continue to raise money for the disaster rather than deal with the complicated issue of our behavior and the role of corporations which creates conditions that change weather patterns. Yet, despite FEMA having noted that they are running out of money to address the crisis after it happened, there are no sweeping changes to address these traumatic events.[120]

Types of Trauma

The word 'trauma' encompasses a vast network of experiences that range from those of an individual to the collective world. Regardless of the source of the trauma, traumatized persons tend to experience similar reactions within their bodies. Therefore, understanding the wider implications of the types of trauma and their potential respective impacts and intersections is significant for the ability to develop programs and skilled responses, and to provide support for TP in recovery.

---

119. Herman, M. D., *Trauma and Recovery*, 1997, 28.
120. Tony Romm, "FEMA Delays $2.8 Billion in Disaster Aid to Keep from Running out of Money," *Washington Post*, September 28, 2023, https://www.washingtonpost.com/business/2023/09/27/government-shutdown-fema-disaster-aid-delays/.

There are three main types of trauma: acute, chronic, and complex with a myriad of subtypes and specificity.

Acute trauma results from a single incident. Examples include natural disasters, accidents, and physical violence (being attacked or mugged *e.g.*). It must be noted and understood that one traumatic incident has the power to completely alter the life of an individual. I have a friend, Emily, who was in a car accident when she was four. Her grandmother was taking her out for lunch when they were hit by a drunk driver. Emily appeared badly injured though it was due to many lacerations that required numerous stitches. She healed quickly after a brief hospital stay. Despite the reality that she was okay and would experience no continuing or long-term issues, her grandmother was so traumatized by the experience, that she never drove again. This is acute trauma.

Chronic trauma is repeated and/or prolonged exposure to dangerous and stressful events such as domestic violence, war, homelessness, chronic illness, and neglect. (This is not an exhaustive list.) Moreover, while emotional neglect and abuse are underreported and do not carry outward visible scars, they are no less damaging; the unseen is not less traumatic. When persons experience repeated exposure to perceived life-threatening events and/or interactions, "the chronic response is often associated with significant impairment and comorbidity."[121]

Two forms of chronic trauma that are helpful to understand; emotional domestic abuse and coercive control. Emotional domestic abuse is used to demean, manipulate, humiliate, and intimidate a person in order to disempower and exert control over them. Despite the lack of physical evidence, the effects of this trauma are long-ranging as this is a constant assault and erosion of one's self-esteem and self-worth with consequences that often include the creation of a psychological dependency on the abuser.

---

121. Feriante and Sharma, "Acute and Chronic Mental Health Trauma."

While emotional domestic abuse is often between romantic partners, it may occur within any intimate relationship including friends, family, and co-workers.

Coercive control "represents the routine patterning of life in a permanently abusive direction; the insinuation of abuse into the everyday fabric of living in a way that incorporates victims' agency in acting and willing counter to their own flourishing."[122] As one works to avoid expected consequences of shaming, blaming, dominating, fear, dependency, and/or exploitation, TP modify their behavior to conform to the exacting demands of the controller. For TP who have endured coercive control, the complete lack of agency has metamorphosed into an existence lacking in authenticity, power, or choice. "Coercive control need not be violent. Neither is it the episodic, incidental *interruption* of everyday normality; it *is* normality."[123] Consequences of coercive control include constant submission, lack of autonomy, the eradication of one's own needs, and the avoidance of affirmation. Finally, coercive control is also known as emotional domestic abuse.

Complex (developmental) trauma is repeated exposure to *varied and multiple* traumatic events of an invasive, interpersonal nature that cause severe distress or fear such as sexual abuse, torture, and chronic abandonment. This type of trauma is distinguished from chronic trauma as it is experienced during the critical developmental stages in childhood and adolescence, thereby disrupting one's emotional, cognitive, and social development and the formation of a sense of self. Complex trauma results in severe injuring to emotional and cognitive reasoning which causes great distress to the Authentic Self. As these events often occur with a caregiver upon whom the child is forced to rely as a primary

---

122. O'Donnell and Cross, *Feminist Trauma Theologies*, 81.
123. O'Donnell and Cross, 81.

source of safety and stability, attachment and trust issues originate as the child has not experienced (or had limited access to) appropriately responsive individuals and healthy relationships. Thus, the effects of these experiences, which are egregious and pervasive, are wide-reaching. Complex trauma has long-term aftereffects on the physical, emotional, cognitive, and spiritual health in adulthood, as well as having economic consequences, and "current data suggest that childhood trauma leads to worse outcomes than trauma experienced in adulthood."[124]

When an acute or chronic trauma occurs in adulthood, there may be inner resources available to assist in recovery. If one has a 'good-enough' childhood or what could be noted as a 'physiologically unharmed' childhood, then as adults, they have a foundation of safety, stability, and inner certitude which can be instrumental in dealing with and healing from traumatic injury. Typically, such people have a stronger support system than those who experienced complex trauma. Those with "good-enough" childhoods have more accessibility to their Authentic Self which can assist and guide in recovery.

Within the three main categories of trauma are specific types of trauma that are significant for their impact on individuals, communities, and the world.

"Historical trauma is multigenerational trauma experienced by a specific cultural, racial, or ethnic group."[125] This cumulative trauma that affects generations is found in systemically oppressed persons who have endured such atrocities as slavery, the violent colonization of Native Americans, the Holocaust, genocide, and forced migration. Because trauma is passed both biologically and epigenetically, "descendants who have not directly experienced a

---

124. Feriante and Sharma.
125. "Historical Trauma," accessed January 3, 2023, https://www.acf.hhs.gov/trauma-toolkit/trauma-concept.

traumatic event can exhibit the signs and symptoms of traumatic injury, such as depression, fixation on trauma, low self-esteem, anger, and self-destructive behavior."[126] Moreover, "current life-span trauma, superimposed upon a traumatic ancestral past creates additional adversity."[127] People of color who experience trauma in addition to their historical trauma must rely on systems of services and support from institutions, communities, and individuals who have been the oppressor and perpetrator and are subsequently increasingly challenged to believe or trust that these systems could be safe enough to support them. Subsequently, they may choose to not seek justice, redress, or treatment.[128]

Collective trauma refers to catastrophic events experienced by a group of people who may or may not be of the same cultural, ethnic, racial, or familial group. These events affect the foundation of the community, city, or country in which they occur and can impact people around the world. Examples of collective trauma include terrorist attacks, mass shootings, pandemics, war, economic crashes, natural disasters, nuclear disasters, and violent political revolutions. Collective trauma is furthermore represented in the collective memory of the group and "is different from individual memory because collective memory persists beyond the lives of the direct survivors of the events and is remembered by group members that may be far removed from the traumatic events in time and space."[129] The subsequent generations of trauma survivors having never witnessed the actual events, reconstruct the

---

126. ibid

127. ibid

128. A. L. Roberts et al., "Race/Ethnic Differences in Exposure to Traumatic Events, Development of Post-Traumatic Stress Disorder, and Treatment-Seeking for Post-Traumatic Stress Disorder in the United States," *Psychological Medicine* 41, no. 1 (January 2011): 71–83, https://doi.org/10.1017/S0033291710000401.

129. Gilad Hirschberger, "Collective Trauma and the Social Construction of Meaning," *Frontiers in Psychology* 9 (August 10, 2018): 1441, https://doi.org/10.3389/fpsyg.2018.01441.

trauma in an attempt to make sense of it and thus may recall and experience it differently than the direct survivors. Therefore, the construction of these past events may take different shapes and forms from generation to generation and one's personal experience may create dissonance and complicate relationships and recovery.[130]

Kai Erickson describes well the effects of collective trauma in his writing about the Buffalo Creek catastrophe.[131] He says of collective trauma:

> It is a "blow to the basic tissues of social life that damages the bonds attaching people together and impairs the prevailing sense of communality. The collective trauma works its way slowly and even insidiously into the aware-ness of those who suffer from it, so it does not have the quality of suddenness normally associated with "trauma." But it is a form of shock all the same, a gradual realization that the community no longer exists as an effective source of support and that an important part of the self has disap-peared… "I" continue to exist, though damaged and maybe even permanently changed. "You" continue to exist, though distant and hard to relate to. But "we" no longer exist as a connected pair or as linked cells in a larger communal body.[132]

---

130. Hirschberger.

131. On the morning of February 26, 1972, in Logan county, West Virginia, three coal slurry dams failed and a tidal wave of approximately 132 million gallons of black waste water came crashing through 16 towns killing 125 people. Over 4,000 were left homeless and 507 houses destroyed. For more information, visit: https://daily.jstor.org/the-tragedy-at-buffalo-creek/ or read Kai Erikson's book, *Everything in Its Path: Destruction of Community in the Buffalo Creek Flood.*

132. Cathy Caruth, ed., *Trauma: Explorations in Memory* (Baltimore: John Hopkins University Press, 1995), 187.

As trauma is understood as an inherently isolating experience, when a community experiences collective trauma, not only is it isolating for the individual but the usual communal spaces that provide opportunities for engagement, healing, stabilization, and skill building no longer exist. Therefore, recovery is challenging, and help from outside the community must be sought.

Transgenerational/intergenerational trauma is similar to historical trauma; however, transgenerational trauma affects a single family across generations versus an entire or specific cultural group. Examples include - extreme poverty, domestic abuse, child abuse and neglect, estrangement, addiction, refugees, and war. The collective suffering is passed biologically, environmentally, epigenetically, and socially. Effects of untreated transgenerational trauma include the passing of trauma responses through the attachment bond between parents and children as well as unchallenged/unhealed beliefs and worldviews.

Vicarious trauma was a term coined by McCann and Pearlman that was initially used to describe the effect of working with traumatized clients and the subsequent effects on the mental health of therapists.[133] Previously, the phenomenon was referred to as secondary traumatic stress, as noted by Dr. Charles Figley (1982).[134] The concept has expanded beyond the originating context to be understood as a traumatic injury resulting from indirect exposure to a traumatic event including witnessing the event, listening to a first-hand narrative, and/or experiencing audio or visual recordings. Though it is often associated with those in the

---

133. I. Lisa McCann and Laurie Anne Pearlman, "Vicarious Traumatization: A Framework for Understanding the Psychological Effects of Working with Victims," *Journal of Traumatic Stress* 3, no. 1 (January 1, 1990): 131–49, https://doi.org/10.1007/bf00975140.

134. Charles Figley and Maryann Abendroth, "Vicarious Trauma and the Therapeutic Relationship" (Researchgate, 2013), https://www.researchgate.net/publication/259609739.

helping professions (first responders, doctors, nurses, therapists *e.g.*) vicarious or secondary trauma may develop in any individual. Journalists, friends, and family members directly supporting TP or documenting their experiences are susceptible to vicarious trauma.

Assessments

There are many assessments available that attempt to quantify the effects of trauma on an individual. These often are used to assist in determining therapeutic interventions as well as to measure for suicidality and safety. One of the most well-known trauma assessments does not provide information on currently experienced effects and/or symptomology. Known as ACEs, the Adverse Childhood Experiences score was a groundbreaking study created by Kaiser Permanente in the early 1990s to study the effects of adverse childhood experiences on health and social well-being as it relates to public health issues. Ten questions are posited regarding one's life experiences before age 18 concerning factors of abuse, household challenges, and neglect.[135] It is used as a risk assessment tool: the higher the ACE score, the increased possibility that one may experience chronic health issues, disease, and early mortality.[136]

What has been discovered in this research is that someone who has experienced 4 or more ACEs has an increased risk of 1.6-fold of developing diabetes, and the risk doubles for cancer and heart disease, quadruples for chronic lung disease, and increases the risk of developing autoimmune diseases. Individuals were seven times more likely to be alcoholic as well as suffer from other

---

135. "About the CDC-Kaiser ACE Study |Violence Prevention|Injury Center|CDC," March 17, 2022, https://www.cdc.gov/violenceprevention/aces/about.html.
136. Dr. Robert Anda, "Why Prevention Matters" (Chicago IL: Doris Duke Charitable Foundation, n.d.).

chronic mental and physical illnesses.[137] Subsequently, a higher ACE score corresponds with chronic depression in adulthood.

For those with an ACE score of four or more, its prevalence is 66 percent in women and 35 percent in men, compared with an overall rate of 12 percent in those with an ACE score of zero. Moreover, self-acknowledged suicide attempts rise exponentially with ACE scores. From a score of zero to a score of six there is about a 5000 percent increased likelihood of suicide attempts. Injection drug use increased exponentially: for those with an ACE score of six or more, the likelihood of IV drug use was 4600 percent greater than in those with a score of zero.[138]

The ACE study exposed that the "gravest and most costly public health issue in the United States is child abuse."[139] The economic costs of higher ACE scores include estimations that annually, traumatic injury costs "as high as $28 billion for chronic back pain for US businesses, $30 - $44 billion for depression and related absenteeism, reduced productivity, and medical expenses, and $246 billion for chemical dependency in the workforce" for those who have experienced trauma.[140] Robert Anda, co-principal and co-author of the ACE study calculated that its overall costs exceeded those of cancer or heart disease and that eradicating child abuse in America would reduce the overall rate of depression by more than half, alcoholism by two-thirds, and suicide, IV drug

137. Veronique Mead, "Adverse Childhood Experiences Increase Risk for Chronic Diseases - It's Not Psychological," PACEsConnection, July 18, 2019, https://www.pacesconnection.com/blog/adverse-childhood-experiences-increase-risk-for-chronic-diseases-it-s-not-psychological.
138. Bessell Van Der Kolk, M.D., *The Body Keeps the Score: Brain, Mind, and Body in the Healing of Trauma*, Reprint edition (New York, NY: Penguin Publishing Group, 2015), 148.
139. Van Der Kolk, M.D., 150.
140. Robert Anda, MD, MS, "The Health and Social Impact of Growing Up with Adverse Childhood Experiences: The Human and Economic Costs of the Status Quo" (Trauma Informed Oregon, n.d.).

use, and domestic violence by three-quarters. It would also have a dramatic effect on workplace performance and vastly decrease the need for incarceration."[141]

The discussion of ACEs thus far is predicated on the assumption that a person is white. Children of color are enduring adverse childhood experiences within the generational embodiment of racial and cultural oppression as well as the direct exposure of macro and micro-level aggressions including structural racism and the consistent disempowerment and disenfranchisement of their being. Daily, children of color experience the assumptions of criminality, meritocracy, lack of representation/environmental microaggressions, as well as the racist claims of color blindness and the ascription of a lack of intelligence. To utilize the ACE's study, one must acknowledge the inherent trauma endured before any additional traumatic events. "If it is not racially just, it is not trauma-informed."[142]

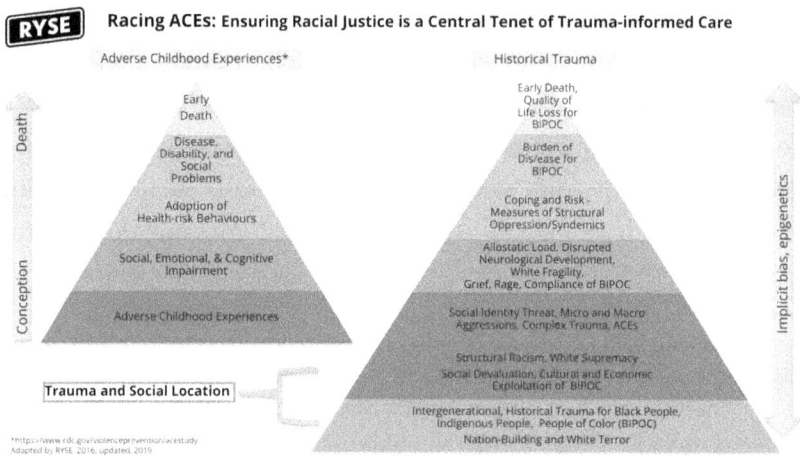

Used with permission RYSE copyright 2023

141. Van Der Kolk, M.D., *The Body Keeps the Score*, 2015, 150.
142. Jana Pressley Psy.D., "The Complexity of Adaptation to Trauma" (Traumatic Stress Certification, Brookline, MA, 2022).

Healing & Recovery

THE HEALING AND RECOVERY PHASE, like all phases of recovery, must be predicated on education, and co-created narrative, and include the provisions of space, time, and necessary accommodations for the traumatized person. Working with, supporting, encouraging, and engaging with TP are not scripted interactions. These are human beings who present in different ways, need a variety of resources, and deserve the utmost care and respect. Having already suffered events so great as to be called trauma and enduring the rewiring of the brain for survival, traumatized persons should not be placed in positions in which retraumatization may occur. Though there are no guarantees in a relationship, every effort must be made to be educated and prepared for the engagement with TP to avoid causing – directly or indirectly – further harm.

If in reading this one feels daunted by the task ahead of them, imagine how a TP must feel trying to share their story or trust someone to ascertain needed resources. What must it be like to be in a body that may feel broken or worse? In this section, you will come to learn more about the neurobiological effects of trauma in the hopes that those engaging with them will have the patience, compassion, and care to create environments in which TP may choose to share their experiences and pursue their healing.

At this point in recovery, the relationship between the witness/journeyer and the TP begins to transition from the immediacy of care to addressing, encouraging, and supporting their long-term needs and goals. This is grueling and difficult work; dismantling and reassembling the mental framework that has been erected by trauma. As TP begin to embody new ways of being, practice new thought patterns, and interact with others, they may desire someone to talk with, who has witnessed their journey thus far and understands – as much as anyone could outside of personal experience – the challenges facing them. For some TP, this is also a time in which relationships may need to change and/or possibly end.

To ponder why some relationships might need to change or even end, I invite you to meet Susan. She is a 55-year-old woman who was sexually assaulted in her teens and went on to have multiple marriages in which she was treated poorly. Her third spouse died by suicide after stalking and tormenting her; telling her that she was the reason this person had to end their life – it was her fault. Susan carried the hallmarks of sexual trauma; feelings of worthlessness, fear, distrust, and the concept that it was her responsibility to please others. When seeking support from her pastor, she was told that God has a plan for her life and that these experiences are opportunities to make her stronger in her faith. To be clear, trauma is not an opportunity, it is a neurobiological wound that needs tending.

However, as Susan engaged in her recovery and experienced healing, not everyone was supportive. She realized that there were people in her life who were used to her being a "victim" or "needy" – labels adhered to her due to the perceptions of those who had not endured trauma. When Susan didn't need to seek shelter at a moment's notice to hide from her former spouse/stalker, or when she no longer needed people to emotionally support her in the same way, some people in her life began to feel unneeded and instead of celebrating Susan's growth and independence, were focused on their own needs of affirmation through service. This did not support Susan and was a stumbling block for her as instead of Susan feeling empowered by her healing, she felt guilty for letting people down. Each person is responsible for their own emotions. If someone is engaging with TP to feel needed and/or important, they will be unable to sufficiently care for and journey with the TP as they heal. The greatest love for others is to want them to be happy and healthy, not for one's own attachment and/or emotional needs to be filled.

Neurobiology

The neurobiological explanations provided do not contain the totality of the specific brain functions related to trauma. The information presented here is to be understood in terms of the brain process most affected by traumatic experiences in order to provide education and engender compassion by recognizing and acknowledging that people's behavior makes sense. As traumatic injury is a physiological response, a foundational understanding of neurobiology is necessary to recognize and attempt to assimilate the experiences of the traumatized person. Finally, neurobiology (as well as medicine in general, psychology, and psychiatry) is a constantly evolving field, with researchers compiling and analyzing more information daily. Thus, the data and research provided herein is the current understanding as of spring 2024.

The brain is an amazing, mysterious structure that protects, animates, and enables living beings. When traumatized people are provided with education on how the brain works, they often respond with awe and a multitude of 'aha' moments. Suddenly, the thoughts, behaviors, and emotions that seem out of control, chaotic, harmful, maddening, or frustrating are transformed into experiences that begin to take shape as puzzle pieces that can consequently be placed and make sense. Neurobiological education doesn't suddenly resolve painful emotions or experiences or render therapy as unneeded or unmerited. However, what occurs is a sliver of hope through which a TP can begin to access and engage in self-compassion and understanding which then fuels the cognitive and emotional energy tank for the grueling work of recovery.[1]

The structure of the brain can be divided into three parts: the forebrain, the midbrain, and the hindbrain.[2] The forebrain contains the cerebral cortex comprised of 4 lobes – frontal, temporal, parietal, and occipital – the gray matter seen when looking at a picture of a brain. It is responsible for thinking and reasoning, judgment, coordinating movement, and problem-solving. The frontal lobes receive and integrate information and attach meaning to it and they are the key structures for abstract thought as well as language. Situated within them are a multitude of brain structures including Broca's area, the anterior cingulate cortex, medial prefrontal cortex, and the dorsolateral prefrontal cortex.[3]

The prefrontal cortex is the processing center for understanding one's surroundings by comparing/cataloging items to past

---

1. Ashutosh Atri and Manoj Sharma, "Psychoeducation: Implications for the Profession of Health Education," *California Journal of Health Promotion* 5, no. 4 (2007): 32–39; Narendra Kumar Singh et al., "Psychoeducation: A Measure to Strengthen Psychiatric Treatment," *Delhi Psychiatry Journal* 14, no. 1 (April 2011): 33–39.

2. Patrick R. Steffen, Dawson Hedges, and Rebekka Matheson, "The Brain Is Adaptive Not Triune: How the Brain Responds to Threat, Challenge, and Change," *Frontiers in Psychiatry* 13 (April 1, 2022), https://doi.org/10.3389/fpsyt.2022.802606.

3. Broca's area was discovered in 1861 by French surgeon Paul Broca and is noted as the area of the brain which controls speech function.

experiences. Understanding that "nothing lasts forever" is the work of the dorsolateral prefrontal cortex, the timekeeper. It tells the brain that experiences are finite and helps one to endure. For TP the dorsolateral prefrontal cortex is offline and thus the traumatic event feels timeless/continuous. "Knowing that whatever is happening is finite and will sooner or later come to an end makes most experiences tolerable. The opposite is also true – situations become intolerable if they feel interminable."[4]

The medial prefrontal cortex (MPFC) provides an aerial view of events and experiences allowing one to observe from above and works in conjunction with the amygdala to keep us safe.[5] When the balance between the amygdala and MPFC is anomalous, the ability to observe and assess information before reacting is greatly decreased and thus, the "inhibitory capacities of the frontal lobe break down."[6] The ventral prefrontal cortex controls regulation, self-awareness, and inhibition/impulse control.

The midbrain is an extremely small part of the brain primarily responsible for the constriction and dilation of the eye and has an essential role in sensory and motor control. Contained in the midbrain is a superhighway that transmits the passage of impulses from the nervous system between the brain and the spinal cord through ascending and descending pathways. Finally, the hindbrain includes the upper part of the spinal cord, the brain stem, and the cerebellum. The body's vital functions – respiration and heart rate – are controlled by the hindbrain.

Deep within the forebrain are the structures that makeup

4. Van Der Kolk, M.D., *The Body Keeps the Score*, 2015, 69.
5. Van Der Kolk, M.D., 62.
6. Van Der Kolk, M.D., 63.

what has been traditionally referenced as the limbic system.[7,8] Bessel Van Der Kolk, trauma expert, termed these affected structures the "emotional brain" which includes the amygdala, hippocampus, thalamus, and hypothalamus.[9,10] These components map the world one inhabits, identifying what feels safe; the things and geography surrounding an individual, discerning what is important versus not important, and scary versus not scary. However, the limbic system is not simply the components: rather, it is a system of intricate communication for information distribution and processing participation for continued existence. It is the unconscious part of the brain over which one has very little control and where trauma primarily resides. To understand how these structures work within the brain and interface with one another, each must be examined individually.

---

7. Current researchers consider it an outdated term as there is not full consensus on the neuroanatomical identification; which structures of the brain should be included. For purposes of ease of information and communication, I will be using the term limbic system as naming all structures constantly is cumbersome for reading.

8. Marcelo R. Roxo et al., "The Limbic System Conception and Its Historical Evolution," *The Scientific World Journal* 11 (December 8, 2011): 2428–41, https://doi.org/10.1100/2011/157150.

9. Van Der Kolk, M.D., *The Body Keeps the Score*, 2015, 57.

10. For more information on the limbic system see Edmund T. Rolls, "Limbic Systems for Emotion and for Memory, but No Single Limbic System," *Cortex*, Special issue: The clinical anatomy of the limbic lobe and connected structures, 62 (January 1, 2015): 119–57, https://doi.org/10.1016/j.cortex.2013.12.005; J. Douglas Bremner, "Traumatic Stress: Effects on the Brain," *Dialogues in Clinical Neuroscience* 8, no. 4 (December 2006): 445–61; Tyler J. Torrico and Sara Abdijadid, "Neuroanatomy, Limbic System," in *StatPearls* (Treasure Island (FL): StatPearls Publishing, 2023), http://www.ncbi.nlm.nih.gov/books/NBK538491/; "Limbic System | Description, Components, Function, History of Study, & Facts | Britannica," December 15, 2023, https://www.britannica.com/science/limbic-system.

The Limbic System

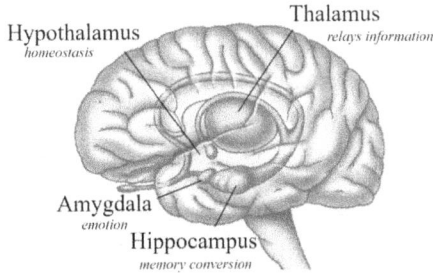

Van Der Kolk, Bessell. 2023

The amygdala is the 'threat detection' center of the body and is best known for the fight/flight/freeze response. It interprets incoming information - discerning if it is relevant for survival. It is most sensitive to danger. Subsequent behavior based upon interpretation is initiated by the amygdala which sends messages to the hypothalamus and brain stem that controls the activation of stress hormones and the autonomic nervous system (ANS). "Because the amygdala processes the information it receives from the thalamus faster than the frontal lobes do, it decides whether incoming information is a threat to survival even before one is consciously aware of danger. By the time a person realizes what is happening, their body may already be on the move."[11] The amygdala is generally hyperfunctional in traumatized persons and is the driving force of PTSD.[12]

Considered the sensory gatekeeper, the thalamus is located near the center of the brain. It receives all sensory information from the surrounding environment, except for smell, and relays

---

11. Van Der Kolk, M.D., *The Body Keeps the Score*, 2015, 61.
12. David M. Diamond and Phillip R. Zoladz, "Dysfunctional or Hyperfunctional? The Amygdala in Posttraumatic Stress Disorder Is the Bull in the Evolutionary China Shop," *Journal of Neuroscience Research* 94 (October 29, 2015): 437–44.

the information to the limbic system and the cerebral cortex through nerve fibers. Trauma completely overwhelms the thalamus and information is not adequately processed and delivered. This glitch in information transmission and processing causes sensations to be recorded in fragments and not situated within time and space which prevents them from being recalled as an integrated whole event. The thalamus is what helps one "distinguish between sensory information that is relevant and information we can safely ignore."[13] If all information is deemed as relevant as with TP, it can cause hyperactivity and overactivation of the limbic system. In addition to real-time/current bodily sensations, when a TP reexperiences a traumatic event whether through thinking, memories, or flashbacks, the somatic experience is activated here.

The hippocampus is the memory system. "It relates new input to past experiences" and is often blocked out in TP.[14] Due to the overwhelming nature of trauma, the information from a memory is not coded correctly and when attempting to recall the event, one may not be able to remember important details. TP often endure frustration, and even fear, when unable to recall details.

Situated directly above the brain stem is the hypothalamus which is responsible for one's housekeeping – sleeping, appetite, regulation of breathing, and heartbeat. Coordinating with the brain stem the hypothalamus maintains the body's homeostasis and directly influences the autonomic nervous system (ANS). "The hypothalamus is critical in initiating hormonal responses to stressful stimuli via the hypothalamic-pituitary-adrenal (HPA) axis."[15] For TP, the brain actuates survival mode by shutting down

13. Van Der Kolk, M.D., *The Body Keeps the Score*, 2015, 70.
14. Van Der Kolk, M.D., 60.
15. Payman Raise-Abdullahi et al., "Hypothalamus and Post-Traumatic Stress Disorder: A Review," *Brain Sciences* 13, no. 7 (June 29, 2023): 1010, https://doi.org/10.3390/brainsci13071010.

all non-essential body and mind processes putting the ANS in 'fight or flight' mode as opposed to 'rest and digest.'[16]

The above findings and information on the brain structures are not simply conjectures or hypotheses but are the result of years of research on the brain and the scientific ability to now visualize (via brain scans, *e.g.*) the differences between non-traumatized persons and those who have experienced trauma. Since the development of functional magnetic resonance imaging (fMRI) in 1990, researchers, neurologists, neurobiologists, psychiatrists, and psychologists have had access to the brain's functioning in previously unimaginable ways.[17] While fMRI has been utilized in all medical and psychological disciplines, the impact of trauma on the brain has been intensely studied, with a notable increase in literature in the last 8 years. A search on PubMed for fMRI and psychological trauma yielded 530 results from between 1992 and 2024 with 89% of the papers having been written in the last eight years. The findings have not only given credence to those suffering from

---

16. The sympathetic nervous system is activated in trauma and causes the 'fight or flight' response which is well-known. However, this means that the parasympathetic nervous system which enacts 'rest and digest' is shut down. Eating and digesting become an issue, sleep is disturbed, heart rate affected, sexual function is impacted. See page 97 for information on the Autonomic Nervous System

17. For further information see Maddalena Boccia et al., "Different Neural Modifications Underpin PTSD after Different Traumatic Events: An fMRI Meta-Analytic Study," *Brain Imaging and Behavior* 10, no. 1 (March 1, 2016): 226–37, https://doi.org/10.1007/s11682-015-9387-3; Federica Meconi et al., "EEG and fMRI Evidence for Autobiographical Memory Reactivation in Empathy," *Human Brain Mapping* 42, no. 14 (October 1, 2021): 4448–64, https://doi.org/10.1002/hbm.25557; Sachiyo Ozawa et al., "Synergistic Effects of Disgust and Anger on Amygdala Activation While Recalling Memories of Interpersonal Stress: An fMRI Study," *International Journal of Psychophysiology: Official Journal of the International Organization of Psychophysiology* 182 (December 2022): 39–46, https://doi.org/10.1016/j.ijpsycho.2022.09.008; Katherine C Hughes and Lisa M Shin, "Functional Neuroimaging Studies of Post-Traumatic Stress Disorder," *Expert Review of Neurotherapeutics* 11, no. 2 (February 2011): 275–85, https://doi.org/10.1586/ern.10.198.

PTSD by elucidating the structural and functional abnormalities and the pathophysiology of PTSD but have informed the treatment of trauma.[18]

Ontological Issues

Ontological questions — who am I, why am I here — are inescapable when dealing with trauma. Does being harmed change who I am? Am I me despite my scars or do my scars make me who I am? These questions exist in all persons, regardless of a faith tradition. What would be expected and assumed to be safe has been proven the opposite; one's world and understanding thereof has been shattered and TP have experienced the subsequent feelings of abandonment, confusion, and fear. Add to the existential angst the issue of why the trauma occurred and the stage is set for an ontological meltdown. How these questions are answered, notwithstanding any direct engagement with spirituality, plays a large part in the recovery of the TP. Nevertheless, how a traumatized person utilizes the relationship with a spiritual source, while seemingly demanding the unanswerable question of why, can be a powerful tool for recovery.

Shelly Rambo's foundational work, *"Resurrecting Wounds,"* deals eloquently with the issue of scars and the Western cultural understanding of healing. Does one need to bear no resemblance to a TP to be declared healed? Must the scars be covered over? Can one be whole while showing a wound? This question of wounding and wholeness is a critical question for TP who often

---

18. Yuval Neria, "Functional Neuroimaging in PTSD: From Discovery of Underlying Mechanisms to Addressing Diagnostic Heterogeneity," *American Journal of Psychiatry* 178, no. 2 (February 2021): 128–35, https://doi.org/10.1176/appi.ajp. 2020.20121727; Akira Kunimatsu et al., "MRI Findings in Posttraumatic Stress Disorder," *Journal of Magnetic Resonance Imaging: JMRI* 52, no. 2 (August 2020): 380–96, https://doi.org/10.1002/jmri.26929.

identify feeling broken; are they worth less than their fellow humans? What is the nature of their being as a wounded individual? While Rambo utilizes work by Jennings to discuss the issue of wounding in the context of race in the United States, I argue that the following applies to all trauma and TP interacting with Christianity: "Christian theology is produced by erasing wounds. It sanitizes and purifies."[19]

Take for instance the concept that everything happens for a reason. If the narrative of God is that "everything happens for a reason", the wound is erased as it is simply a part of the plan – such as the rising of the sun in the morning.[20] However, this reduces the victim to the target of an insidious plan to harm them. Yet, it is expected that the TP would simply move forward with this knowledge. For some Christians, not only does 'everything happen for a reason' but suffering is Christlike.[21] These theologies shape ontological understanding and the recovery from trauma. When I shared this manuscript with a friend and colleague, she wrote in the margins – is this meaning-making real? Can you provide stories?

Sadly, yes. I have many stories of people I have known and worked with who shaped their understanding of themselves by the framework that the trauma was 'planned' by God to bring one closer to God through suffering. Yet, as evidenced by their struggle to 'overcome' the trauma (rather than work through it to heal), these theologies were not supportive and inspiring but further mired down the TP in shame for their understandable and expected emotions of anger, sadness, inequity, and heartbreak that the trauma occurred. How can one heal, and does one even need

---

19. Rambo, Shelly. *Resurrecting Wounds*. Baylor University Press, 2017. P. 76
20. Eph 1:11, Lam 3:37, Job 37:13, Prov 16:4, Prov 16:33, Eccl 3:1
21. 1 Peter 4:1, 2 Cor 4:17, 1 Peter 2:19-21, Romans 5:3, 2 Tim 3:12, Col 1:24, James 1:12

to heal, if the trauma is a part of the plan and is to be used? If suffering is useful, why should it be quelled?

The understanding of ontology is critical for trauma work as in the research conducted for this work, 81% of those who identified as being traumatized noted that spirituality was meaningful for their recovery and 67% noted that the source of spiritual connection informs the way they think about their Authentic Self. Accordingly, spiritual care providers when invited to work with TP should encourage conversation and consider reflection on the disempowering of the perpetrator and the care of the Holy Mystery exploring it not as an arbiter of violence or as controlling and enacting the violence but as one who holds and witnesses the unfathomable, unspeakable, receiving that which is too deep for words. Ontological wounds require careful stitching as the connection to others and the self-compassion that comes with being rooted in a greater love or purpose may be a powerful tool in recovery.

To be clear, this is but a very high-level overview of ontological issues for entire books that could, and have been written on the subject as it pertains to trauma. My aim was not to address every eventuality and argue my theological standpoint but rather to encourage readers to examine *their* understanding, engagement, and theology of being and its relationship to trauma.

Effects of Trauma and Dysregulation

Trauma is not a one-size-fits-all experience or recovery. There are similar reactions and patterns and while the neurobiology of trauma helps us understand how the brain functions and processes information, the expressions of traumatic experiences, emotional pain and anger, and the grief that accompanies it are individual. If one is simply looking for a checklist of expected and/or possible behavior and how to interact with a person, one will be unable to do the work of providing trauma-informed care. At its core, it is creative and dedicated work that requires the co-creation of narratives, trust, and adaptability. Before providing support to TP directly, through programming, or in any other capacity, there must be a foundational understanding of the effects of trauma with which TP live. Because the actions of traumatized people may appear out of sync with the persons and culture around them, it is critical to remember that *"traumatized persons and their actions make sense - their behavior happens for a reason."*[22]

Although the behaviors of TP may be clinically labeled the same, they present and are experienced by others dissimilarly, having been uniquely developed and honed for survival in different environments. However, the behaviors are no longer necessary and thus have become impediments. Part of the work in recovery is to identify those behaviors and the activating moments and begin the psychological and somatic work to develop different, healthy, and currently appropriate responses. It is critical that traumatized persons not be shamed and/or embarrassed (either by self or others) for any behavior utilized for survival.

While adaptive behaviors may no longer be necessary, the mind and body accomplished an unimaginable feat of enduring despite staggering odds and crippling pain – emotionally, psychologically, spiritually, and/or physically. TP deserve compassion from others and themselves for the ways in which they had to survive – regardless of whether the behavior is what they would choose *now*.

Many physiological responses are automatic - once the brain detects danger, it alerts the amygdala and uses the preprogrammed response of fight/flight/freeze for survival. This system serves us well in situations of imminent danger such as house fires, encountering a rattlesnake, or rescuing a toddler before they touch a stove.

---

22. Pressley Psy.D., "The Complexity of Adaptation to Trauma."

One's responses happen so quickly that "by the time we are fully aware of our situation, our body may already be on the move."[23] However, when people have experienced a traumatic event, their bodies continue to produce stress chemicals long after the event has ended:

> Extensive neurophysiological studies have demonstrated abnormal reactivity in patients with PTSD based on physiological measures such as heart rate, skin conductance, facial electromyogram, and cortical electroencephalographic event-related potentials.[24]

This increased chemical level causes responses to stimuli to often be hyperreactive producing what is understood/experienced as dysregulation.

Dysregulation is the difficulty of controlling or inability to control one's emotions and reactions to internal or external stimuli and is often a sign of psychological distress. What makes the dysregulated behavior notable is that the emotions and reactions are deemed by others as disproportionate to the surrounding observable stimuli. Yet, dysregulation isn't only observed by others. TP are keenly aware of the behaviors of those surrounding them, noting how different they are, which causes them to feel dysregulated, often perceiving that the emotional, cognitive, and psychological homeostasis is akilter in their bodies. For many this only increases the internal emotional distress as they recognize their bodies and emotions are reacting, their cognition slowing or stunted yet they still may not understand why.

Every person experiences chaos and responds according to their perspicacity and cognitive and emotional framework.

---

23. Van Der Kolk, M.D., *The Body Keeps the Score*, 2015, 53.
24. Kunimatsu et al., "MRI Findings in Posttraumatic Stress Disorder."

Sometimes these responses and reactions are labeled as outbursts. Adults as well as children are subject to outbursts, but these behaviors tend to be overlooked if it is expected and/or age-appropriate, or if the behavior is within what is socially acceptable and/or personally tolerable. Such outbursts tend to come in many forms from anger and frustration to crying and lamenting, to complete overwhelm and shut down. Some may even appreciate the outburst as some adults can mask it in the form of particularly poignant sarcasm or humorous rambling diatribes. One only needs to look through a social media platform to note the numerous memes addressing overwhelm, overwork, or simply over 'it'.

During transitions such as changing jobs, purchasing a home, moving to a new apartment, dealing with a sick relative or friend, the death of a loved one, or simply the daily chaos of the dryer breaking, wet clothes, coffee spills, and transportation issues, people experience and exhibit a range of substantial emotions. The display of emotions during these experiences is usually understood and tolerated as the antagonist (event) is public/visible. However, when a traumatized person exhibits emotions and/or reactions, their antagonist is not visible; the trauma is stored in their bodies and the memory or incident is not provided to the person with whom they are engaging. None of the average chaos begins to compare to the level of internal pain and challenges the TP is experiencing – presenting them as hyperactive (over the top) or hypoactive (seemingly barely able to connect to their environment). Recall that trauma is not simply the event but the physiological reaction to the event. Consequently, the behavior of the TP is out-of-sync compared to those surrounding them which brings attention to their presence and their dysregulation.

Yet, just as some outbursts are more socially acceptable, some dysregulated behavior of traumatized persons is also experienced as or considered more acceptable and subsequently overlooked. For instance, over-functioning and perfectionism are often categorized as perseverance, pluck, or grit whereas the inability to work, engage in basic self-care (hygiene), or the numbing of pain through substance use/abuse – food, drugs, alcohol – i.e. under-functioning, is considered lazy, unmotivated, weak, and lacking perseverance.[25] These opposing characterizations are both of traumatized people, yet their dysregulation appears in stark contrast to one another. "It is sobering to realize that many of the personality traits we have come to believe *are us*, and perhaps even take pride in, actually bear the scars of where we lost connection to ourselves, way back when."[26] This is important as over-functioning and perfectionism etc. are traits praised in American society but are, nonetheless, often traits of deep pain, shame, and feelings of unworthiness.

Current culture praises overachievers and perfectionists and though these behaviors do not appear as necessarily harmful or dysregulated, they can be symptoms of trauma and equally as self-harming as other behaviors. Potentially, communities and individuals participate in reinforcing trauma narratives and creating more harm when they praise and exemplify those who are perfectionists and overachievers as pillars of society. This narrative often mirrors, in its expectations, abusive parents. The child who is beaten for a B+ and told they are stupid and worthless or who misses a spot on the table when wiping it off thus internalizes the requirement of perfection to have worth.

To be clear, over-functioning is not a healthy regulation. The definition of addiction "is a compulsive, chronic, physiological or psychological need for a habit-forming substance, behavior, or activity having harmful physical, psychological, or social effects

---

25. Overworking and overfunctioning are addictions akin to substance abuse though socially acceptable. https://www.theatlantic.com/health/archive/2017/02/do-some-trauma-survivors-cope-by-overworking/516540/
26. Maté and Maté, *The Myth of Normal: Trauma, Illness & Healing in a Toxic Culture*, 109.

and typically causing well-defined symptoms (such as anxiety, irritability, tremors, or nausea) upon withdrawal or abstinence."[27] Over-functioning is a physiological and psychological effort to avoid and/or numb the pain, impeding emotional and somatic responses, and can be as addictive as substance abuse. Furthermore, it is known that overworking causes health issues and elicits symptoms when stopped.[28] It is imperative to remember that not all behavior that is harmful appears as such.

Those who appear traumatized are often treated with disdain, especially when others who suffered similar experiences appear "fine". For those whose traumatic event(s) are known and yet they *still* appear fine, people make assumptions of resiliency and strength.[29] As Kate Bowler says, "I have still, somehow, clung to the idea that I am able to save myself. To my friends and family, I sugarcoat the truth with spiritual sounding assurances and good cheer."[30] Those who behave and cope like Bowler are more socially acceptable. Their pain is tolerable for those around them

27. "Definition of ADDICTION," December 8, 2023, https://www.merriam-webster.com/dictionary/addiction.

28. Tanya Paperny, "Do Some Trauma Survivors Cope by Overworking?," *The Atlantic* (blog), February 16, 2017, https://www.theatlantic.com/health/archive/2017/02/do-some-trauma-survivors-cope-by-overworking/516540/; Kapo Wong, Alan H. S. Chan, and S. C. Ngan, "The Effect of Long Working Hours and Overtime on Occupational Health: A Meta-Analysis of Evidence from 1998 to 2018," *International Journal of Environmental Research and Public Health* 16, no. 12 (June 2019): 2102, https://doi.org/10.3390/ijerph16122102; "Long Working Hours and Health," *The Lancet Regional Health – Western Pacific* 11 (June 1, 2021), https://doi.org/10.1016/j.lanwpc.2021.100199.

29. Keisha "TK" Dutes et al., "Why You Should Stop Complimenting People for Being 'Resilient,'" *NPR*, August 25, 2022, https://www.npr.org/2022/08/16/1117725653/why-being-resilient-might-matter-less-than-you-think; "How Patience Can Be a Better Balm for Trauma than Resilience | Aeon Essays," Aeon, accessed January 5, 2024, https://aeon.co/essays/how-patience-can-be-a-better-balm-for-trauma-than-resilience.

30. Kate Bowler, *Everything Happens for a Reason* Random House, New York, 2018, p. 101.

because they hide it, and so those who conceal their pain, hardship, or reactions from or to their traumatic event, are given the high praise of being identified as resilient. As a culture, Americans have glorified resilience – making it the word of the year – and seemingly embodying it as 'getting over something'.[31] However, Oxford first notes resiliency as "the capacity to withstand" and TP have withstood more than can be imagined: thus, regardless of their dysregulation, they are incredibly resilient.

Traumatized persons who are hyporeactive, incredibly withdrawn, or nonengaged often fall through the cracks and off the radar of those who may be able to provide assistance; they are either dismissed for their perceived inadequacies or are unnoticed and/or ostensibly forgettable and are thus ostracized. In an era and culture of demanding attention, constant motion, and multitasking, focus is pulled in multiple directions and those who do not demand attention often do not receive it. Paradoxically, those who are hyperreactive and frequently and/or publicly display emotional outbursts including crying, yelling, depression, sadness, or anger are often labeled as attention-seeking and/or controlling and are consequently considered mentally unstable and also ostracized.

The ability to recognize behaviors without judging; to understand their origin, and to use this understanding as an aid in identifying those who may need support is an important component in providing trauma-informed care. It is worth pausing to note who is actively engaged in one's spiritual community. Does a person who is hyper or hypo-reactive come to mind? How is this person received in the community? Is it known if they have a history of trauma? Has there been castigation because of their

---

31. Bryan Robinson, Ph.D, "Why The Word For 2021 Is 'Resilience' And How It Affects Mental Health," Forbes, accessed January 6, 2024, https://www.forbes.com/sites/bryanrobinson/2020/12/06/why-the-word-for-2021-is-resilience-and-how-it-affects-mental-health/.

behaviors/responses? These are questions that are critical to be mentally attended to as one continues to learn and begins to apply objectives.

"What is considered normal and natural are established not by what is good for people, but by what is expected of them, which traits and attitudes serve the maintenance of the culture."[32] Thus, society determines what is tolerated and accepted by what they can withstand in their window of tolerance. As Gabor Maté, a leading expert in trauma articulates, the 'maintenance of the culture' is not about the health and well-being of individuals but rather the ascribing to indoctrinated theories of self-reliance, rugged individualism, and the "American dream" which says if one works hard, one will be rewarded. When what is "socially acceptable" or socially sanctioned aligns with the (harmful and racist) 'pull oneself up by one's bootstraps' ideals of the United States and Western world, at risk is normalizing trauma responses when they conform.

Culturally, the industrial age has moved us from a cooperative society to a competitive society in which the collective good is less about the wholeness of the community based upon the best interests of individuals than the ability to attain personal wealth and status. The added pressure and shame of societal expectations upon TP contributes to the harm they have previously experienced and further isolates them from the community. One cannot overcome traumatic injury by sheer determination or individual grit, or every single TP would have been able to immediately recover. For it is only in dauntless perseverance that they were able to survive. Recovery requires community, compassion, and care.

Returning to dysregulation, it is crucial to recall that "there is no such thing as a 'bad' response; there are only adaptive

---

32. Maté and Maté, *The Myth of Normal: Trauma, Illness & Healing in a Toxic Culture*, 202.

responses."[33] The nervous system is focused on survival and any actions of the TP are an outgrowth of that rugged subsistence. The work of the TP and those who support them is to move from critical evaluation of emotions and behaviors to understanding and respecting their function and usefulness in survival; extending grace, compassion, and acceptance which empowers self-healing. The next section will provide information on the adaptive responses and effects of trauma (symptoms) that are experienced as dysregulated behavior which are often encountered in working with TP.

Traumatized people experience a fragmentation of the self that occurs as they are unable to integrate memories and present experiences into a coherent narrative. This fragmentation leaves one unable to fully inhabit their body, mind, and soul which becomes not only out of sync but in some cases, TP cannot even define 'sync'. Pierre Janet "proposed that traumatic recall remains insistent and unchanged to the precise extent that it has never, from the beginning, been fully integrated into understanding. The traumatic injury is the confrontation with an event that, in its unexpectedness or horror, cannot be placed within the schemes of prior knowledge." Thus, it cannot become "integrated into a completed story of the past."[34]

The memory system for traumatized persons is offline and the inability to recall creates immense problems as society expects linear thought and scrutinizes anything that strays from it, thus labeling it as 'false' or 'fake'. For traumatized persons who may be trying to seek justice, to tell their story, or simply to make sense of their personal timeline and experiences, this can be maddening as

---

33. Stephen W. Porges, *The Polyvagal Theory: Neurophysiological Foundations of Emotions Attachment Communication Self-Regulation* (New York: W. W. Norton & Company, 2011), 45.
34. Caruth, *Trauma: Explorations in Memory*, 153.

well as terrifying. How memory works for TP is that it does not return synchronously and may only materialize in bodily sensations, images, or sounds in their memory as an incomplete picture such as a sofa, a sunset, or a siren. One may not be able to identify why they feel terrified, sad, and/or activated within their body – nor to connect the sensation or image to an event; it is the ghostly artifact of a memory. Although the memory is somatically awakened, addressing or resolving it is difficult when one doesn't know the etiology. In recovery, while it may be understood that it is less about the traumatic details than the emerging and recurring emotions and sensations, that doesn't necessarily assist one's cognitive mind to understand. For TP, it often feels as if they could know the whole picture, they could understand. Yet, there is no explanation or picture available that would explain the trauma in a way that would provide immediate relief. As will be discussed later, this can be a powerful space for SIC/SAP to engage with TP and affirm their story and experiences. One should not require a linear timeline of events or the story – in part or whole – to observe and recognize deep pain and provide compassion, safety, and affirmation.

As trauma is remembered in the body and traditional memory is inaccessible, the responses and reactions of TP may be confusing and/or upsetting to those around them. Exploring a few of the ways in which the symptoms of the psychological chaos of traumatic injury present is imperative for providing quality, helpful, and unharming trauma-informed care.

Dissociation

Dissociation (also known as self-fragmentation) is an emotional, cognitive, and/or physical detachment from one's current reality. This can cause disconnection from one's sense of self, security, thoughts, feelings, and emotions as well as an inability to recall information. When one experiences something so insufferable, overwhelming, and distressing, the only way for the brain to defend and protect the Authentic Self is to detach. "This altered state of consciousness might be regarded as one of nature's small mercies, a protection against unbearable pain."[35] If TP were forced to experience the intensity of the betrayal, the magnitude of the harm, and the extremity of sadness and rage while enduring the event, it would be, in my experience, unsurvivable.

Donald Kalsched explores the merits of dissociation as he relates it to the crushing pain of early relational trauma (child abuse and/or neglect by a caretaker) in which the actions and effects are so astoundingly stultifying and horrifying that they "threaten to shatter the child to its very core" – threatens to extinguish that "vital spark" of the person so crucial for the experience of aliveness and so central to the later experience of "feeling real."[36] To subvert the demise, children dissociate in a life-saving act. "It prevents annihilation of the unit self, substituting multiplicity and an archetypal story that implicitly holds the parts together."[37]

Trauma causes an estrangement from one's core identity – their Authentic Self – as an act of protection. While the defense mechanism of dissociation saves and protects the Authentic Self, lost are the experiences, healthy relationships, spiritual, emotional, and mental activities, and health that create a whole living experience. Dissociation allows a person to continue living while only merely surviving for they are not present to time and activity and are unable to engage and exist as their Authentic Self. This is experienced both in the function of dissociation and narrative.

---

35. Judith Herman, M. D., *Trauma and Recovery* (New York, New York: Basic Books, 1997), 43.
36. Kalsched, *Trauma and the Soul*, 11.
37. Kalsched, 11.

Narrative

Every person has a narrative which may also be known as the lens or framework through which they receive information, engage with others, and perceive the world. It is created by experiences, culture, spirituality, ethnicity, and societal expectations and/or assumptions as well as internalizing the words and actions of those in their immediate circle of influence including those who have caused traumatic harm. "The mind is a meaning-making machine. It will generate stories that "make sense" of the emotions that, at a vulnerable time, it could not contain and perhaps still cannot."[38] This is especially true with child abuse, domestic abuse, and other chronic abuses. For instance, if told often enough that one is worthless or shown through actions that one is disposable, it becomes nearly impossible to believe otherwise and it institutes the framework – the narrative - by which TP engage the world.

One's narrative defines how one observes and scrutinizes themselves. The "writing" of one's narrative may not be written by the individual and in traumatic injury, as noted previously, is often constructed by the words and stories imposed by the perpetrator/abuser regardless of whether the narrative is true or an adequate reflection of one's Authentic Self. For those who have been abused as children or chronically as adults, the perpetrator often utilizes psychological control to dominate and thus the narrative constructed by the TP is in another's voice. Moreover, TP may not even be aware that the narrative or story to which they cling is not, in fact, their own.[39] Consequently, when TP attempt to engage with others, or even themselves, they do so through the narrative they have come to embody regardless of who composed

---

38. Maté and Maté, *The Myth of Normal: Trauma, Illness & Healing in a Toxic Culture*, 257.

39. The exposing and rewriting of narrative is accomplished through therapy and trauma recovery.

it. Additionally, some narratives are not necessarily the nonfiction stories of their lives but are rather the stories created to cope with the indescribable pain.

For example, a young girl who has been sexually abused by her father cannot comprehend how or why those who are supposed to love her seemingly do not. Children are born with an innate desire to be loved and to give love. Thus, not only biologically but culturally in television, books, and movies, children receive the message that parents/caretakers are supposed to love them. When that is not experienced, the girl has two options for emotional survival. She can either believe that these people are evil and malicious and subsequently live in the constant threat of annihilation and feeling entirely alone in a large, frightening world or instead, in an act that provides a sense of control, she believes she is to blame for their behavior. Therefore, as painful as it is, she chooses to blame herself as that is the marginally better option and her narrative becomes one in which she is bad, unworthy, undeserving, and the cause of their behavior. They would love her if she would _____. That created narrative then influences all relationships, experiences, and emotions.

Immobilization

Trauma is an immobilizing experience with no place to flee and/or no ability (literally) to do so. "Immobilization is the root of trauma. Being able to move and *do* something to protect oneself is a critical factor in determining whether or not a horrible experience will leave long-lasting scars."[40] Within traumatic experiences and subsequent dysregulation, the development of immobilization becomes apparent. For children experiencing trauma, they are immobilized in that they depend on their caretakers for food,

---

40. Van Der Kolk, M.D., *The Body Keeps the Score*, 2015, 55.

shelter, and other necessities. It is not an option for them to flee; often the abuser has groomed the child to accept what is happening and in fact, be *more* dependent upon them. In the experience of domestic violence, there is the emotional and psychological fear of leaving, the issue of grooming, and the perpetrator often having control of finances, cars, phones, etc. For other types of trauma, immobilization is experienced in a multitude of forms including abject fear or literal entrapment (car accident, natural disaster, mass shooting). However, the experience of immobilization is psychological as well.

The feeling of immobilization may also continue in recovery, as TP experience another insidious aspect of traumatic injury - the inability to articulate their emotions, experiences, and sensations. As Van Der Kolk writes, "Traumatized people suffer speechless terror."[41] This phenomenon is known as 'alexithymia'; the difficulty of recognizing emotions and articulation. It is experienced as an immobilization of words in that they cannot be formed, accessed, or even uttered. While it is known that Broca's area in the frontal cortex is affected by trauma, it must also be acknowledged that language has limitations and there are no words that can describe the terror and torment of rape, incest, war, torture, or natural and/or ecological disasters. How does one ever piece together words for experiences that defy logic and language? Thus, acknowledging the confines of communication in combination with the neurophysiological limitations of one's brain to access words or language, TP experience a profound inability to explain and describe their emotions and experiences.

If an organism is stuck in survival mode, its energies are focused on fighting off unseen enemies, which leaves no

---

41. Bessel van der Kolk, "In Terror's Grip: Healing the Ravages of Trauma," *Cerebrum* 4 (January 1, 2002).

room for nurture, care, and love. For us humans, it means that as long as the mind is defending itself against invisible assaults, our closest bonds are threatened, along with our ability to imagine, plan, play, learn, and pay attention to other people's needs.[42]

And what cannot be conveyed to the other, cannot be conveyed to the self.[43]

Social Isolation/Withdrawal

As noted by Herman, "The core experiences of psychological trauma are disempowerment and disconnection from others."[44] Many TP have previously experienced social isolation as perpetrators threaten and coerce victims not to disclose the abuse or else they will be dangerously harmed or even killed. Post-traumatically, individuals again experience social isolation/withdrawal and personal disrepute for a myriad of reasons including the inability to communicate that which has neither adequate nor accessible language. Consequently, this inhibits and/or disempowers TP to share their stories and experiences thus excluding them from receiving comfort, acceptance, and community support.

Seemingly, much of what is labeled and experienced as dysregulation is connected by the "inarticulable dimension of pain."[45] If one cannot articulate, how can one heal, explain, seek help, or recover? While it is an arduous task, through the use of IFS, EMDR, somatic work, and psychotherapy (talk therapy), TP begin to create a language for their experience. Those who journey

---

42. Van Der Kolk, M.D., *The Body Keeps the Score*, 2015, 76.
43. John Bowlby, psychologist who developed attachment theory, has said, "What cannot be communicated to the (m)other cannot be communicated to the self."
44. Herman, M. D., *Trauma and Recovery*, 1997, 133.
45. Rambo, "Trauma and Faith," 237.

with the TP are privy to that language and their proximity affords them a better chance of understanding. It will NEVER capture the story, the horror, the pain, the grief, the loss, but the work of the witness and those who journey with the TP is not to exact a story but to live into the depth of pain that knows no bounds and still witness the Authentic Self within.

Therefore, surviving becomes not simply an act of continuing to breathe but of learning to live in the inarticulate. Of recognizing the hovering between life and death so often experienced by TP as they are neither living in the past nor the present; their brain is unable to recognize the traumatic event has ended nor to fully engage in the present. Survival becomes the work of learning to live with the activators and the demands of the brain to focus on the pain and horror of the past as it still feels present, which thus disrupts daily living. Recovery is not a journey to a destination; it is a way of existing in a world in which there are no words, in which the pain – physical, emotional, and spiritual – is so great as to feel absolutely crushing and at times impossible to endure, a way of existing in a space that is not what one would choose but of what is imposed upon them. Recovery is learning to live with the "persistence of death in the experience of *living on*."[46] Within the 'living on' as Rambo notes, is the reality faced by TP, as noted above, one does not know when the activations of one's traumatic injury will arise and thwart, upend, and possibly destroy the careful survivalist work to which the TP has engaged.

By learning the neurobiology and attempting to understand what is known of the machinations of the brain, people are better prepared and able to advocate with and for and create space with and for traumatized persons; designing programs that can attempt to meet the needs of the TP and the community. Choosing to educate oneself is a radical act of solidarity that says, 'I will do my

---

46. Rambo, 239.

best to not inflict more harm. I am working to be a safe person for you to trust'. The willingness to learn may offer a TP reason to trust that the witness can handle hard truths, endure the experience of their pain, and respond and react with compassion. Finally, individuals and communities must be mindful to not conflate behavior with the authentic self. "Because post-traumatic symptoms are so persistent and so wide-ranging, they may be mistaken for enduring characteristics of the victim's personality."[47]

All the effects noted are psychological and physical adaptations that were utilized for survival and thus these tools need to be appreciated for the context in which they were formed and for their ingenuity. To appreciate these does not mean to accept the behavior and/or dysregulation that may accompany it but to have compassion that the traumatized person survived and clearly has the capacity to develop tools that are better suited to their current environment. However, without being provided and afforded the space and guidance to develop other tools, they are left navigating a new system with an outdated operating system. This is another opportunity for SIC to offer compassion, grace, and patience as TP develop and practice a new way of being in the world. SIC can be the safe space in which TP may practice their new skills and engage via a healthy framework and SIC that develop relationships with mental health practices may be able to provide referrals to those seeking help. Finally, an act of radical hospitality and solidarity with TP may be to assist with financial expenses for those needing mental health professionals or other professional services (somatics, massage, advocacy).

Autonomic Nervous System

As should be clear, the effects of trauma are ubiquitous. The good

---

47. Herman, M. D., *Trauma and Recovery*, 1997, 49.

news is that the adaptability of the body and mind for survival speaks to the current capacity of a traumatized person's plasticity to learn and develop a skillset to cope, heal, and thrive.

The autonomic nervous system (ANS) is foundational to that work; bodies are designed to respond to stimuli via a superhighway of nerves that distributes information to organs, appendages, etc. called the Autonomic Nervous System (ANS) which is a component of the larger emotional processing system. The ANS doesn't distinguish between good and bad input; it simply acts to manage risk and seek safety and is "a component of the peripheral nervous system that regulates involuntary physiological processes including heart rate, blood pressure, respiration, digestion, and sexual arousal" as well as other functions.[48] It is comprised of the sympathetic and parasympathetic nervous systems that are separate but have complementary roles. The sympathetic nervous system (SNS) is responsible for reacting to threats and carrying signals that put the body's systems on alert. Its counterpart, the parasympathetic nervous system (PNS) carries signals that return those systems to their standard activity levels. The nervous system craves predictability and is interrupted by trauma.

The SNS activates the well-known "fight, flight, or freeze" response:

If the amygdala senses a threat...it sends an instant message down to the hypothalamus and the brain stem, recruiting the stress-hormone system and the ANS to orchestrate a whole-body response...by trigger[ing] the release of powerful stress hormones, including cortisol and adrenaline, which increase heart rate, blood pressure, and

48. Joshua A. Waxenbaum, Vamsi Reddy, and Matthew Varacallo, "Anatomy, Autonomic Nervous System," in *StatPearls* (Treasure Island (FL): StatPearls Publishing, 2023), http://www.ncbi.nlm.nih.gov/books/NBK539845/.

the rate of breathing, preparing us to fight back or run away.[49]

In non-traumatized persons after a threat, the body usually returns to its non-danger/normal state fairly quickly. This is not true for TP as they remain in a chemically altered state.

Non-traumatized persons are capable of perceiving and receiving information as a threat or innocuous communication. Yet, one of the greatest difficulties that TP experience is the inability to distinguish between types of threats as the amygdala and thalamus are unable to decipher between real (current) and perceived (past) threats. Therefore, the body constantly remains in a state of hyper or hypo arousal.

This indecipherable information and reactivity not only cause a multitude of issues in navigating daily living, but also challenges relationships and attachments through miscommunication, perceived slights, and assumption of ill-intention. TP are not simply overwhelmed by the physical threats but are often left feeling alone in their journey as they cannot read, decipher, or trust their interpretation of the words and actions of those closest to them.

Balancing the SNS is the PNS that relaxes the body after periods of stress or danger and controls the body during times of rest.[50] Thus, the rhyming phrases "rest and digest" or "feed and breed" are easy ways to remember what the PNS does.197F[51] When the SNS enacts a "fight or flight" response, the parasympathetic nervous system reacts by triggering "the release of acetylcholine to put a brake on arousal, slowing the heart down, relaxing muscles, and returning breathing to normal."[52] For TP, an aspect

---

49. Van Der Kolk, M.D., *The Body Keeps the Score*, 2015, 60.
50. ibid
51. ibid
52. Van Der Kolk, M.D., *The Body Keeps the Score*, 2015, 79.

of the work of recovery is to develop tools used to activate the PNS in times of crisis, anxiety, and distress to navigate the effects of traumatic injury and take control of one's body. As will be discussed later, activating the PNS can be experienced via somatic exercises which can be easily adapted and used in rituals and gatherings within SIC.

Moral Injury

While moral injury (MI) is not categorized as a trauma in that it does not involve a threat to one's life and is not a physiological response, morally injurious experiences are a threat to one's deeply held beliefs, credos, theology, and spirit and can result in a deep emotional, psychological, and spiritual injury. Until recently, those with moral injuries tended to be diagnosed with PTSD and consequently treated with corresponding care as many of the symptoms appear in similar ways. However, the etiology of those symptoms is different and requires a distinct response. This injury is discussed within the confines of a trauma-informed care model, as people may witness those with moral injury and assume (reasonably) that they are dealing with a traumatic injury. It is important to understand the distinction as well as to recognize that the diagnostic for moral injury includes a spiritual wounding.

Accompanying the concept of a protected/unharmed Self posited by Schwartz, Jung, and others, and claimed within this work, moral injury (MI) provides a distinct elucidation of the Authentic Self and a further example of its protection and intactness. Understanding moral injury allows for a window into the Authentic Self and additional justification of the separation between the Authentic Self and bodily experiences.

The term moral injury was developed in the mid-1990s by Jonathan Shay to help explain the psychological, spiritual, and emotional issues veterans were experiencing that were overlooked by traditional PTSD treatment. He first discussed it in his book, '*Achilles in Vietnam*', Shay defined it as, "a betrayal of what's right, by someone who holds legitimate authority, in a high stakes situation."[53,54] Almost 30 years later, "moral injury" has not garnered a unified definition. In 2009, Litz furthered the foundational definition, expanding it to "perpetrating, failing to prevent, or bearing witness to, or learning about acts that transgress deeply held moral beliefs and expectations."[55] A more comprehensive understanding of MI was provided by Jinkerson in 2016 which included specific diagnostic criteria: "Moral injury is a particular type of psychological trauma characterized by intense guilt, shame, and spiritual crisis, which can develop when one violates his or her moral beliefs, is betrayed, or witnesses trusted individuals committing atrocities... These experiences cause significant moral dissonance, which if unresolved, leads to the development of its core symptoms."[56] These include shame, guilt, anxiety, withdrawal, intrusive thoughts, painful recall, self-harming behaviors, and suicidality.[57] "Moral injury is essentially an existential-ontological wound that can have lasting psychological, biological, spiritual, behavioral, and social consequences."[58]

Symptomatically, MI may appear similar to PTSD, and

---

53. Jonathan Shay, *Achilles in Vietnam : Combat Trauma and the Undoing of Character* (Atheneum, 1994).

54. Jonathan Shay, "Moral Injury," *Psychoanalytic Psychology* 31, no. 2 (April 2014): 182–91, https://doi.org/10.1037/a0036090.

55. Brett T. Litz et al., "Moral Injury and Moral Repair in War Veterans: A Preliminary Model and Intervention Strategy," *Clinical Psychology Review* 29, no. 8 (January 1, 2009): 695, https://doi.org/10.1016/j.cpr.2009.07.003.

56. Jeremy D. Jinkerson, "Defining and Assessing Moral Injury: A Syndrome Perspective," *Traumatology* 22, no. 2 (June 2016): 122, https://doi.org/10.1037/trm0000069.

57. Litz et al., "Moral Injury and Moral Repair in War Veterans," 700–701.

58. Timothy J. Hodgson and Lindsay B. Carey, "Moral Injury and Definitional Clarity: Betrayal, Spirituality and the Role of Chaplains," *Journal of Religion and Health* 56, no. 4 (August 1, 2017): 1224.

therefore an assumption could be made that it is a trauma. What distinguishes moral injury from trauma – specifically PTSD — is that they are mechanistically different in their neurophysiological basis. "Psychological trauma is an affliction of the powerless. At the moment of trauma, the victim is rendered helpless by over-whelming force."[59] PTSD is a physiological disorder resulting from constant fear, threats, and/or belief that one is in imminent mortal danger which causes the body to produce chemicals such as cortisol and norepinephrine while MI is evidenced not by fear and subsequent chemical alterations but by the "negative self-referen-tial emotions" of guilt and shame.[60] Research presented by Barnes, et al, on the underlying neurobiology of moral injury notes, "Whether a moral injury develops is determined by how the indi-vidual interprets the potentially injurious event. The appraisal process determines whether the event generates significant disso-nance with the individual's belief system and worldview."[61]

Recent studies using fMRI to examine the neurobiology of MI and PTSD reveal that there is "little or no overlap" in the areas of the brain that are activated in response to the corresponding expe-rience.[62] "One study has compared resting-state regional cerebral metabolic rate between veterans with PTSD grouped by whether the index trauma was danger - and/or - fear-based, (i.e., life threat to self or other) or non-danger-based (i.e., witnessing violence, trau-matic loss, moral injury by self or others). Danger and/or fear-

---

59. Herman, M. D., *Trauma and Recovery*, 1997, 33.
60. Haleigh A. Barnes Ph.D., Robin A. Hurley, M.D., and Katherine H. Taber, Ph.D., "Moral Injury and PTSD: Often Co-Occurring Yet Mechanistically Different | The Journal of Neuropsychiatry and Clinical Neurosciences," Spring 2019, https://neuro.psychiatryonline.org/doi/full/10.1176/appi.neuropsych.19020036; Bremner, "Traumatic Stress."
61. Barnes Ph.D., Hurley, M.D., and Taber, Ph.D., "Moral Injury and PTSD: Often Co-Occurring Yet Mechanistically Different | The Journal of Neuropsychi-atry and Clinical Neurosciences."
62. Barnes Ph.D., Hurley, M.D., and Taber, Ph.D., 98.

based traumas were associated with higher metabolism in the amygdala, whereas non-danger-based traumas were associated with higher metabolism in the precuneus."[63] Thus, MI is not caused by a physiological response but occurs in the cognitive and emotional self-assessment of an event. In Brock's book, *Soul Repair,* a veteran offered this distinction between PTSD and MI; "PTSD is a breach of trust with the world. Moral injury, however, is the violation of a moral agreement he had with his internal world, his moral identity."[64] Moral injury is separate from or in addition to PTSD and trauma and therefore, if the mechanism that "causes" PTSD is the constant state of fear, and morally injured people do not experience that, then any recovery work must address either and/or *both* injuries.

Yet, akin to trauma, a moral injury is not necessarily developed simply because one experiences a potentially morally injurious event. Determinants of developing a moral injury include how an individual interprets the event as well as their social determinants of health (SDoH).[65, 66] Additionally, just as in trauma, there is a factor that cannot be qualified or quantified that impacts the experience of the individual: resiliency. This does not mean that one who experiences PTSD, or a moral injury is not resilient. It simply means that some people, regardless of the trauma or the moral

---

63. Barnes Ph.D., Hurley, M.D., and Taber, Ph.D., 99.

64. Rita Nakashima Brock and Gabriel Lettini, *Soul Repair: Recovering from Moral Injury after War* (Boston, MA: Beacon Press, 2012), 87.

65. Lauren M. Borges et al., "The Role of Social Determinants of Health in Moral Injury: Implications and Future Directions," *Current Treatment Options in Psychiatry* 9, no. 3 (September 1, 2022): 202–14, https://doi.org/10.1007/s40501-022-00272-4.

66. Social Determinants of Health (SDOH) are "nonmedical factors that influence health outcomes. They are the conditions in which people are born, grow, work, live, and age, and the wider set of forces and systems shaping the conditions of daily life." For further information see, www.cdc.gov/about/sdoh

injury, do not experience the same level of emotional, spiritual, and psychological disturbance as others.

While MI and PTSD share similar symptoms of depression, anxiety, anger, re-experiencing of events, and self-harm (including substance abuse, social problems, and suicidality), the core symptoms of MI are guilt, shame, spiritual crisis, and a loss of trust in self, others, and/or transcendental beings.[67] However, MI and PTSD have in common the possibility of dissociation and/or detachment. During the potentially morally injurious experience, one may disengage from the event to comply with the expected behavior (in terms of military personnel or dissociation in sexual abuse/rape) or acquiesce to the forced actions (coercion). For military personnel, being told to shoot a child by a superior officer, and being trained that is it morally justified, causes a severing of one's own emotions from the event.[68]

It is critical to understand the concerted effort required to disconnect and/or override the Authentic Self to engage in actions that are anathema to the moral principles held by the individual. As MI developed from veterans' experiences, it is within the military that the moral disengagement training will be viewed and analyzed, beginning with the history of combat killing and the subsequent military policies and alterations to them.

"In World War II, almost 75 percent of combat soldiers did not fire directly at the enemy, even when their own lives were at risk. In his landmark 1947 study, the official U.S. Army historian Brigadier General L.S.A. Marshall revealed that despite training, propaganda, and social sanctions, soldiers retained a deep inhibition when it came to taking human lives."[69] Though Marshall's methodology was criticized, Lt. Col. Dave Grossman discusses the

---

67. Jinkerson, "Defining and Assessing Moral Injury."
68. Brock and Lettini, *Soul Repair: Recovering from Moral Injury after War.*
69. Brock and Lettini, 17.

corroborating studies that continue to evidence "that the vast majority of combatants throughout history, at the moment of truth when they could and should kill the enemy, have found themselves to be "conscientious objectors".[70] It is not clear that there was an abrogating issue created by the lack of 'firing at the enemy' nor that there would have been more lives spared. However, the military developed "reflexive fire training" to overcome the reluctance to killing; conditioning soldiers to shoot before thinking.[71] Similar to the muscle memory created by a musician playing scales or a person writing their alphabet; it is accomplished without thinking. "By the time a soldier does kill in combat, he has rehearsed the process so many times that he can, at one level, deny to himself that he is actually killing another human being."[72]

After this new training protocol, shooting was raised to "50 or 60 percent in Korea and 85 to 90 percent in Vietnam."[73] Major Pete Kilner, in the documentary *Soldiers of Conscience*, acknowledges, "the problem with reflexive fire training is that it does bypass, in some sense, [the soldiers'] moral decision-making process."[74] Moreover, "such training is believed to have increased the number of kills in OIF (Operations Iraqi Freedom) such that 40-65% of soldiers reported killing enemy combatants."[75] Speaking of the reflexive fire training, Herm, a veteran says he "still remembers the shock of having to shout, "Kill! Kill! Kill! Kill without mercy."[76] Other stories of the intensity and pervasiveness of this training include that of Chas Davis "who was appalled by

70. Lt. Col. Dave Grossman, "Hope on the Battlefield," Greater Good, n.d., https://greatergood.berkeley.edu/article/item/hope_on_the_battlefield.
71. Grossman.
72. Grossman.
73. Brock and Lettini, *Soul Repair: Recovering from Moral Injury after War*, 18.
74. Brock and Lettini, 18.
75. Jinkerson, "Defining and Assessing Moral Injury," 123.
76. Brock and Lettini, *Soul Repair: Recovering from Moral Injury after War*, 22.

having to sing "Sniper Wonderland" as part of a military drill."[77,][78]

Despite the consistency of training and the subsequent ability to override one's Authentic Self, there is a "demonstrable fact that within most people is an intense resistance to killing other people. A resistance so strong that, in many circumstances, soldiers on the battlefield will die before they can overcome it."[79] The infliction of harm upon the Authentic Self when it is forced to detach from bodily reactions and responses not only causes untold emotional and spiritual pain but again points to the intact soul. This story clearly illustrates the experience:

> At one point in his tour, Camilo's squad faced a crowd of protestors. He had his gun sights on an adolescent young man who appeared to have a grenade in his hand. Camilo was ordered to shoot. He had no awareness of firing, but when he took shelter in a closet by himself and examined his gun magazine, he counted eleven bullets missing. He still has no memory of the shooting. All he remembers is the young man standing and then lying dead in a pool of blood in the dirt. He was appalled that his ability to decide what to do had been taken away by his training.[80]

Morally injured persons are filled with negative self-referential emotions of guilt and shame as they cannot assimilate their

77. Brock and Lettini, 101.
78. "See the little girl with the puppy; Lock and load a hollow pointed round... Take the shot and maybe if you're lucky; You'll watch their lifeless bodies hit the ground...Through the fields we'll be walkin'; 'Cross the rooftops we'll be stalkin'... One shot one kill from the top of the hill...Walkin' in a sniper wonderland." Brock and Lettini, 101.
79. Grossman, "Hope on the Battlefield."
80. Brock and Lettini, *Soul Repair: Recovering from Moral Injury after War*, 34.

actions with their beliefs and ethical constructs of the Authentic Self. How can such moral harm be accountable in an individual who has essentially had their decision-making process extracted from them via constant desensitization and conditioning? Nevertheless, those who have endured morally injurious events in the military, bear the scars. "Severe psychological trauma becomes a distinct possibility when military training overrides safeguards against killing."[81]

Interestingly, "feelings of guilt, shame, and contrition were once considered the feelings of a normal ethical person" and yet are now seen within military circles as a weakness or a psychological disorder.[82] The chasm between the Authentic Self and the industrialization of war is great and soldiers who have MI require no less compassion than those who have PTSD. The complication in providing care and compassion is that if one has engaged in killing another, most average citizens will be unable to imagine such a scenario and are likely to dismiss the extreme pain of the individual out of their own great discomfort.

As Rambo has discussed the importance of journeying with those in the liminal spaces in which neither death nor life are clear – such as in the extreme pain of moral injury – she emphasizes that one cannot heal without relationship and community. An insidious aspect of moral injury is the inability to share with others what has happened due to the "shame and concern about adverse impact or repercussions."[83] When persons are required to engage in acts that cause moral injury and are disconnected from their Authentic Self, those who have led them into these spaces and/or forced them to act cause a fracturing of trust with others.[84] In trauma and MI, recovery and healing do not happen alone and

---

81. Grossman, "Hope on the Battlefield."
82. Brock and Lettini, *Soul Repair: Recovering from Moral Injury after War*, 51.
83. Litz et al., "Moral Injury and Moral Repair in War Veterans," 696.
84. Mariam Kvitsiani et al., "Dynamic Model of Moral Injury," *European Journal*

thus the issues of trust and attachment can hamper and halt recovery efforts. "Shame is fundamentally related to expected negative evaluation by valued others."[85] It often leads one to sever relationships and/or greatly curtail them as the assumption of the morally injured is that they would or could be misunderstood, rejected, and even completely shunned or estranged, and consequently they isolate from friends and community which then leads to further emotional pain and even suicidality.

While moral injury was conceptualized in the context of veterans and military issues, recent research has furthered the application of the concept to include civilian populations including healthcare workers, refugees, teachers, law enforcement, educators, and child protection services/social workers.[86] For example, medical personnel determining patient appropriateness for care, which patient receives procedure/component (vents/dialysis) when in short supply, etc., providers must complete the task at hand and attend to the patient, being told they are 'morally justified' in their actions.[87] Returning to Shay's initial conceptualization of MI, a component of the injury is the fracturing of trust when "someone who holds legitimate authority" expects one to

of Trauma & Dissociation 7, no. 1 (2023), https://doi.org/10.1016/j.ejtd.2023.100313; Shay, "Moral Injury."

85. Litz et al., "Moral Injury and Moral Repair in War Veterans," 699.

86. Stephen M. Campbell, Connie M. Ulrich, and Christine Grady, "A Broader Understanding of Moral Distress.," *The American Journal of Bioethics: AJOB* 16, no. 12 (2016): 2–9; Harold G. Koenig and Faten Al Zaben, "Moral Injury: An Increasingly Recognized and Widespread Syndrome," *Journal of Religion and Health* 60, no. 5 (October 1, 2021): 2989–3011, https://doi.org/10.1007/s10943-021-01328-0; Kvitsiani et al., "Dynamic Model of Moral Injury."

87. Priya-Lena Riedel et al., "A Scoping Review of Moral Stressors, Moral Distress and Moral Injury in Healthcare Workers during COVID-19," *International Journal of Environmental Research and Public Health* 19, no. 3 (February 1, 2022): 1666, https://doi.org/10.3390/ijerph19031666; Sarah Rabin et al., "Moral Injuries in Healthcare Workers: What Causes Them and What to Do About Them?," *Journal of Healthcare Leadership* 15 (2023): 153–60, https://doi.org/10.2147/JHL.S396659.

complete an action in opposition to one's Authentic Self.[88] Whether that is your commanding officer, Chief Medical Officer, or Board of Directors, the moral justification offered by another person does not soothe the Authentic Self and is a component of moral injury.[89]

Additionally, MI also applies to those who have experienced sexual abuse, assault, and/or rape. Bodies are biologically programmed to respond to stimuli. When the brain does not control or is unable to intervene in the body's response, the result is shame as the Authentic Self is not represented in the behavior. Regardless of how the moral injury was acquired, the experience leads not only to incredible shame, guilt, spiritual and ontological crisis but the added burdens of experiencing a loss of self-trust, including worry of how one's behavior will emerge in the future - "the feeling that similar or other morally unjustified behavior could occur at any moment."[90] It must be noted that moral injury cannot affect a sociopath or a psychopath, for their Authentic Self does not experience the assumptions or understanding of right and wrong morality.[91]

In the research and examinations of moral injury, there is a presupposition that an individual is worthwhile and good, and that the world is benevolent and meaningful.[92] Thus, the question of the Authentic Self could be ostensibly answered in that actions that are harmful, injurious, or unkind are automatically anathema to the Authentic Self. This professedly universal tenet, or, at the

---

88. Shay, "Moral Injury."
89. Brock and Lettini, *Soul Repair: Recovering from Moral Injury after War*, 50.
90. Kvitsiani et al., "Dynamic Model of Moral Injury," 4.
91. Brock and Lettini, *Soul Repair: Recovering from Moral Injury after War*, 50.
92. Litz discusses the issue that shame are "signs of an intact conscience and self- and other-expectations about goodness, humanity, and justice. In other words, injury is only possible if acts of transgression produce dissonance (conflict), and dissonance is only possible if the service member has an intact moral belief system" (701)

very least, universal assumption within psychotherapy, speaks to the idea that the Authentic Self is the best of a person. Their behavior may not reflect that which is thus the cause of emotional, psychological, and spiritual distress. "Moral injury involves an act of transgression that creates dissonance and conflict because it violates assumptions and beliefs about what is right and wrong and personal goodness."[93]

If moral injury includes the "unsuccessful accommodation of these behaviors to existing moral schemes", then the soul while aching for the behavior, is not damaged as the person is experiencing pain *because* their behavior did not match their Authentic Self.[94] The soul isn't what acts but what guides. The brain reacts before the soul can make decisions.

Finally, one aspect of moral injury that should be noted is the fracturing of relationships out of fear of retaliation or repudiation. Currently, Surgeon General - Dr. Vivek Murthy - has declared an epidemic of loneliness, citing "physical health consequences of poor or insufficient connection include a 29% increased risk of heart disease, a 32% increased risk of stroke, and a 50% increased risk of developing dementia for older adults. Additionally, lacking social connection increases the risk of premature death by more than 60%."[95] It is clear relationships are essential for human functioning;

The shame of moral injury as it relates to relationships only solidifies the concept of an Authentic Self which is separate from and/or protected from bodily trauma or actions. MI and its

93. Litz et al., "Moral Injury and Moral Repair in War Veterans," 698.
94. Kvitsiani et al., "Dynamic Model of Moral Injury." p. 698
95. Office of the Assistant Secretary for Health (OASH), "New Surgeon General Advisory Raises Alarm about the Devastating Impact of the Epidemic of Loneliness and Isolation in the United States," Text, May 3, 2023, https://www.hhs.gov/about/news/2023/05/03/new-surgeon-general-advisory-raises-alarm-about-devastating-impact-epidemic-loneliness-isolation-united-states.html.

subsequent shame keep others from knowing and/or witnessing the Authentic Self. The pain is because the Authentic Self knows it has worth and value and wants to be seen. "Don't be afraid of the pain you're in – it's the good part wanting out."[96] Moral injury demonstrates definitively that the soul is in anguish because of engaged behaviors that are anathema to the Authentic Self.

Witness

The term 'witness' has a variety of meanings and usages to examine before locating the term in trauma recovery. In Christian circles, witness has meant to demonstrate in word and deed the works of God as well as seeking out and sharing the good news of Jesus' life and ministry by converting others to Christianity. While this supposedly is providing attestation or fact of the personal knowledge and experiences one claims to have of God, the attempts of conversion have a history rooted in colonization, slavery, and more recently, judgment, hate, and shunning against the LGBTQ community.[97] Therefore, some may find the word 'witness' activating of prior trauma and it is imperative if the word is to be used in trauma recovery literature or support, that a clear definition and boundary must be set and provided.

Additionally, witness is a legal term to define when one has been a spectator to an event – usually a crime – and can provide testimony through corroboration and/or validation. Since the Holocaust, the concept of bearing witness has also been connected

---

96. Personal conversation with Dr. Rita Nakashima Brock regarding moral injury, 1/24/2024.

97. To be clear, many denominations and millions of Christians around the world affirm the image of God in all persons regardless of race, gender, or sexual orientation and are actively working to repair damage that has been wrought. For examples, see http://jubileepractice.org, http://belovedarise.org, http://mlp.org, https://www.poorpeoplescampaign.org

to the work of social justice and the obligation to uphold stories, people, and events to ensure the repugnance, horror, or perniciousness of an event or experience is not forgotten as well as a deterrent to repetition.[98] Subsequently, witnessing is thus an act of solidarity with the harmed as Holocaust survivor Elie Wiesel notes, saying it "is a relationship to radical suffering – a relationship to events that fall outside the sphere of what is ethically imaginable...to stand in a place where you cannot see clearly and where the evidence of what took place is not fully available to you."[99] For those who are willing to witness the traumatic injury experienced by others, is to bring the full meaning of the word to the relationship. To attest personal knowledge of what they know and believe to be true, to reflect what they see in the other – perhaps to one who does not believe the same thing (bearing witness to the worth of one who does not believe they have worth), and to embody the testament to a radical suffering that surpasses one's capacity to fully understand. As Rambo notes, "Witness... describes a way of being oriented to what remains, to the suffering that does not go away."[100]

My use and understanding of the term and concept of witness emerges from and is an outgrowth of Shelly Rambo's foundational work on the use of witness in trauma literature and recovery as well as the historical use in areas of social justice as it intersects with my professional and personal development and reflects the experiences of my work with traumatized persons. My definition has an additional rootedness as the use of the term witness in my work underpins not only my theological and moral understanding but is established in and encompasses the belief that the

---

98. Rambo, "Trauma and Faith," 241.
99. Shelly Rambo, *Spirit and Trauma: A Theology of Remaining*, First edition. (Westminster John Knox Press, 2010), 23.
100. Rambo, 26.

recognition of the Authentic Self is critical for the work of trauma recovery and healing.

Rambo places the use of witness (in trauma literature) at the intersection of history and theology noting two things that define the understanding - "the communal dimension of faith" and "the importance of embodied faith."[101] I concur with these concepts that witnessing occurs in community and is not only a theoretical or emotional response but an embodied action and have placed my practice intending to assist witnesses to be empowered, educated, and motivated to care for traumatized persons. Yet, I believe these concepts must include and speak of and to the AS. Thus, my definition of witness in trauma recovery is one who journeys with, and to whom has been entrusted to behold yet never know or understand, the most hidden and ineffably painful part(s) of a traumatized person and their lives in a relationship of unwavering support in which the witness attends to the Authentic Self in the depths of inarticulable suffering as well as attests to its phenomenal resiliency.

The importance of the relationship between TP and witness is essential. Every psychologist, psychiatrist, therapist, researcher, and TP that I have encountered acknowledges that healing and recovery cannot occur without it. "The core experiences of psychological trauma are disempowerment and disconnection from others. Recovery is based upon the empowerment of the survivor and the creation of new connections. Recovery can take place only within the context of relationships; it cannot occur in isolation."[102] In trauma, people lose their ability for relationships. What was thought to be safe has been exposed as an untruth and subsequently, relationships have been terminated. As many TP are in a constant state of hyperawareness, they are often unable to

---

101. Rambo, "Trauma and Faith," 241.
102. Herman, M. D., *Trauma and Recovery*, 1997, 133.

adequately assess safety and thus engage in protective behavior which may include isolation and cutoff.

Within the relationship with the witness, TP have the opportunity to experience safety and observe and engage in healthy interactions, responses, and reactions, as well as relational repair. These acts of witness *from* the traumatized person are a heavy lift. Not only are their relational experiences being changed but their brain is undergoing a reconstruction beyond imagination. At work is a literal rewiring of the brain including the creation of new neural pathways. TP are persevering through intentional remembering (usually in therapeutic spaces) and the intrusion of memories – some (or all) of which may provide previously unknown information that is beyond the comprehensible and causes immense distress. Additionally, they are being asked to challenge existing narratives, care for their bodies, attend to somatic issues, and endure the harrowing emotions as they arise. These are but a few of the experiences of recovery that occur while the TP continues with the everyday demands of living.

For the witness, the work is also exhausting and transformational – to minimize the importance and contribution is to ill-prepare those who wish to accompany traumatized persons. It is uncomfortable, at times distressingly so, to observe unimaginable pain, grief, destruction, disgust, and/or horror. Witnessing is not merely the ability to be physically present; it also requires emotional, spiritual, and even physical preparation. One must ensure that one can be a vessel to receive what a traumatized person needs to share, unburden, and expunge. This necessitates attuned listening, presence, and the ability to remain in palpable pain without acquiescing to the human need to fix - spitting out random cliches and platitudes like a broken fortune teller.

Foundationally, the first requirement of a witness is to believe the TP. Witness implies belief. Traumatized persons deserve affirmation when they share their stories and unquestioning support regardless of unanswered questions, timelines that seem to contradict, or hearing details seemingly so horrendous as to be implausible. It is the responsibility of those who have been entrusted with the harrowing story to hold it. Indeed, the job of the witness is not to fact-check the narrative or to make sense of the traumatic event(s), but to believe that it happened. This is imperative because "belief mediates action."[103] Needed and required action may not be immediately apparent but will emerge and the traumatized person deserves not simply a sounding board but a living being who will engage in the work with them.[104] Furthermore, the courage required to share the traumatic experience/injury and the hope extended to the witness can be irrevocably damaged by an act of disbelief or doubt. This damage may permanently affect a traumatized person and further support a narrative of their own self-doubt or unworthiness.

When witnessing and experiencing dysregulated people, one without trauma training may label their behavior as dramatic, over the top, attention seeking, overly withdrawn, or that of a 'control freak.' One's discomfort with the actions of the other is what leads to this judgment. Thus, another requirement of those who want to provide trauma-informed care and journeying is the ability and commitment to move from judgment to compassion. Compassion incites curiosity: "I wonder why someone would behave in that way. To live in that body with those thoughts/behaviors must be challenging/exhausting/difficult." Beginning in compassion, the caregiver and community are thus positioned to listen, engage, and

---

103. O'Donnell and Cross, *Feminist Trauma Theologies*, 44.

104. "Advances in the field occur only when they are supported by a political movement powerful enough to legitimate an alliance between investigators and patients and to counteract the ordinary social processes of silencing and denial. In the absence of strong political movements for human rights, the active process of bearing witness inevitably gives way to the active process of forgetting. Repression, dissociation, and denial are phenomena of social as well as individual consciousness." Herman, *Trauma and Recovery*, 9

respond. What may be considered or judged as dysregulation is actually survival – learned behavior required to endure. As Jana Pressley says, "Traumatized people make sense! All developmental adaptations are functional in the context in which they initially developed."[105]

Additionally, to be fully available to a traumatized person, one must have examined one's beliefs and capabilities as well as gathered knowledge so as not to inflict harm unintentionally. What does the witness personally believe about theodicy? Can they ensure their belief system will not be imposed upon another? What does the witness understand and believe about trauma, traumatic injury, and recovery? Have they received training? This does not necessitate obtaining a Ph.D. in psychology but rather an awareness of one's boundaries, scope of practice, and a willingness to engage others and ensure the TP is receiving the care needed. There is no place in trauma recovery for ego or territorialism. Those with God complexes or who long to be a solitary hero will not serve TP well.

Importantly, traumatic recovery requires the witness to inhabit the messiness of bodily experience. Snot, tears, screams, crying, cold hands, tremors, and palpable silence are entrusted to those who witness. Acknowledging their ears may take in the sounds of the words, the cries, and the silence but it is felt deep within; the reverberations of the waves pinging between ribs and heart and stomach within the listener. If such intensity is experienced in simply witnessing, this should provide deeper compassion, empathy, and determination for appropriate advocacy as the full weight of traumatic events and injury surpasses comprehension. "Bearing witness .... is to feel God's presence and God's absence at the same time. It is to hear stories that unsettle and to view profoundly

---

105. Pressley Psy.D., "The Complexity of Adaptation to Trauma."

disturbing scenes. It is to realize the very liminal spaces and edges of faith, beyond where we can even imagine them."[106]

Rambo notes the relationship between the witness and TP that both are transformed and engage in a "co-birth of an experience" regarding the TP's "difficult past".[107] While Rambo writes beautifully, challengingly, and compellingly on the work of witnessing as being present to the traumatized person, even amidst the concept of "co-birth," it is categorized as a relationship of one giving and another receiving. Thus, I believe she may have overlooked a critical aspect of the relationship. I argue that the act of witness is a symbiotic relationship.

In an interview with Janine Benyus, Krista Tippett was inquiring about biomimicry and, as she describes it, "a radical way of approaching the gravest of our problems by attending to how original vitality functions."[108] As the interview progressed, the poetic, powerful, and profound ways in which Benyus described biomimicry, though she was talking about design and structural implications of the work, began to take shape for implications in trauma recovery regarding the interdependence and attachment required for TP to heal. One cannot heal alone.

The importance of the symbiotic relationship in recovery cannot be underscored enough. Traumatized persons are disconnected from themselves and often their surroundings and require reconnection to facilitate healing. When Janine began to poetically describe the symbiotic relationship between humans and leaves - it was an awakening moment to contemplate trauma recovery as a symbiotic relationship (and the concept of witness) as

---

106. Karen O'Donnell and Katie Cross, eds., *Bearing Witness: Intersectional Perspectives on Trauma Theology* (London, UK: SCM Press, 2022), 4.

107. Rambo, "Trauma and Faith," 241.

108. "Janine Benyus — Biomimicry, an Operating Manual for Earthlings," The On Being Project, accessed October 30, 2023, https://onbeing.org/programs/janine-benyus-biomimicry-an-operating-manual-for-earthlings/.

it pertains to caring for a traumatized person AND the act of witness required *of* a traumatized person. Just as there is a symbiotic relationship evident in nature so too is there in recovery. Specifically, one must bear witness to that which has been unseen, unknown, unclaimed, unheard, and unloved. In response, the traumatized person too has the work of bearing witness – to an image of themselves that perhaps they have never been privileged to see as a person of intrinsic worth, undefined by the narratives, words, and actions of others.

As Benyus describes leaves and photosynthesis, she says,

This little wishbone-shaped molecule that grabs light photons, two photons femtoseconds apart and takes our out-breath — carbon dioxide, and water, and some minerals — and makes sugars and starches and then gives us back oxygen. So, for a biologist, there's nothing more poetic really than photosynthesis. It's just so beautiful in its symbiotic exchange: you give me carbon dioxide and I'll breathe out some oxygen for you.[109]

In this eloquent explanation, it became obvious that in discussing witness, there is transformation in both persons and a rebirthing and healing which requires the witness to receive the stories and information shared by the TP as well as reflect the Authentic Self to the TP. Reciprocally, the traumatized person is also a witness to a radically different schema of engaging with and relating to themselves and the world through the person journeying with them. The witness says to the TP, 'You give me your wounds and I will reflect to you the Authentic Self I see which may seem hidden beneath them'. The TP offers the witness the

---

109. "Janine Benyus — Biomimicry, an Operating Manual for Earthlings."

trust and sacred gift of a story that may be hidden in the dark and often allows the witness the first glimpses of the Authentic Self.

Therefore, the relationship is one rooted in compassion, steadfastness, nonjudgement, and grace, and by these behaviors and consistent journeying, the TP will (hopefully) be able to see themselves through the eyes of the witness not hidden behind the maelstrom of trauma responses including the harmful (and understandable) self-evaluation as a fractured, broken, shame-filled individual but rather as a person bearing the unspeakable marks of traumatic injury which has not destroyed their Authentic Self. The witness not only watches the AS emerge but are themselves transformed as they have witnessed a liminal space in which one is never the same.

Thus, the importance of witness is not only to what can be known but to what is unknown. Spiritually, it is the space in which individuals dwell in the liminal spaces between life and death; the unending facet of the traumatic event and the death of what was and the current trajectory of life – neither space being fully inhabited. As trauma is an ontological wound, the issues of spirituality and being as oriented to something greater are necessary to explore and engage. For those who choose to be witnesses journeying alongside TP, the credo espoused is critically important to ensure further harm is not committed. Spiritually integrated communities and persons should be prepared to address these questions and beforehand, intentionally reflect on the intersections of trauma and one's credo or theology - regardless of any organized religion.

Rambo's ability to contextualize the experience of journeying in the middle, precariously balanced between life and death is a profound concept and gift to trauma literature, recovery, and the spiritual dimension of faith. In addition to her two books, she wrote an article that situates her work within the theology of resurrection and the story of the hemorrhaging woman which provides important insight and opportunities for engagement regarding the concept of resurrection as related to recovery.[110,111] Addressed herein is the importance of her conceptualization as well as the divergence of my own work and understanding.

In Christianity, there is a theological emphasis and interpretation of the death of Jesus (the cross) and the resurrection which purposes the life of Jesus as one of divine suffering and redemption followed by complete resolution of pain. The corollary leads people to believe that suffering is warranted, idealized as a deeper connection to God, and thus to be endured. This dichotomic concept of suffering and healing does not speak to the experience of traumatized persons. First, the suffering they endure is not divinely appointed nor is it purposeful. Second, in trauma, one is as Rambo describes, "living in the middle between death and life."[112] As the past is unending and the present unattainable, there is no opportunity for, or experience of, resurrection. "In the aftermath of trauma, death, and life no longer stand in opposition. Instead, death haunts life. The challenge for those who take seriously the problem of trauma is to witness traumatic injury in all its complexities – to account for the ongoing experience of death in life."[113]

Theologians in the twentieth century have questioned the symbolic use of the cross as a symbol of redemption considering the oppression and physical abuse of people of color and colonization, the objectification, suppression, and harm against women, and the white supremacist ideologies that are seemingly inherent in evangelical Christianity.[114] It is imperative if one is endeavoring to work with and provide support to TP that one not perpetuate

---

110. Matthew 5:25-34
111. Rambo, *Resurrecting Wounds*.
112. Rambo, "Trauma and Faith," 239.
113. Rambo, *Spirit and Trauma*, 3.
114. For further discussion see works by James Come, Kristin Kobes De Mez, Kathryn Tanner, Tim Alberta

trauma and harm; intentionality is expected and required. For if a witness is observed disenfranchising and obfuscating, in words or actions, the experiences of the marginalized (or any person), TP internalize the message that the witness is capable of and willing to cause harm and extrapolates that they are therefore unsafe. The hypocrisy of providing trauma-informed care while continuing the harmful rhetoric or actions against other marginalized communities discredits and upends anything of value to which one is attempting. SIC have an ethical imperative to do no harm.

Issues of overcoming and resurrection require discussion for it is not a complete line of demarcation and triumph between life and death, pain and healing, wounded and unmarked, as that would omit the experience of the traumatized. "In a posttraumatic age, they [life and death] exist simultaneously rather than sequentially."[115] TP do not live in the past or the present. They live in the liminal space, the 'Holy Saturday' between death and resurrection. This space becomes tenuous, difficult, and discomforting for those who have not been traumatized as it is unimaginable to be neither here nor there when a non-traumatized brain knows that the current moment is 'real'. "Insofar as resurrection is proclaimed as life conquering or life victorious over death, it does not speak to the realities of traumatic suffering."[116]

Resurrection in the context of trauma recovery is a way of existing in the liminal space in which wounds are neither fresh nor healed. It is "a practice of witnessing that senses life arising amidst what remains. The middle story is not a story of rising out of the depths but a transformation of the depths themselves."[117] This practice of remaining with TP as they ascertain what living on will entail and what must be left behind to do so, is a sacrosanct

---

115. Rambo, *Resurrecting Wounds*, 7.
116. Rambo, *Spirit and Trauma*, 7.
117. Rambo, 172.

covenant in which both TP and witness embody the space and experience transformation. There is not the erasure of wounds but a claiming and naming of the Authentic Self as wounds turn to scars and traumatized persons forever live with a reminder and yet are invited to recognize the scar as a symbol of not only the nearness of death but the testament to resurrection and living on.

In Rambo's work, she notes John Calvin's urging of the erasure of wounds to triumph over death. Such erasure is harmful; Rambo reclaims the wounds stating,

> The danger in erasing these wounds is that the erasure occludes a testimony to what is most difficult about traumatic histories, whether personal or collective: that the wounds remain. And yet to reorient the logic of wounds toward the after-living requires care and attention. To think about these wounds differently is to draw from Calvin's thought for what Calvin could not bring into view. Resurrection wounds provide a curious constellation for conceiving of life that is marked by wounds but recreated through them.[118]

Spiritually integrated communities – in whatever manner that presents and is shaped, defined, and described – are known for being spaces in which, regardless of tradition, the importance of connectedness and community are upheld. All faith traditions see humanity as being created for relationships. Moreover, all psychological and psychiatric science is predicated on the need for connectivity and relationships. As a basic tenet of humanity, facilitating healthy relationships is a primary way in which spiritual communities can exercise great care and support for TP. This requires strategic development and intentional examination of

---

118. Rambo, *Resurrecting Wounds*, 42.

current structures and behaviors within the community to attempt to create a safe space for TP. To begin, understanding systems and their function is foundational.

Systems

As SIC consider engaging in trauma-informed care, in addition to the obligation and need for education on trauma, a primary work is understanding how communities and individuals function. This systemic approach is best explained through Bowen Family Systems Theory. Following is a brief primer.

Systems affect the individual, family, organization, community, country, and world; existing at micro, mezzo, and macro levels and are integral to understanding trauma impacts and recovery. Throughout his career which began in the 1940s at the Menninger Clinic, Dr. Murray Bowen pioneered the theory of 'family systems' which utilizes "systems thinking to describe the complex interactions in the unit."[119] Bowen's groundbreaking work taught that the automatic emotional processes of groups can be better analyzed, understood, and changed by understanding the self as part of a unit that functions in certain ways.[120] Through that experience, one takes on certain behaviors, as understood and influenced by the system they experienced in their formative years.

Every individual is part of a system and carries with them the marks of that system – communication, expectations, responses, reactions, norms, etc. "Systems thinking strives to look at the

---

119. Michael E. Kerr, M.D., *One Family's Story: A Primer on Bowen Theory* (Washington, D.C.: Center for the Study of Family, 2013), 1.
120. While Dr. Murray used the term 'family', due to the multitude of issues arising in trauma regarding the family, I have chosen to use the other word that he employs, 'unit' in order to not place the context in something that may be painful and/or triggering as well as ostracizing..

emotional process going on among people...to better manage oneself and one's contribution to the situation."[121] When an individual is unaware of the influences upon their own system or their impact on other systems, it is difficult to engage in healthy communication. Additionally, boundary setting – a critically important aspect of recovery for TP and those who journey with them – may be difficult to utilize. In trauma, as in all change, if someone is becoming healthier, more differentiated, and more able to function in regulated ways that allow their Authentic Self to appear, systems will also be affected by positive change.

"In thinking systems, the focus is on the *whole* relationship system, how emotions circulate through it and the different processes or patterns that arise automatically in the process."[122] This is observable in an example of anxiety. What causes one to be anxious spreads through the group and increases anxiety in others. At times, the spreading of anxiety is overt, such as when one announces a tragedy like a sudden car accident or house fire, and the group or community all react. However, there are times when the anxiety that spreads is less overt. When someone unknown comes into the group or organization. Everyone may be welcoming and kind but the anxiety of interacting with a new person may be increasing beneath the visible surface which may affect interactions. It is important to recall that every person's response will be different but nevertheless, they are affected by the emotions/actions/experiences of each one within the group. Though this may seem rather obvious, individuals often do not recognize the depth of emotions activated within themselves when they are experiencing the anxiety of another.

How one responds to anxiety – fusion, triangling, conflict,

---

121. Roberta M. Gilbert M.D., *The Eight Concepts of Bowen Theory* (Lake Frederick, Virginia: Leading Systems Press, 2004), 2.
122. Gilbert M.D., 6.

distancing, and/or under/over-functioning – creates patterns of behavior that are carried into every relationship or system of which one is a part. It is only in recognizing these patterns and learning how systems interact and function that one can fully engage in healthy and thoughtful ways. The concept and understanding of systems are critical to understanding the impact of witnessing trauma, the effect of trauma on the system, and how the system is responding to the experiences and reactivity/reactions of the TP. Additionally, organizations function in patterns of behavior that respond to stimuli. Thus, not only is it pertinent to understand the individual and their functioning within a system but to analyze the organization, group, community, and their responsive vs. reactive ability.

Trauma affects systems; the internal system as noted in IFS and the systems to which individuals engage, participate, and belong. Most people are aware of the issue of triangulation, though the act of triangulating is different from the notion of triangles that Bowen develops in Family Systems Theory.[123] Triangles are the smallest stable unit of an emotional system – the smallest stable relationship system. As Bowen states "A three-person system is one triangle, a four-person system is four primary triangles, a five-person system is nine primary triangles, etc. In addition, there are a variety of secondary triangles when two or more may band together for one corner of a triangle for one emotional issue, while the configuration shifts on another issue."[124]

An example of the function of triangles is as follows. If someone comes into one's office extremely upset and needs to talk, those two people create a system for the time they are together,

---

123. Bringing a third party into a relationship and/or conflict in order to manipulate another to take a side by avoiding direct interaction with the person in the originating conflict. It is a common tactic to help one feel in control, have a sense of power, and experience being heard/seen.
124. Gilbert M.D., *The Eight Concepts of Bowen Theory*, 44.

thus impacting one another. When the upset person leaves, the other person may return to the equilibrium of their own system or not. If they take the conversation home and share with their partner that they had a difficult interaction, three systems converge and this triangle, completely ubiquitous and often used to help diffuse anxiety, either does so and allows a return to the homeostasis of the individuals and system *or* the partner takes on the anxiety and then that system is affected.

If one goes to work the next day and is anxious/worried about their partner because of the previous day, their work system is affected. This is now called 'interlocking triangles'. The importance of understanding how systems impact and influence one another is critical to working with traumatized persons for trauma *is* unsettling. It *is* upsetting. It *is* sad, angering, enraging, and crushing at times. It is almost inhuman to hear the story of one's trauma and NOT have a reaction. The question being, is the system to which one is working within able to handle the emotional needs of the TP? Is the system equipped to provide support to the witness? Is the internal system of the witness able to handle both the TP's and their own reactions? How do others within the witness's and TP's work, family, and community system respond? What tools does a person possess to return to equilibrium? These questions are at the heart of mutually influencing relationships and their ability to withstand anxiety.

Systems are not simply created by a triangle of individuals in relationships. Organizations are a system, a board of directors or deacons, church council, session, choir, garden group, running club, etc. are each a system within other systems. Therefore, the questions that need to be addressed are not only of the individual but of the community and groups within it.

Systems (and the people within them) tend to fall into functional ruts – we've always done it this way. Not only is that obvious in a church or organizational setting, but it is true within the individual system as well. For instance, if one has always identified themselves as a helper and has been in a relationship in which they can engage in that manner but the person they have become close with no longer needs them to function in that capacity, the inability of the helper to function differently within their internal and external systems may cause a relational break. Systems must be analyzed for their current capacity and characteristics of their functioning. Where are the strengths and weaknesses within the systems? Who are the leaders and/or to whom do people defer? Why? Is this healthy? What is the general reactivity of the system? Who or what tends to most influence the system?

Finally, one may assume that participating in the TP's recovery (which may subsequently cause a reduction in PTSD systems such as flashbacks, hyper/hypo activity, etc.) would positively affect the system, but that is not a guarantee. Sometimes systems thrive on reactivity and emotions. If this is the case and the positive change causes negative functioning, TP may also have to deal with the realization that their recovery may structurally change their world at an incredibly crucial juncture thereby causing distress and possibly thwarting any positive healing. Thus, it is critical that persons and/or organizations take inventory and be aware of the ways in which their systems function before taking on the question of whether or not to develop programming and/or intentional outreach to traumatized persons.

Justice & Reconciliation

HEALING IS NOT AN ENDPOINT; it does not have a definitive moment after which everything is 'okay'. Recovery is a way of living post-trauma that empowers one to deal with the dysregulation in body, mind, and spirit, set and enact healthy engagement with self, others, and the world, and choose to tend to the wounds when they are enflamed with self-compassion and care.

I wish I could tell you there is a moment when healing occurs and the TP never has to deal with the effects of the trauma again. But I would be lying. Or that there is an easy way through the pain. But again, that would be a lie. It is crucially important to be clear that healing is painful. It is some of the most difficult work one will ever endeavor. Yet, this is not a solo voyage. While the work may only be done by the traumatized person and each achievement is theirs alone, they can accomplish the work of recovery because of relationships.

Rooting the work of the spiritually integrated and aware in the presumption that the Authentic Self is protected by the brain and the body which experience the unmitigated pain, the power of spiritually integrated communities to be ideal supports and positive influences resides in their capacity to engage TP in ritual, community, and intentionality to create space for trauma healing. Moreover, standing against a consumerist/capitalist society focused on individual productivity and financial/material worth and alongside the TP who does not have to "perform" to be cared for, welcomed, and loved is a radical act of solidarity and a visible witness to the community and world that TP deserve to recover. This underscores the imperative of understanding the effects of trauma as neurobiological expressions and not those of the Authentic Self.

Work of Spiritually Integrated Communities/Persons

Trauma recovery is an arduous, multifaceted, herculean challenge coexisting with unimaginable pain which requires an attentive, prudent, educated, and compassionate response. Yet, before responding to and engaging with TP, the question must be asked and answered, why does one and/or an organization want to become intentionally involved in trauma-informed care and/or recovery? Trauma work requires a commitment to examine the self and the community as ontological questions are not only individual in nature. These may include why does the SIC exist? What brought it into being? Why is it still functioning? What is its purpose? Has the role/purpose/function of the SIC changed over time? If so, how? Is the desire to engage in trauma-informed care and/or recovery reflective of the whole? If not, who or what faction of people is requesting this, and who might be affected by this change? Will individuals as well as the community be able to tolerate the level of intentionality and/or change required? What practices will be instituted to ensure that all feel heard and seen?

Many of these questions are best accomplished through the examination of systems as noted previously.[1]

It would be insufficient and irresponsible to attempt to care for the most vulnerable without ensuring their safety to the best of the ability of the organization and individual; the outlined questions must be answered not only by leadership but discerned as a group. The undertaking of providing trauma-informed care and recovery cannot simply be another designation, award, or logo for the bulletin, website, newsletter, or church/company t-shirt. This work requires fundamental change and is not for the marginally committed. Continuing to root this endeavor in recognizing the Authentic Self and the spiritual component of all persons, trauma-informed programming which facilitates care and recovery will be examined and presented through the framework of the Christian tradition. However, the reader will engage in tangible experiences and opportunities to observe the necessary endeavors and practices to prepare and the applicability thereof thus one can extrapolate and implement these concepts in their particular community and/or context.

"It is not enough for theology to state that survivors ought to be believed. We are obliged to construct embodied practices of belief that bear full witness to what it means to live as a person who has experience the world's attempt to erase them."[2]

Nevertheless, research, conversations, and stories reveal that churches, spiritually integrated communities, and pastors are unprepared to construct embodied practices nor adept in

---

1. It is also imperative that if a community discern to engage in the work of providing trauma-informed care that attention is paid to those who did not want to participate in such initiatives. How will their emotions and experiences be addressed so as to not undermine other efforts as well as to ensure they are cared for during this time of transition. Will there be additional listening sessions? Are there specific concerns that could be addressed which may assist in the decision to participate in the trauma-informed initiatives?

2. O'Donnell and Cross, *Feminist Trauma Theologies*, 55.

theological or spiritual constructs for the work of providing trauma-informed care regardless of desire or commitment. Until recently, most seminary graduates were not receiving any specific education on trauma-informed care. Within the confines of the research survey I conducted, out of 37 respondents who identified as spiritual leaders, 92% believed that churches and/or spiritual communities were neither prepared nor adept at dealing with and addressing trauma. However, when asked if one's faith community engages in intentional actions to assist traumatized persons to integrate and feel welcome and safe in their community, 43% answered 'yes'. When asked to describe how the practice came to be, it is clear that there is a lack of understanding of what trauma is; of the 15 who provided written answers, 13 identified actions or practices that were not trauma-informed nor were they addressing trauma as the responses included such things as 'creating safe space for neurodivergent persons'. While that is a wonderful, intentional act, neurodivergent persons are not traumatized merely by their status as neurodivergent persons.[3] Additionally, while it is caring that 'help can be requested', as noted by two people, TP struggle to ask for help for a variety of reasons previously discussed including stigma, fear, and feeling unworthy. Thus, obvious and accessible information is necessary to ensure intent and communication. Not only are leaders and churches unprepared, but so too are many of the organizations with whom they work and/or partner.

Having worked as an executive director of a community nonprofit for seven years as well as consulting with a variety of community non-profit organizations providing frontline care for food insecurity, unhoused persons, medical access, mental health, education, and support for LGBTQ persons, I have witnessed

---

3. Some neurodivergent persons may have experienced trauma but neurodivergence is not a trauma nor a reaction to trauma.

firsthand the lack of training and resources these organizations have been provided thus ill-equipping them to offer necessary care. Many of these vitally important institutions are underfunded and additionally might rely on volunteers who may have little training and/or exposure to vulnerable populations. The impetus of any person or entity to provide care (usually) emerges from a place of ethical conviction that should be honored. However, those who have experienced trauma require more than heartfelt desire as their needs are multilayered and complex. Yet, without heart and conviction, this work is null. Therefore, it is easy to teach trauma-informed care to those who desire to learn. Because of the inherent existential ontological questions in trauma, SIC and SAP are ideally situated to respond, engage, and journey to and with TP.

The impetus to care for traumatized persons is an outgrowth of what is often deemed an ethical responsibility though each person and/or organization may define that differently. Assuming that a SIC and/or SAP has discerned to move forward in providing care, it is necessary to identify why the engagement of those most harmed and marginalized is reputed as obligatory and essential; what is the root of the ethical imperative. What does one's faith tradition, spiritual practice, credo of organization, and/or individual spirituality assert regarding the ethics of caring for others? The identifying philosophy, credo, or statement of purpose that reflects the ethical imperative should be visibly posted as a mark of encouragement and accountability. Not only does this serve as consolation and incentive in challenging moments, but it is also a conspicuous commitment to traumatized persons of the ethics and promise of the relationship.

"Trauma is always an existential process of responding to the ontological anxieties inherent in threats to existence, selfhood, and relationship and spiritual security."[4] As people have diverse cultural, spiritual, and philosophical experiences and ideas, their worldview shapes their understanding of trauma. It is imperative to providing ethical care that one be mindful of their biases and beliefs. Thus, the examination of the witness and/or organizational theology or credo as the guiding imperative must include issues of theodicy, vision, and equity.[5]

Furthermore, "belief mediates action."[6] When persons and organizations claim to believe the stories that traumatized persons disclose yet do not engage in concerted efforts to work towards justice, create safe space, and/or directly support TP, the message may be received that the harrowing event is not either believed or deemed insufficient as to warrant action. The lack of action is often experienced and internalized by TP as a reflection of their worth; they are not worth the effort required to make a difference. This is why it is imperative that if one is intentionally engaging in this work, they are prepared to act, in whatever way they are able, to stand on the side of those who have been harmed and declare them worthy, believed, and deserving of justice, care, and affirmation.

Theology and Theodicy

When examining the interactions, programming, and rituals that spiritually integrated communities engage and offer, it is important to do so through the lens of trauma-sensitive theology. Baldwin

---

4. Steven J. Sandage et al., "Anxiety, Relational Trauma, and Suffering," in *Relational Spirituality in Psychotherapy: Healing Suffering and Promoting Growth* (Washington, DC, US: American Psychological Association, 2020), 89, https://doi.org/10.1037/0000174-005.
5. For further study, see *Bible Through the Lens of Trauma* – Elizabeth Boase and Christopher G. Frechette, *Trauma Sensitive Theologies* – Jennifer Baldwin
6. O'Donnell and Cross, *Feminist Trauma Theologies*, 44.

defines this as, "a theoretical lens, ethical commitment, and guide for praxis that extends in most areas of pastoral care, practical theology, pastoral counseling, liturgy, homiletics, and care for souls, minds, and bodies."[7] The need for a trauma-informed hermeneutic is vitally important to develop to adequately assimilate information and provide thorough and conscientious care. This must include and be built upon one's personal and institutional ethics and credo as well as the incorporation of knowledge of trauma including the neurobiological responses, and the emotional, psychological, and spiritual effects. A trauma-informed hermeneutic provides a lens through which information is filtered thereby affecting how one interprets and responds to TP.[8]

For instance, a well-developed trauma-informed hermeneutical lens assists in questions of theodicy such as "Why do bad things happen" and "What is the justification for doing good in the presence of evil" as these are universal regardless of the notion of any deity.[9] This subject is pivotal to working with TP as humans are inherently wired to engage in meaning-making; it is a predictable and reasonable question for TP to ask as to why this happened to them. If one has not examined their understanding and beliefs, they cannot respond deliberately and with care.

It is human nature to want to acknowledge the pain of an individual. People generally are uncomfortable sitting in the palpable pain of another without offering an antidote or platitude. "What doesn't kill you makes you stronger." "If anyone can do this, you can!" "Anything is possible if you believe!" Pithy aphorisms that

7. Jennifer Baldwin, *Trauma-Sensitive Theology: Thinking Theologically in the Era of Trauma* (Eugene, Oregon: Cascade Books, 2018), 6.
8. Elizabeth Boase and Christopher G Frechette, eds., *Bible Through the Lens of Trauma* (Atlanta: SBL Press, 2016); Baldwin, *Trauma-Sensitive Theology*, 2018.
9. Theodicy: is the justifying of God; theos (God) dikē (justice); More broadly, it is understood as the question as to why bad things happen. See also, *The Oxford Handbook of Systemic Theology*, edited by John Webster, Kathryn Tanner, Iain Torrance 2007. P. 191-192

dispense and invoke 'truth' of what has been imposed upon people for generations often create harm and pain, and fracture relationships when doled out like cold water on a hot day as all the words and phrases seemingly were crafted for those not living in the liminal space between life and death, with the Authentic Self obscured by a wounded brain and an injured heart.

While these sayings may all contain a thread of truth, they constrain and oblige the traumatized person into a position of untenable guilt and shame, as if they would merely try harder, they could feel better. If they simply believed in themselves, this would not be happening. Yet, reactions to the trauma are not purely a matter of self-confidence or determination, the brain has been rewired. Trauma contains psychological and emotional injuries that have often stripped away the ability to embrace any sense of confidence or worth.

Therefore, offering words or quotes in the guise of spirituality and/or religion may cause additional harm as it may plausibly be interpreted as issuing claims of a deity (deities) and speaking on their behalf. "God does not give you more than you can handle."[10] "All things work for good for those who love God."[11] "With God, all things are possible."[12] "God has a plan for your life!"[13] Within these quips - scripture references taken out of context - it is thus implied that God is testing and/or teaching one with a specific purpose for life. A specific purpose for the trauma. As Rambo notes, "This theo-logic is unsettling for what it demands of human persons and what it implies about God's nature. It is also insufficient, given the scale of violence and suffering present in our world."

Theologically, justifying the pain one is experiencing by

---

10. 1 Corinthians 10:13
11. Romans 8:28
12. Matthew 19:26
13. Jeremiah 29:11

acquiescing to the concept that God has caused/allowed these situations to teach and/or to challenge individuals so that God can use them for some greater purpose causes incredible emotional, psychological, and spiritual distress; it is an impediment to recovery for how could one cry out, lament, long for healing, or seek comfort when the thing for which they require and deserve compassion, relief, and solace has been announced as a planned action against them for an unknown reason. "The traumatic event challenges an ordinary person to become a theologian, a philosopher, and a jurist. The survivor is called upon to articulate the values and beliefs that [they] once held, and that the trauma destroyed. [They] stand mute before the emptiness of evil, feeling the insufficiency of any known systems of explanation."[14]

The implications wrought by this thinking about God's character are harmful at best and, at worst, deadly. Most TP experience suicidal ideation and have an increased risk of completed suicide.[15] If one believes themselves unworthy of protection and so dispensable as for a God to cause this, it is not a psychological leap to recognize the damage inherent in such theologies. This underscores the requirement for one's theology to be examined before engaging with traumatized persons. An examined, trauma-informed theology prepares the witness to assimilate the information being offered in the story shared by the TP and respond with care and grace, centered on the tenet of doing no harm and extending compassion and the ability to sit in the incredible discomfort of there being no discernable reason that would ever excuse the insidiousness and pain of trauma.

Within Christianity in some traditions and denominations, the sole focus on the resurrection of Jesus as a triumph over death as

---

14. Herman, M. D., *Trauma and Recovery*, 1997, 178.
15. Verity Fox et al., "Suicide Risk in People with Post-Traumatic Stress Disorder: A Cohort Study of 3.1 Million People in Sweden," *Journal of Affective Disorders* 279 (January 15, 2021): 609–16, https://doi.org/10.1016/j.jad.2020.10.009.

the central tenet with an impetus to not only overcome suffering and adversity but to accept these as a marker of being "Christlike" has caused harm. These pains are taught that they will be healed in the afterlife, aka, heaven but must be endured now. "This thrust toward life can foster Christian triumphalism and supercessionism. If redemption is depicted as a happy or victorious ending in which life wins out over death, or in which death is somehow concluded/ended, such a depiction runs the risk of glossing over a more mixed experience of death and life."[16] TP do not have the luxury of waiting for their pain to be abated in an afterlife for they are barely surviving the current one. They do not fully inhabit death nor resurrection as they live in the liminal space between what was and what is: otherwise known as healing/recovery. Finally, should resurrection only be framed as the conquering of death or might it more faithfully resemble the ability to live with the scars?

"Survivors of trauma, and especially complex trauma, often carry intense feelings of justifiable rage within themselves. They are likely to direct those feelings not only at the perpetrators but also at those whom they perceive to have had the power to help them but did not, especially at God."[17] The question of theodicy cannot be easily engaged nor answered: for no two religions, groups, or individuals answer it exactly the same. It is an endless issue that keeps theologians employed. One cannot ever sufficiently answer the questions of 'why do bad things happen' or 'why did God let this happen' that would explain or justify why some people are raped, tortured, or enslaved. There are no reasons that would ever rationalize, vindicate, or defend the actions or events that have caused the egregious pain of traumatic injury. Yet, the question will always exist and if left unaddressed, becomes an

---

16. Rambo, *Spirit and Trauma*, 7.
17. Boase and Frechette, *Bible Through the Lens of Trauma*, 77.

iron bar wedged into the cog of spirituality and healing. What is most pertinent for TP is that, as spiritual care providers and those invested in their healing, they work not to provide fortune-teller responses but rather sit with the imposing reality that words are insufficient and explanations unfathomable that would soothe the traumatic injury.[18]

Reflecting upon my own experiences as a traumatized person and as one who has studied theology and trauma, I feel I must note the abject, indescribable pain and spiritual fracturing that occurs by receiving a theological explanation that is centered in the concept that God is "in control" and/or "has a plan". Speaking from a Christian perspective, I do not believe that everything happens for a reason. For what reason would God ever decide the rape of a child is necessary? The shooting at a school? The terrorist bombing at a marathon? What God would decide that being beaten and emotionally abused daily by a narcissist is the course of life they want for you? What God would condone slavery? Endorse genocide? Plan for murder?

For more than 30 years, I believed what I had been taught as a child and that was reinforced in my teenage years in foster care when I was required to attend an evangelical church – hearing constantly and consistently that 'God had a plan' and that 'everything happens for a reason'. This fracture between myself and the Holy Mystery caused me to lose my ability to connect to the care and love that others offered as I continued to wonder what I had done wrong for my trauma to be a part of a plan. Without engaging in lofty theological arguments akin to my seminary days, I offer the words of nurse Julienne in Call the Midwife which I believe to be true: "God isn't in the event. God is in the response to

---

18. I have coined these aphorisms and platitudes as 'fortune teller' responses as they are reminiscent of the words provided by fortune teller machines, fortune cookies, and cute sayings on tea bags.

the event. In the love that is shown and the care that is given."[19] I invite you to ponder your responses to the theodicy questions of why. Are your answers sufficient in that if you put yourself in the shoes of the TP, would you be happy to receive them? Would they be words of comfort and empowerment? Would they hold space for the unanswerable "reason" of trauma?

Providing care to TP requires the ability to espouse a theology that reflects the reality of trauma in all its facets, emotional, spiritual, cognitive, and psychological pain, and the physiological changes. One must be prepared to enter the liminal space in which the trauma feels ongoing thus one lives in the death of what was while also inhabiting the present which cannot be fully experienced, the liminal space of surviving. James Derrida provides an etymology of the word survive translating it from the French *survivre*, noting "if directly translated, it means "over living" or "living on".[20] Traumatized persons experience the living on within the context of crisis, grief, and death. Any theology or credo that cannot reflect the reality of existing in the liminal space or of the never-ending unanswerable question of why while affirming the Authentic Self will only cause harm and should be reevaluated.

Finally, one may assume that this question would only be asked by those who believe in a higher power or energy within the universe; inferring that atheists do not wonder why bad things happen. However, this question is universal, transcending any formal religious identity or spirituality as humans seek to understand why and to explain the pain. Lament is universal. The cry of why and how could this be is heard in every language and culture. It is imperative that those who recognize the Authentic Self and work to care for the spirit of the TP – regardless of race or religion - are prepared for this conversation if/when it arises so that they

---

19. "Call The Midwife" (BBC, February 8, 2015).
20. Rambo, "Trauma and Faith," 239.

may assist them in discovering what their AS fears, worries, assumes, or believes about the answer as to why and to situate their answer in a place of empowerment and self-affirmation; they did not deserve this and are worthy of experiencing healing.

The Story of the Hemorrhaging Woman

Within Christianity, there is a story about a woman and her encounter with Jesus that exemplifies the power of interaction between traumatized persons and those who are witnesses to their experience. The story reads, "Now there was a woman who had been suffering from hemorrhages for twelve years; and though she had spent all she had on physicians, no one could cure her. She came up behind him [Jesus] and touched the fringe of his clothes, and immediately her hemorrhage stopped. Then Jesus asked, "Who touched me?" When all denied it, Peter said, "Master, the crowds surround you and press in on you." But Jesus said, "Someone touched me; for I noticed the power had gone out from me." When the woman saw that she could not remain hidden, she came trembling; and falling down before him, she declared in the presence of all the people why she had touched him, and how she had been immediately healed. He said to her, "Daughter, your faith has made you well; go in peace."[21]

Though one may read this and assume the emphasis is on miraculous healing, through a trauma-informed hermeneutic, one observes the power of witness, self-determination, and the internal healing that may occur in the intersection of these. Shelly Rambo has written a profound article on this passage which is worthy of examination. She roots her premise by "allowing the experience of

---

21. Luke 8:43-48

radical suffering to inform and reshape the category of faith" of which she asserts that "faith is a witnessed movement".[22]

It is significant that the encounter of healing between the woman and Jesus was not after facts had been gathered, checked, assessed, or interpreted, nor did the woman identify herself as being in pain and/or needing healing; her self-determination was the locus. Too often people believe they are entitled to or required to know the story before the need is addressed. While TP yearn to tell their stories and witnesses should be prepared to listen, it is a space of privilege not entitlement. Trauma-informed care requires that TP are emotionally embraced and affirmed without requesting the reasons why they are experiencing the emotions/feelings etc. This is not to say that if one is facilitating connecting a traumatized person with services that they should not attempt to ascertain pertinent details to provide assistance but rather that the story of the trauma is not necessary to provide compassion and support and should not be expected.

Like many TP, the hemorrhaging woman had exhausted her resources having "spent all she had on physicians."[23] She had been excluded from her community as during that time, a menstruating woman would have been considered unclean and disallowed to be physically amidst the community. Additionally, she would not have been permitted to partake in any rituals or gatherings. Thus, she arrives at the place in which people had gathered around Jesus destitute and ostracized, taking an enormous risk in being in public. With nothing further to lose and only hope, she seeks healing, "believing that the brush of his cloak will be enough to heal her."[24] As Judith Herman would say, "Recovery is the empowerment of the survivor."[25]

---

22. Rambo, "Trauma and Faith," 234.
23. Luke 8:43
24. Rambo, "Trauma and Faith," 244.
25. Herman, M. D., *Trauma and Recovery*, 1997, 133.

One of the most compelling aspects of this story is that it is the woman who facilitates her own healing. Jesus is not, in fact, the healer; he "occupies the particular space of witness."[26] He is a witness to the healing experienced by this woman. He felt something happen when she touched his cloak, but he did not initiate the healing, nor did he purposefully engage in it. As Rambo states, "The woman's body feels life again and Jesus is not making it happen; he is not even aware of what has happened."[27]

While some may read that she "came trembling and falling down before him" as an act of fear, arguably, this could be an act of shock, relief, and joy; she has bravely initiated her healing. This woman had been ostracized for 12 years, left destitute with no resources, has dealt with all the health issues accompanying the hemorrhage, and suddenly, is healed. The physiological response must have been unimaginably powerful to feel the hemorrhage stop. Yet, that isn't the end of the story. Courageously, she tells Jesus why she sought him out and touched his cloak: the whole, messy story. He doesn't interrupt and asks her to refrain from such a discussion in public. He doesn't mitigate her words or her experiences. Jesus listens. "The roots of resilience...are to be found in the sense of being understood by and existing in the mind and heart of a loving, attuned, and self-possessed other."[28] This taboo subject is laid bare after which, to a woman who is an outcast, Jesus publicly calls her 'daughter'. In one sentence she is affirmed and transformed from alone and ostracized to cherished and treasured; her worth is declared in the midst of all the people. She is claimed. She is worthy. She is beloved.

Thus far, Rambo's work is in sync with my own analysis, yet I diverge from Rambo's regarding the emphasis on bodily touch. She

26. Rambo, "Trauma and Faith," 246.
27. Rambo, 248.
28. Van Der Kolk, M.D., *The Body Keeps the Score*, 2015, 107.

emphasizes the profundity in the bodily encounter between the hemorrhaging woman and Jesus that begins the story. While the significance of bodily touch is remarkable as it is understood that trauma is a wound held within the body, I argue that the act of witness is enough to empower and hold space for the TP to engage in the work necessary for recovery. Thus, I contend that as Jesus had no knowledge of what was happening, it was not in the touching of the cloak through which the woman was healed but, in her self-determination and bravery to seek restoration. This is reflected as her Authentic Self is affirmed when Jesus calls her "daughter". While the story as it is written ends with her healing, it is dubious to assume that nothing transpired post her encounter with Jesus. I would argue that her work was just beginning, as she doubtless then returned to fractured relationships (as she had been ostracized), financial ruin, and the experience of recovery through post-traumatic living in a body that bore the memories and scars but was led by the Authentic Self.

Another reason for the divergence in Rambo's work is concern that the emphasis will be placed upon bodily touch and external healing which could create unsafe actions for TP. Not all TP (or any person) tolerate nor desire physical touch and it is inappropriate and harmful to touch another person without their consent. Caregivers must be cautious about interpreting this story to believe that physical touch is required. Trauma healing cannot solely be experienced externally through an act of another, and such concepts may set up an unreasonable hope placed upon spiritual leaders and therapists to "fix" the pain. Traumatic healing and recovery is an internal endeavor that, while it is assisted by others, cannot be accomplished through a single outside source but requires a multitude of strategies including mental health interventions, somatics, rituals, and the act of witnessing which beholds the inarticulable pain of trauma and affirms the Authentic Self. A body may feel transformed simply by those who surround it with love, acceptance, and grace without direct touch.

As Gabor Maté states, "No one can plot somebody else's course of healing, because that's not how healing works. There are no road maps for something that must find its individual arc. We can, however, sketch out the territory, describe it, familiarize ourselves with it, prepare to meet its challenge." This is the work of those who choose to journey with traumatized persons. Therefore, having created a framework grounded in the science of trauma, identifying the need for a trauma-informed hermeneutic lens and the importance of educating witnesses, a sketch of TIC is emerging and the need for a plan of care. In the following section are action items to assist in the implementation of trauma-informed care and recovery engagement and programming. It is not an exhaustive list but rather practical guidance and generative information to begin this critical work.

Action: Relationships

One cannot heal without the engagement of social support, relationships, and healthy attachments. This is especially true for traumatized persons as there is a fundamental lack of safety and a fracturing of relationships within traumatic injury; "what has been broken relationally must be repaired relationally."[29] TP, especially those who have experienced interpersonal violence, have learned that relationships cannot be trusted, even the most sacred (parent, spouse, child), and therefore will need emotional accommodations including patience, grace, tolerance, and a commitment to stay in the relationship regardless of the challenges - even if that means setting difficult boundaries. This is not to say that if a relationship is unsafe or causing harm, it should continue. However,

29. Kalsched, *Trauma and the Soul*, 13.

traumatized persons have difficulty with closeness as it has been unsafe, and they will need to develop tolerance and trust with a caring confidante as TP often vacillate between needing closeness and distance; sometimes pushing others away in painful acts as an unconscious test of whether the person will remain. It is the task of the witness to be steadfast as the TP works to build trust and learn, develop, and practice new ways of engaging.

Another aspect of the vacillating need between closeness and distance is the TP's need to reestablish autonomy and self-control. TP have often been stripped of those empowerments and rights. While being close to someone may be dangerous, it may also be the only way for TP to experience positive feedback as their inner dialogue/narrative may not be capable – yet – of providing positive self-care and/or affirmation. A primary imperative of their healing is that TP deserve the opportunity to learn relational repair. This is the intentional work of dealing with miscommunication, perceived offenses, and hurt feelings which lead to distress and relationship ruptures. Ideally, repair will take place when the rupture occurs. If one has been in relationships that did not engage in repair but instead operated through threats, coercion, or being ignored or dismissed, TP were likely unable or unallowed to express their emotions, concerns, or negative experiences in the relationship and the concept of repair will be quite foreign.

Kellyanne Rugenstein, a psychotherapist specializing in marriage and family therapy with over 25 years of experience explains the foundations of relational repair:

> The most common human relationship tripwire in communication is the tension between what the speaker intends, and the listener interprets. The speaker may say something with every good intention and the other hears it with every bad connotation one could think of. This happens in most communication people engage in on a

daily basis. We are not trained or practiced to seek clarity but rather, one moves forward assuming they know what the person meant. When one walks away from the conversation hurt, angry, or feeling misheard, something has gone awry and a reparative conversation is in order – if the parties can tolerate the anxiety and conflict that may arise from such a conversation.[30]

Not only does this reparative work strengthen and benefit relationships and allow for healing but also models behaviors that TP will be able to implement in all areas of their life including within themselves as they work with their wounded parts.

It is essential to recall that while people have daily miscommunication due to a perceived understanding of intention that may not be correct, TP have the added struggle of listening to another through the lens and narrative they have adopted or has been forced upon them which may be the voice of their perpetrator. While it is not the sole responsibility of the witness to ensure that TP are safe in the relationship, they do bear a large portion as their brain is operating without the impediments of trauma. Traumatized persons all have things that cause activation (triggers) of their traumatic injury and there are many times that they may not even realize the activators. It is incumbent upon both the witness and TP to address the tripwire and/or miscommunication and share their intention. While the witness, nor the TP for that matter, may know why something caused anxiety, irritation, and heartache, the important aspect of repair is sharing the intention with which something was said or done as it is imperative to learn how to communicate and not assume.

Witnesses should understand and recognize that for a TP to

30. Kellyanne Rugenstein Ph.D., "Personal Conversation Regarding Communication Dynamics and Their Impact on Relationship," January 31, 2024.

disclose to them, if they choose, what the activator was is an incredible act of bravery and trust and they should be acknowledged for this. It should not be overlooked. Moving forward, the witness has the knowledge and ability to avoid actions, words, or behaviors that may/will cause activation within the TP, it is also the responsibility of the TP to begin to understand and manage their activators. Witnesses may support the TP once they have identified the activator as they learn to navigate new relationships and ways of relating to the world.

> For TP, the work of discerning and learning that other people have good intentions and are not acting maliciously takes time and repetition. Moreover, neither person will be able to adjust how they engage in an instant. The mutuality lies in the idea that one will try to avoid the triggering and the TP will try not to react to it. In this effort, both parties grow and the relationship deepens due to the mutual respect afforded each other for their effort and understanding.[31]

Additionally, secure, trustworthy relationships require internal and external systems of safety surrounding the individuals and/or programs with which TP engage. "Establishing a safe environment requires not only the mobilization of caring people but also the development of a plan for future protection."[32] What are the policies currently in place to protect marginalized people including traumatized persons and also children, LGBTQ, and BIPOC? Are there policies regarding sexual abuse, exploitation, harassment, or being alone with other people? What, if any, continuing education

---

31. Rugenstein Ph.D., "Personal Conversation Regarding Communication Dynamics and Their Impact on Relationship," January 31, 2024.
32. Herman, M. D., *Trauma and Recovery*, 1997, 164.

requirements are there? Is there a policy and plan of action regarding suicidality and suicidal behavior? Are these policies known and/or accessible?

An aspect of the creation and implementation of policies for safety is the importance of noting if the current resources available to TP are equally accessible to all in need who have been traumatized or if there are issues of systemic oppression, race, or gender identity that would be barriers to engaging in programs. If there are impediments identified, what are they and how can they be remediated? Building safety includes creating a wide net and therefore it is important to identify existing resources in the community that one may employ and/or partner with to provide care. The duplication of resources is a waste of time, money, and talent. Are there mental health professionals within the community to whom one could refer? Are there trauma recovery groups, in person or online, that could be offered as another resource? Are there individuals or organizations committed to justice in which TP may engage should they choose to pursue legal avenues? Trauma recovery requires multiple therapeutic interventions – a spiritually integrated community or person cannot undertake this alone. Multi-focal modalities and therapy interventions are required. Harm will be done if one entity believes they can "heal" the injury or "solve" the crisis.[33] Individuals and organizations need to build strong relationships amongst those serving TP to create a network and not a single outlet. No one organization or person can provide all the necessary care.

Many of the resources that TP deserve and require are often inaccessible due to the financial resources that adequate care necessitates. While not every organization may have the monetary assets to provide funding for essential treatment and resources, it is ethically imperative to work with organizations and discern ways

---

33. Herman, M. D., 169.

of ensuring care is provided regardless of the cost. From a Christian ethic and framework, one is called to stand against consumerist and capitalist exchanges in which only those with financial means receive care. Trauma recovery is not a luxury but a human right and a necessity for the good of humanity.

Action: Communication

One of the most important aspects of providing trauma-informed care is competent communication which requires preparation on behalf of the witness. Foremost is to ready oneself to receive any information the TP may want to share including their experiences of trauma.[34] This may occur before a relationship is established which requires a herculean act of courage from the TP and is imperative that such courage is met with compassion, nonjudgement, and respect. Without this, a relationship would be nearly impossible to form. Recognize that disclosing one's story is a radical act of trust by the TP and a fracturing of the relationship could occur if one is unable to withstand experiencing the trauma as told through the story of the TP and therefore attempts to subvert, alter the conversation, or even look away. Empathic presence and listening are necessary skills, not the interrogation of the TP regarding their story. To that end, interrupting is unacceptable. Full stop. It is a dismissive act that inflicts harm and asserts authoritarian power. 'Clarifying questions' may also be inappropriate and/or harmful. The witness must decide if they are asking questions because *they* want more information or if it is necessary to provide care. Humans tend to be inquisitive – nosy – and one's trauma is not available for voyeurism. The goal isn't to know every

---

34. For further conversation, see *Trauma Sensitive Theology*, Jennifer Baldwin. p 75, Defining and Assessing the Syndrome of Moral Injury, Litz et. al.

detail of how they were wounded but to honor them and work with the TP for their healing.

Consequently, practice should be undertaken by those who plan on engaging with TP, ideally in groups, to read stories (fiction or nonfiction) or transcripts of interviews that detail trauma and respond to the person reading/telling the story. This exercise of listening to another a few feet away transforms the experience from one in which a person may remain detached (watching television, reading a book) to the palpable pain encountered in a "real-life" setting thus providing the witness with the opportunity to practice experiencing vicarious pain, discomfort, shock, and horror in a safe setting to hone the necessary skills of listening and responding. If this exercise seems odd, perhaps think of it this way: the first time you watch a horror movie or psychological thriller, you may have jumped, startled, or even cried out when something unexpected happened. The next time you watched it, and after that, you were more prepared for that part and your body knew what to do.

Upon hearing a painful story, one feels an imperative to soothe the pain yet there are no words that could ever adequately address the atrocity. The best anyone can offer is empathic listening that honors and reflects the current expressions and experiences as shared by the traumatized person. In her book, Everything Happens for a Reason and Other Lies I've Loved, Kate Bowler tackles head-on what I denote as fortune-teller responses. "Be grateful you don't have to live that way anymore." "Be grateful you survived." "You are a miracle." "Your attitude determines your destiny."[35] These phrases and pithy aphorisms are ultimately an attempt by the listener to make the pain palatable for them. The TP knows, endures, and is ensconced in their suffering. It cannot be made more palatable for them by simple quips. These fortune-

---

35. Bowler, *Everything Happens for a Reason*, 118.

teller responses may come from a genuine desire and effort to build one up but become weights and responsibilities that often invoke shame and feelings of worthlessness when TP cannot – or should not – abide/embody them.

A phrase that I cannot discourage strongly enough is, "I understand." Unless you have experienced the exact same trauma, you cannot understand. And even those who have experienced the same or similar trauma, have limited understanding for they are not in the body of the other person. Appropriate words of care may include, "Thank you for trusting me with your story." "I hear your pain." "I see you and your (bravery/heartache/pain/courage/endurance)." "I am sorry you experienced such trauma."

Continuing to critically consider communication, one must recall that a challenge of traumatic injury is the lack of ability and/or language to share what is happening. Zora Neale Hurston wrote, "There is no greater agony than bearing an untold story inside of you."[36] One can only imagine having to contain the story of inconceivable and indescribable horror which cannot be communicated as it may not have been safe to tell, there are no adequate words to convey the pain, and if TP want to share their story, they may feel societal or personal pressure to use sanitized and/or conventionally appropriate language to explain what they are feeling. Traumatized persons cannot begin to heal until they are given a safe space to tell their story without repercussions and allowed to use the words they want and *need* to paint the picture of their torment; thus, to not make it palatable for another. Witnesses need to be prepared "to see life through the wounds of death."[37] While one may not be comfortable with profanity (or what they may deem as vulgar slang) or the graphic images to

---

36. Zora Neale Hurston, *Dust Tracks on a Road: An Autobiography* (New York: Arno Press, 1969), 220–21.
37. Rambo, *Spirit and Trauma*, 72.

explain one's pain, TP must be encouraged, allowed, and empowered to utilize the language they need and can access to tell their story. It is not a function of the witness to police their words; attempting to do so may not only cause shame but incite frustration, dismissal, and fracture trust.

Within communication one must consider that 55% is nonverbal.[38] Therefore, while the words used are critical, it is foundational to this work that the Authentic Self be declared worthy – in word and action – because TP may be unable to hear, embody, or hold the truth of their worth for themselves until they are farther in their recovery.[39] This essential ethic is the responsibility of the witness and community to consistently communicate in word and deed the reflection of the Authentic Self and to uphold the truth that all religions and spirituality espouse – each human is beloved and has worth. Communicating this message effectively includes the nonverbal language of presence and deep listening, keeping appointments, accepting feedback without defensiveness, body language – not crossing arms or sitting/standing closed – and creating an atmosphere and physical space that is safe and calming. The combined effect of verbal and nonverbal affirmation of the Authentic Self allows the TP to begin to recognize their reflection in the words and actions of the other and empowers them to begin to embrace themselves with compassion, grace, acceptance, and awe.

Retraumatization is a constant issue and poor/uncareful communication is one of the fastest ways that TP may experience it. All those working with TP must take necessary precautions and steps to not retraumatize the person with whom they are working.

---

38. "How Much of Communication Is Nonverbal? | UT Permian Basin Online," November 3, 2020, https://online.utpb.edu/about-us/articles/communication/how-much-of-communication-is-nonverbal.
39. Baldwin, *Trauma-Sensitive Theology*, 2018, 60.

Here is a list of things to consider. This is not an exhaustive list but is generative for your work.

- Be clear from the onset regarding communication. If you say that you will 'text later' be specific. Time is not always linear for TP so what may feel like a few hours to a non-traumatized person may feel like a day for TP.
- Be consistent in communication. Depending on your relationship and role, it may be helpful and appropriate to have a set time to check-in. I'll text you on Wednesday mornings. This does not mean you cannot text or talk at other times, but to establish trust, you should follow through each Wednesday even if there isn't anything new to share.
- Remember that being asked to tell one's story repeatedly is traumatizing/retraumatizing.
- Be mindful of where you are meeting the TP. Is this a safe space? Is it in the same space as the traumatizing event? Who owns the space – are they allies? Does the TP have direct access to an exit or are they backed into a corner? For instance, if someone was harmed by clergy, meeting in a church could be very retraumatizing. If someone has survived a natural disaster such as a tornado in which their family was killed, meeting in a room with a bulletin board filled with pictures of the local clean-up efforts might not be helpful. Finally, within the space, is it confidential? Can others overhear what the TP may say? Who is seeing them there? Who do they have to pass on the way out of the building? Just because someone shares their trauma with one person does not mean they are okay with others knowing they are experiencing pain.

How to talk to TP

- Validate their feelings
- Don't tell them how they are feeling or should be feeling
- Don't take credit for being a decent human being - there are no prizes for doing what should be done
- Do not lie to them
- Listen: do not interrupt, do not 'mansplain'
- Do not take credit for their success
- Do not uplift yourself in any way that may cause feelings or responses of indebtedness.
- Do not say 'I understand'
- You do not need to match the intensity of their reactions/emotions to be a support. This takes away from their process. Your job is to be a non-anxious presence. Empathy/sympathy/compassion are good. If they are at a 10, you do not need to be at a 10.
- Empower by asking what they need.
- Do not give false hope.
- No voyeurism - curious questions are good but are they necessary? Are they serving your curiosity for details or to know/support the person?
- Know your own biases. Notice the 'curious' questions that arise and examine them - they may reveal more about oneself.

Action: Public Discourse and Response

Traumatic recovery requires a response from the witness and/or the community. This does not mean that the individual story of the TP is publicly shared unless they choose, however, there are many pathways for community response. Simply the act of acknowledging that trauma happens and naming the types and affected individuals and communities is the first step.[40] Admitting that some systemic problems and failures harm TP and prevent/obstruct/make access to recovery difficult. Further discernment will be required for every SIC has differing obstacles and assets with which to contend and use to engage and support TP yet they cannot recover without belonging which requires being claimed. "We believe we can only do things because we have people around to whom we belong."[41]

One of the most powerful ways in which SIC can engage in the work of caring for TP is to create an environment in which trauma is not ignored, truncated, attempted to be made palatable, or spoken of only behind closed doors. "The experience of traumatic suffering is intensified by the invisibility and unspeakable nature of violence. A witnessing presence in trauma will make visible what is rendered invisible."[42] Therefore, public action and acknowledgment are essential to providing trauma-informed care. This requires a commitment to acknowledge trauma in what is taught, and for faith-based organizations, what is preached. For example, within the Presbyterian Church (USA), of which I am an ordained clergy, pastors have discretion as to what text is chosen for the use of sermons. While it is imperative to consider one's audience – children in attendance for example – there are ways of addressing trauma in the biblical texts as well as in the world. Pastors can arrange to have an activity or something outside of the sanctuary or worship space for children so that a forthright conversation/sermon can be offered. They should also alert the

---

40. These are to be generalized acknowledgements. *E.g.* "those who have experienced sexual assault", "People of Color".
41. Bessell Van Der Kolk, M.D., "Trauma, Body, and the Brain" (Kripalu, August 1, 2023).
42. Rambo, *Spirit and Trauma*, 123.

congregation as to what the content will be to ensure no one is unprepared and thereby activated by the material.

Visibility and action do not exist only in preaching, teaching, or in the curriculum of the organization and any current programs but are also achieved by collaborating with organizations and/or acquiring speakers to facilitate informational discussions, lead presentations, and/or book or lecture series. Providing resources as well as specific programming on issues of traumatic injury, recovery, and/or prevention is another means of bringing to light that which is often hidden. It is worth noting that these events and activities are important to follow through with regardless of the number of attendees as the success of the event cannot strictly be qualified by the attendance; changing one person's life may change the world. Consider that when notification of the events is shared via social media or old-fashioned pamphlets and fliers, not only does this make a public claim as to the importance of this subject but it is a communication to traumatized persons that there are allies in their community. Thus, one does not know the total impact of these types of visible actions.

Another mode of engaging in public action is by developing relationships with organizations that support TP (including therapists, recovery centers, shelters, yoga studios, massage therapists *e.g.*) and publicly acknowledging these alliances. SIC may also choose to provide funding to organizations that are engaged in the work of trauma recovery and prevention. The honesty, transparency, and forthrightness with which SIC engage regarding the reality of trauma in communities is critically important to helping to reduce the stigma of traumatic injury and subsequent responses. It also works to announce an ethical imperative, open dialogue, and motivate/inspire others to become involved in prevention and intervention. Situating the paradigm in an ethic of action, it is essential to recall that "so much of what makes people either well or not is not coming from within themselves, it's coming from their circumstances. It makes [one] think much more about social justice and the bigger issues that go beyond individuals."[43]

Many communities have assembled public gatherings and actions such as 'Take Back the Night', walk to end suicide, Black Lives Matter rallies, Juneteenth gatherings, campaigns to bring awareness to child abuse, and food collection boxes to support those with food insecurity. These are but a few of the gatherings which address, in some form, a trauma. Within these, the importance of intentional presence cannot be underscored enough. If attending, let it be known in one's spiritually integrated community and, at the event be sure to share any resources and/or opportunities that one's SIC provides. Most importantly, announce through words and/or presence (wearing a t-shirt or pin from one's SIC) that there are safe, welcoming, and intentional places for TP.

Story of Thomas

There is another story in Christianity that seems befitting in the context of creating a paradigm for SIC in which to engage. This pericope, situated within the ethic of action, speaks to the reality of how diverse individuals' experience of trauma is and how it is processed. In this story, each person has experienced a traumatic event in the crucifixion of Jesus. The disciples watched their beloved friend and mentor executed in an unspeakably heinous manner. Their grief was compounded by the injustice of his murder. Suddenly, they are confronted with the concept that life continues in an unfathomable way in Jesus' resurrection. This profoundly speaks to the experience of TP as they live through something so immensely overwhelming that their brains are rewired. They feel the weight of the trauma as they experience

---

43. Maté and Maté, *The Myth of Normal: Trauma, Illness & Healing in a Toxic Culture*, 59.

grief, confusion, anger, shock, and unspeakable pain. Then suddenly, a witness, therapist, spiritual care provider, friend, or loved one comes alongside and announces to them that what they believed was the end, is in fact, not. That there is life *after* the traumatic event and injury.

In the Gospel of John, after Jesus is resurrected, he appears to his 12 disciples but Thomas, one of them, is not there. The other disciples tell Thomas that they have seen Jesus and the story of Thomas begins with him speaking to the disciples. "Unless I see the mark of the nails in his hands, and put my finger in the mark of the nails and my hand in his side, I will not believe. A week later his disciples were again in the house, and Thomas was with them. Although the doors were shut, Jesus came and stood among them and said, "Peace be with you." Then he said to Thomas, "Put your finger here and see my hands. Reach out your hand and put it in my side. Do not doubt but believe." Thomas answered him, "My Lord and my God!" Jesus said to him, "Have you believed because you have seen me? Blessed are those who have not seen and yet have come to believe."[44]

Thomas has been traumatized. His reactions make sense. He watched Jesus die. And now, according to tradition, Jesus is standing before him. Regardless of whether one believes in the resurrection or its possibility, the story is the interaction between a TP and their friend. Jesus's response in offering Thomas the ability to touch the wounds denotes his understanding, compassion, grace, and empathy recognizing Thomas as one who is hurting, distrustful, and unable to orient to the here and now as they remain in the tyranny of nonlinear time; as a traumatized person who may need more than words. Traditionally this story is used to elevate those who believe without proof – as if their faith is

---

44. John 20:25-29

morally superior – and shame those who doubt; thus, the designation of "doubting Thomas".

In simply labeling Thomas as a doubter, the profundity of the encounter is obscured which would ostensibly be a result of theological history attempting to shame Thomas and erase the wounds as found in John Calvin's commentary on this passage in *Commentaire sure L'Évangile selon Saint Jean*. He writes, "The stupidity of Thomas was astonishing and monstrous; for he was not satisfied with merely beholding Christ but wished to have his hands also as witnesses of Christ's resurrection."[45] Continuing, Calvin advocates that the wounds on Jesus then disappear as he excludes two verses that speak to the compassion and understanding of Jesus when he encourages and welcomes Thomas to touch his wounds. "The danger in erasing these wounds is that the erasure occludes a testimony to what is most difficult about traumatic histories, whether personal or collective: that the wounds remain."[46, 47]

In reading this story through a trauma-informed theology, Jesus recognized Thomas's distress, pain, and traumatic injury. He immediately responded with compassion and encouragement – do what you need to find peace, to trust me, to believe that this trauma will not be death. Furthermore, I would assert that Jesus was admonishing the disciples gathered there that they have the privilege of not 'needing' to see the wounds. This is a 'blessing' and should not be taken for granted. Blessed are those who do not have traumatic injury for they have the privilege of being able to hear and to believe. Blessed are those who do not feel fractured and have not experienced the depth of pain that causes them to be unable to trust. Blessed are those who have not seen the totality of

---

45. Rambo, *Resurrecting Wounds*, 22.
46. Rambo, 42.
47. For further discussion of scars and wounds see also, O'Donnell, Karen, *Feminist Trauma Theologies* (SCM Press, 2020) p. 275-281

injury and pain in Thomas' life which would break one's heart open.

Sometimes like Thomas, TP will need proof – possibly including bodily action – and there is no shame in that as they have experienced unimaginable harm and fracturing and subsequently do not have the emotional capacity to trust and may, like Thomas, require more than just the word of another to believe. For the witness, simple things such as eye contact when traumatized persons tell of the horror and shame, announce to the TP that the witness is not afraid to look, to 'touch' the wound; that it is not so hideous as to obscure or distort the Authentic Self and its worthiness. Moreover, as Thomas is confronted with Jesus' resurrection, altering Thomas's understanding of death and his internal experience with traumatic injury, so too, are TP confronted with the concept that there is life after what they experienced as an event so egregious that it felt or feels like death. The traumatic event or injury does not define them, nor do the scars or marks of it need to be erased. It is their history and their future. It speaks to the death incurred and the resurrection awaited.

Resurrection is the act of restoring life: reanimating, regenerating, and reviving. Trauma recovery is resurrection. "Resurrection wounds provide a curious constellation for conceiving of life that is marked by wounds but recreated through them."[48] The mind and body are revived, reanimated, and the Authentic Self resurrected from the obscure hidden space it occupied for safety. Returning to Thomas's story, yes, blessed are those who have not been traumatized and do not need proof. Blessed are those who are unable to comprehend traumatic injury for their life of safe and loving experiences are not outweighed by negative ones. Blessed are those who do not ache, who can imagine a future, and who can engage fully in the present. And Jesus' model for

---

48. Rambo, *Resurrecting Wounds*, 42.

responding to the TP - yes. Yes. Yes. Yes, we will give you proof. We will stand by you while you examine us. We will not judge you for needing proof, for needing assurance and reassurance. We honor your scars and wounds not as signs of death but as testaments of survival, endurance, persistence, perseverance, and resurrection.

Action: Creating Trauma-Informed Programming

Imagination

An insidious aspect of trauma is that one's imagination is thwarted and inaccessible. Although this may not immediately seem pertinent, one cannot heal without imagination for it is a critical aspect of mental flexibility. "Imagination gives us the opportunity to envision new possibilities – it is an essential launchpad for making our hopes come true. Without imagination, there is no hope, no chance to envision a better future, no place to go, no goal to reach."[49] Therefore, the invitation to engage in the healing of imagination is a significant and necessary component of trauma-informed and is stimulated by the play instinct.328F[50] Play is vital to recovery. Moreover, to engage in imagination, one must feel safe. "If an organism is stuck in survival mode, its energies are focused on fighting off unseen enemies, which leaves no room for nurture, care, and love. For us humans, it means that as long as the mind is defending itself against invisible assaults, our closest bonds are

---

49. Van Der Kolk, M.D., *The Body Keeps the Score*, 2015, 17.
50. "Carl Jung: The Dynamic Principle Of Fantasy Is Play...Quotations - Carl Jung Depth Psychology," accessed March 5, 2024, https://carljungdepthpsycholo gysite.blog/2020/11/09/carl-jung-the-dynamic-principle-of-fantasy-is-play-2/.

threatened, along with our ability to imagine, plan, play, learn, and pay attention to other people's needs."[51]

Thus, the potential for spiritually integrated communities to engage in imaginative encounters is limitless. This spans from arranging and hosting game nights (board games, team games, etc.) to endeavoring to bring curiosity and wonder to interactions such as noting the new buds on a plant or the flowers in bloom. Imagination is utilized in the stories told and the texts shared in the community. In the Jewish tradition, there is a mode of interpretation known as 'midrash' which asks questions of the text using what Dr. Wil Gafney, a womanist biblical scholar, notes as the 'sanctified imagination'.[52] "It is the fertile creative space where the preacher-interpreter enters the text, particularly the spaces in the text, and fills them out with missing details: names, back stories, detailed descriptions of the scene and characters, and so on."[53]

When imagination is engaged with spiritual texts, TP may locate themselves within the stories and feel connected. The 'sanctified imagination' encourages curiosity within traumatized persons as they dream, wonder, and imagine the whole story thus stimulating their ability to creatively consider more than they currently know and subsequently consider their healing. Furthermore, one cannot engage in their spirituality without it. As Christena Cleveland states, "Imagination is theology. We can only believe what we can imagine."[54] Thus, if one has only been taught about a punishing God that is causing harm in the recovery of trauma, one cannot imagine anything else without being invited to do so.

The importance of imagination in recovery is that one cannot

51. Van Der Kolk, M.D., *The Body Keeps the Score*, 2015, 76.
52. Dr. Wilda Gafney, *Womanist Midrash* (Louisville, KY: Westminster John Knox Press, 2017), 3.
53. Gafney, 3.
54. Christena Cleveland, *God Is a Black Woman* (HarperOne, 2022).

heal if one cannot imagine one's life not centered on the traumatic event and injury. TP cannot imagine (and thus engage) in healthy relationships, activities, hobbies, etc. if they cannot envision what that might entail.

Art of Lament

A powerful aspect of spirituality is the art of lament which has been engaged for thousands of years. "Lament calls the individual and community to examine the work of reconciliation between those who live under suffering with those who live in celebration. Lamentations challenges the celebratory assumptions with the reality of suffering."[55] It is the desperate plea to be heard, the space of the most unmitigated grief, and the outcry for justice; recovery cannot happen without lament as the TP require support from others to mourn the tragedy within the requisite relationship.[56] "You have to mourn otherwise all that sadness is simply multiplying inside of you and holding you back. It is okay to cry. In fact, it is required."[57] When TP are expected to move into recovery without lament, that expectation is imposed by those who have the privilege of ignoring or silencing that which they do not wish to acknowledge. TP do not have that luxury. Moreover, "failure to complete the normal process of grieving perpetuates the traumatic reaction."[58]

Within Christianity, the Bible is filled with stories and acts of lament from the Psalms to an entire book, Lamentations. Chan-Rah notes lament as a "response to the reality of suffering and

55. Soong-Chan Rah, *Prophetic Lament: A Call for Justice in Troubled Times* (Downers Grove, Illinois: InterVarsity Press, 2015), 69.
56. Van Der Kolk, M.D., *The Body Keeps the Score*, 2015, 133.
57. Rebecca McCullough, Psychotherapist, Discussion on Lament and PTSD, February 22, 2024.
58. Herman, M. D., *Trauma and Recovery*, 1997, 69.

engages God in the context of pain and trouble. The hope of lament is that God would respond to human suffering that is wholeheartedly communicated through lament."[59] It serves not only as a way of engaging God/Holy Mystery (in a spiritual tradition) but of bringing the community into a consciousness of the stories and pain that affect the universal energy connecting all persons. It is important to recognize the importance of lament for all TP regardless of spiritual tradition. One cannot heal without crying out for what was, what was lost, what never will be, what never was, and how the future has been altered.

Lament should not be conflated with divine punishment but may be used in the context of righteous anger for the harrowing actions and subsequent pain experienced.[60] Frechette discusses the use of lament and the importance of attending to suffering though cautions, "contemporary trauma survivors may be apt to appropriate the motif of suffering as divine punishment in a way that confirms their sense that they lack dignity." This is incredibly detrimental to the psyche and emotional and spiritual health of the traumatized person. TP are seeking meaning and for those whose religious understanding is one of a punitive God, or who are culturally aware of such beliefs and have adopted them, (or fear there is truth to them), the conceptualization of punishment not only stalls healing but is traumatic in and of itself. When TP engage in these conversations with witnesses/spiritual care providers/therapists etc. who do not have training and/or who have not considered their own understanding, additional traumatization is quite possible.

TP have every right to feel anger – even rage – for the gross

---

59. Rah, *Prophetic Lament*, 21.
60. For further discussion see: Christopher G Frechette, "Two Biblical Motifs of Divine Violence as Resources for Meaning-Making in Engaging Self-Blame and Rage after Traumatization," *Pastoral Psychology* 66, no. 2 (April 2017): 246–47, https://doi.org/10.1007/s11089-016-0745-x.

injustice and inconceivable damage they have suffered, yet it is a secondary emotion. What is beneath anger is the emotion necessary to attend and that is usually sadness – lament. However, the concept of righteous anger is an aspect of lament that should be explored (if appropriate) and within the Christian tradition, multiple texts speak to the rage of injustice. One of the best examples is the imprecatory Psalms. These are psalms that speak to the unmitigated pain humans experience due to the actions of others and the desire for revenge – both personally and in divine punishment – of the perpetrator. The importance of communal engagement is foundational as the psalms were utilized and shared during worship; therefore, what affected one affected all. Thus, what can be gleaned from these is that for thousands of years, individuals have needed to share their grief, to lament publicly so that the community supports them, and these psalms provide contextual symbols for processing the pain.

Though the witness may be uncomfortable with the words of revenge and/or the desire thereof, to speak the desire for revenge is an absolute need of the TP and it also engages the imagination which is critical for healing. In speaking the revenge fantasy or desire for divine retribution, anger, and rage may be expelled thus allowing for the sadness and the act of lament to be engaged. Witnesses should recall that anger is (usually) experienced as less vulnerable than sadness. Consequently, it is often easier for TP to share and when their expressions can be witnessed without judgment, a framework of trust is developed. Lament speaks to the desire for healing and right relationships.

Regardless of religious or spiritual affiliation, the act of lament is an essential experience required for healing. The example of the imprecatory Psalms brings to light the truth of family systems theory that what affects one, affects all. Therefore, spiritually integrated communities are ideal partners for TP to engage as they are practiced in the art of rituals that address these emotions.

Ritual

Humans have used rituals since the beginning of time as a way of connecting and creating meaning. While rituals have a connotation of religiosity, they are not limited to religion and are found in all cultures, traditions, and most families. Any act that is executed in a repeatedly consistent manner, a "normal protocol," is a ritual; everything can be ritualized which allows for imagination in the creation of them to provide trauma-informed care.[61] This is extremely important as the act of ritual allows TP to sync their bodies with one another and integrate into the present moment. "Our sense of agency, how much we feel in control, is defined by our relationship with our bodies and its rhythms... This is the opposite of dissociation, of being "out of body" and making yourself disappear."[62] In a ritual, all are invited to participate at the same time, engaging in the same behavior thus allowing the TP to mirror others.

> Trauma-oriented interventions that focus exclusively on the cognitive dimension of traumatic memory without corresponding care for the multiple ways in which the body holds traumatic response are doomed to be ineffective in the long run. Traumatic experiences cannot be processed solely by means of intellect or faith. Strategies for resolving the consequences of trauma must include the body.[63]

Within a church service, all stand, sit, pray, listen, and sing at the same time; therefore, ideally and with intention, TP can exist

61. "Definition of RITUAL," March 4, 2024, https://www.merriam-webster.com/dictionary/ritual.
62. Van Der Kolk, M.D., *The Body Keeps the Score*, 2015, 333.
63. Baldwin, *Trauma-Sensitive Theology*, 2018, 7.

in their current space and time as their body is moving with another in real-time; they have the opportunity to be rooted in the present. These simple, collective movements are powerful, nonintrusive forms of grounding and centering. As TP often feel out of sync, moving together draws them into the community and allows them to participate regardless of how they may be feeling. There are a plethora of options for spiritual communities to create meaningful rituals such as baptism, services of lament, longing, hope, the longest night, memorials, anointing, naming, healing, *etc.* "Religious ritual can cultivate safety, nurture social bonds, and foster both discursive and nondiscursive modes of representing collective suffering."[64] These must be cultivated with intentionality and awareness of the needs of the TP, the capacity of the community to be present and engage, and the ensuring of additional resources should they be necessary.

Every interaction, program, service, and/or activity can contain elements of ritual to assist in the healing of the TP, and organizations and individuals are invited to think beyond conventional ideas and incorporate meaningful, intentional engagement. "Rituals can facilitate the movement from wounding to resiliency if conducted with intentional care and compassionate holding by a community."[65] For example, in a community garden there are often gatherings for planting, weeding, and harvesting. Rituals could include each person noting something they see that was not there last time before attending to the garden inviting curiosity, wonder, and awe which are critical elements of imagination. Something as simple as when they have completed their tasks if there is a communal sink, they may pass the soap to the next person. Another ritual that is easy to implement is taking a minute at the beginning or end of a gathering to take one minute and

---

64. Boase and Frechette, *Bible Through the Lens of Trauma*, 10.
65. Baldwin, *Trauma-Sensitive Theology*, 2018, 57.

breathe together, centering and grounding oneself in the present. While the actions may sound rather benign and, for some, silly, these types of intentional moments, movements, and interactions are profound grounding opportunities for TP as they are consistent acts that build trust and allow TP to begin to anticipate good experiences and emotions as well as creating habits – rituals – they can implement in other parts of their lives. Traumatized persons' lives have been so emotionally and psychologically disrupted that they do not have the capacity to find equilibrium. Rituals help instill the idea of rhythm which provides external resources for countering internal chaos.

An aspect of ritual is discerning if it is a synchronous or relational act - it is important to discern when planning or developing a ritual if one would need to know another to participate. Synchrony is the act of being in sync with another through external movements co-occurring at the same time yet independent of a relationship. For instance, acts in worship (standing, sitting, praying), singing in a choir, dancing, yoga, etc. all can be engaged without a personal relationship with another. These synchronous acts invite individuals into a space of safety in that they are tethered to the present time through shared experiences. Additionally, synchronic events allow TP to observe others in safe spaces and choose to explore relationships that may then develop and allow them to also add the tool of co-regulation which is a dynamic process of interaction between individuals that contributes to emotional stability and differs from synchrony in that being in sync can be experienced individually.

For those engaging in co-regulation, the relationship is one in which the emotions and reactions of another assist in the regulation of one's emotional state. This may be experienced positively or negatively depending upon the mental health of an individual and one's ability to differentiate. In trauma recovery, it is an intentional act by the witness to assist TP in coping with the overwhelming emotions by reflecting to them empathy, calm, and consistency. In the act of a ritual, there are a myriad of opportunities for TP and witness to engage and for TP to learn, develop, and hone additional resources. Not only do rituals contain the possibility of emotional, physical, and spiritual outlets but also the hope of reconnection to one's AS and the wider world.

Mindfulness

Practicing mindfulness calms down the sympathetic nervous system and subsequently one is less likely to enter into fight-or-flight. Many SIC practice intentional mindfulness and for those who do not, it can be easily implemented. There are many benefits to TP and the entire community as one learns to self-ground and to attain equanimity which is important as TP often experience wide emotional swings in recovery. For those who have not practiced, finding a qualified mindfulness coach is incredibly helpful in teaching the practice. Moreover, it is easily accessible in a group and can also be provided with guided meditation which helps keep all participants grounded and feeling safe. Mindfulness builds community and the skills learned including intentionality, awareness, and equanimity are then able to evoke these traits and strongly assist in supporting traumatized persons.

Note on Investigations/Accusations

What happens when the trauma happens within the community and requires an immediate response? Who should respond? What should the response be? These are among the many, many questions asked when the unthinkable happens.

First, the response should always be to believe the victim. Period. Statistically, the rate of false accusations is incredibly low with research showing that approximately 2-5% of accusations of sexual assault are false.[66]

Second, every organization should have a policy in place for responding to allegations of sexual assault/abuse within the organization. This should be reviewed yearly and training for all should be mandatory yearly as well. When a crisis happens and a person brings forth an accusation either current or past that has not been dealt with, that is not the time to try and "figure things out". The victim needs the series of events to happen smoothly and expediently. Depending upon your organization, some questions to consider are:

    a. Do the police need to be contacted? If so, does the victim want someone to be with them? If so, who will go? *Does this person have training to do so?*

    b. What is the polity of the organization? Who will initiate a response team? Who will lead an investigation? Who will contact the accused? Will the accused be removed from any position at the organization pending an investigation? How will be victim be protected from retaliation?

    c. Who will journey with the victim? What services will be offered to them and will their cost be covered by the organization? For how long? Is there a financial cap? These may include but are not limited to counseling, physical health care (massage, somatic work), and advocacy.

This is but a <u>miniscule</u> glimpse into the work required to

---

66. de Zutter, André, Robert Horselenberg, and Peter J van Kopen, "The Prevalence of False Allegations of Rape in the United States from 2006-2010," *Journal of Forensic Psychology* 2, no. 2 (March 20, 2017).

address new/current accusations and more information is available in the workbook. However, these questions must be considered if an organization declares itself trauma-informed.

Conclusion

This is the tip of an iceberg: what you have learned is enough to prepare you to learn more and that isn't an easy thing to hear. Most people want to read a book, take a class, and "know" it; before moving on. But trauma isn't stagnant. Even the most educated clinicians continue to grow in their understanding of the complexity of trauma, how to address it, and how the brain is affected. The good news is that you have taken a step towards providing trauma-informed care and hopefully empowering TP in their recovery.

There is no way to erase trauma. It would be unethical, unprofessional, and inhumane to ignore the pain that TP experience nor to acknowledge that their pain impacts others. This is the systemic piece of trauma: it radiates and all are affected. However, trauma does not break an individual. Their brains change and adapt for survival. TP protect their Authentic Selves. We can attempt to ease the pain but daily, forever, it will have an impact. Yet we must not only assume the negative regarding impacts. Yes, it is an unspeakably horrendous experience to be traumatized. There is no acceptable reason for the event. However, TP are often highly compassionate, aware, and empowering individuals of whom all around them benefit. This does NOT make the trauma acceptable. It means that TP cannot be discounted or assumed to only bring challenges. Recognizing the intrinsic, super-human strength of TP and how they positively affect systems is vitally important to creating narratives of inclusion, acceptance, and validation.

I write as one who cannot be silent, as one who dreams of a different way of living for traumatized people; accepted, understood, embraced, affirmed, encouraged, and empowered. The harm done by churches must be called into accountability for there are far too many wounded, far too many currently being harmed, far too many ignored, silenced, and marginalized by a contorted gospel which is only good news for white men and one of subjugation for the rest. I write as one who has experienced the first-hand harm done by churches who keep silent as the Lutheran church intervened and supported my biological father when I disclosed that he had been raping me for 10 years. I write as one who has experienced the harm done when a (colleague) pastor rapes teenage boys and then manipulates many in a community to support them sending fractures into a community and ending friendships. I write as one who has helped churches come to terms with the abuse in their churches; as an advocate for trauma-informed care, victims, and the innocent.

I write as a traumatized person who, despite working with others, did not recognize the depth of my own trauma until it almost cost me my life. I have experienced trauma in almost all facets and still learn from others daily.

Throughout this book, evidence has been presented on the neurobiological effects of trauma and their relation to the Authentic Soul and the protection of the AS is, I argue, obvious and thus worthy of uncovering and/or recovering. It cannot be underscored enough that the work of healing must be done in encounters with those who can reflect the Authentic Self of the individual, not the narrative placed upon them by perpetrators, societal or religious expectations, nor the experience of trauma and/or moral injury. Trauma and moral injury are isolating experiences that require the injured individual to have an "equally intense real-time encounter with a countervailing experience."[67] Spiritually integrated communities have the opportunity to be that

---

67. Litz et al., "Moral Injury and Moral Repair in War Veterans," 701.

'countervailing experience' which is a catalyst to healing for traumatized persons.

Statistically, the research conducted and presented lends credence to the need for SIC to engage in this work as 81% of self-identified traumatized persons note that there is a spiritual support or connection that is meaningful for their recovery. Moreover, 67% identify that the source of the spiritual connection informs the way they think about the protected part of themselves (the AS). Within my own practice and experience, it has been obvious that the pain of trauma is intricately linked to the understanding of one's spirituality regardless of religiosity or practice; all have an Authentic Self that cannot be duplicated and is the vital source of life. Thus, for SIC to not address trauma is to ignore the plight of the wounded and to continue to engage in the systematic oppression of the marginalized whether in overt or covert ways.

Thus, the totality of the information herein was important to read and comprehend to the best of one's ability as the work is too serious to engage without a solid foundation and framework. The are no shortcuts to providing trauma-informed care. The work required of SIC and SAP to prepare to be witnesses is but a pittance compared to the work that TP must do to engage in survival, healing, and recovery. However, I acknowledge that no single article, book, class, or even degree could encompass the totality of information and thus the importance of continuing education to learn and grow is imperative. May it be unambiguous that the effects of trauma and moral injury would both be assisted by the words and behaviors of the spiritually aware being those of grace, compassion, understanding, and nonjudgment.

Appendix: Research And Methodology

Overview

The purpose of this study is to gauge understanding of the Self as identified in Internal Family Systems (IFS) regarding its impact on the healing, emotional safety, and empowerment of traumatized persons and the connection between the concepts of 'Self' and soul. Does the concept of a protected soul, an Authentic Self, impact healing? The study was approved by the Drew University Institutional Review Board.

Goals

Each distinct target group provided unique opportunities to gather information that would provide a comprehensive picture of the concepts of 'Self' and the impacts of healing. These groups would identify strengths and weaknesses in the education currently held regarding the provision of trauma-informed care within spiritually integrated communities and individuals. Thus, with those who identified as having experienced trauma, the questions of whether they knew of the concept of a protected soul and their interactions (if any) with spiritual communities and/or spiritual care providers were integral to the study. For the leaders in spiritual communities and mental health providers, the intention was to gauge their level of education with the material as well as their comfort in presenting it.

Method and Procedures

Three different surveys were designed to gather information on the understanding and/or awareness of the concept of the soul (self) in trauma recovery as it relates to the emotional safety of traumatized persons and its impact on trauma recovery and healing through the experiences of the traumatized person, the spiritual care provider, and the mental health provider. Individuals were empowered to identify and self-select one or more surveys to complete consisting of between 14 and 22 questions with an estimation of completion at approximately 10-20 minutes. The surveys were distributed online via emails and Facebook and a link to the survey was displayed on posters at a counseling center that serves both traumatized persons and clergy. The opportunity to take the surveys was available for 60 days.

The program used to collect data, REDCap, did not collect any identifiable information including a user's IP address. The researcher had taken all reasonable measures to protect the participant's identity and responses. The data collected was SSL encrypted, and stored on a password-protected database, and IP addresses were not collected. As email and the internet are not 100% secure it was also suggested that participants clear the computer's cache and browser history to protect their privacy after completing the survey. The survey results are kept on a password-protected, two-factor authentication, cloud storage.

Background

In the 1980's Dr. Richard Schwartz developed Internal Family Systems as a psychological model for therapy and paradigm of emotions. He proposed that parts of the self interact within and, when engaged, lead to self-healing and therefore "live lives of wisdom and clarity."[1] While this model was not developed strictly to address trauma, the power of IFS to assist traumatized persons in their recovery is well documented.[2] Building upon his work which identifies the 'Self' as undamaged in trauma, this study seeks to assess if that information is important and/or useful to the traumatized person in their recovery. As asserted that the 'Self' is akin to the soul, this study seeks to explore whether the connection to spirituality may be another source of healing.[3] Does the concept of the Self as being protected in trauma provide comfort and/or encouragement to traumatized persons?

Participants

Participants were anonymous adult volunteers who received no compensation for the study. They were recruited through social media and direct email (blind copy to a list of colleagues) and were asked to self-identify as one or more of the following: a traumatized person and/or one who provides care to a traumatized persons, specifically a spiritual care provider and/or a mental health clinician, and to complete the corresponding survey based

1. "About IFS," June 5, 2023, https://www.foundationifs.org/about/about-ifs.
2. Hilary B. Hodgdon et al., "Internal Family Systems (Ifs) Therapy for Posttraumatic Stress Disorder (Ptsd) among Survivors of Multiple Childhood Trauma: A Pilot Effectiveness Study," *Journal of Aggression, Maltreatment & Trauma*, December 26, 2021, https://doi.org/10.1080/10926771.2021.2013375.
3. Schwartz and Falconer, *Many Minds, One Self*, 4.

upon their self-identifying criteria. Individuals were invited to complete any/all surveys applicable.

Before agreeing to participate, participants were provided with the purpose, intent, duration, risks/benefits, a confidentiality statement, and informed of the voluntary nature of the study as required documentation from Drew. They were that there were psychological risks posed due to the content of the questions regarding trauma and the processing thereof and the possibility of activating memories. After receiving all the information, participants provided their consent by clicking a box to continue to the study. Additionally, participants were provided with resources for emotional support at the end of the survey.

Data Collection

The program used to collect data, REDCap, does not collect any identifiable information including a user's IP address. All reasonable measures were taken to protect identity and responses. The data collected is SSL encrypted, and stored on a password-protected database, and IP addresses are not collected. The survey results are kept on a password-protected, two-factor authentication, cloud storage. As email and the internet are not 100% secure it was also suggested to the participants that they clear the computer's cache and browser history to protect their privacy after completing the survey.

Questions

Designed to gain insight into current understanding of the Authentic Self as it applies to trauma and a traumatized person's experience both generally and specific to any interaction with communities and/or persons who are identified as being in a spiritual nature, the questions attempt to reflect the myriad of ways that the Authentic Self has been used in spirituality, mental health, and trauma literature.

Data Analysis

- 42 Persons completed the traumatized person survey
  - 71% responded that they believed there is a part of them that remains/remained protected from the perpetrator
    - 31% of the total participants agreed with Schwartz's definition (provided) of the self
  - 81% identified a spiritual support or connection that is meaningful for their trauma recovery
  - 67% noted that the source of spiritual connection informs the way they think about their protected part
  - 90% identified that they have experienced feelings of being broken as a result of the trauma they experienced
    - Of these, 62% identified the soul as what felt broken
  - 55% answered affirmatively that knowing leading trauma experts believe the Self cannot be damaged felt empowering to their recovery.
- 9 persons completed the mental healthcare provider survey
  - 56% of respondents believed that the Self cannot be broken by trauma
  - 33% had studied Internal Family Systems (IFS)
  - 100% of respondents agreed that the Self to which Schwartz refers in IFS may also be understood as the soul (definition from Schwartz provided)

- o 89% were open to discussing the sacred/spiritual with their clients if the client raised the connection
- 37 persons completed the spiritual care provider survey
  - o 41% of respondents agreed/affirmed Schwartz's definition of Self (provided)
  - o 49% noted that they had training in trauma-informed care
  - o 92% of respondents did not believe that churches or spiritual communities were adequately prepared and equipped to deal with and address trauma
    - 43% responded that their faith community engaged in intentional activities to assist and integrate traumatized persons to feel safe and welcome in their community
      - 43% answered in writing how the practice came to be

This information provided critical data, both challenging expectations as well as confirming professional experiences and assumptions regarding the authenticity and protection of the Self, and current education and engagement of spiritual communities regarding traumatized people. The respondents' answer regarding a part of them remaining protected was surprising and encouraging as much of the current literature and personal experience with TP does not correspond with that affirmation. Therefore, more information gathering is needed, which would best be achieved in narrative interviews. While TP respondents noted the protection, 90% still reported feeling broken. Thus, the question must be asked, what is the corollary, if any, between those two concepts/experiences?

Based on their answers, spiritual care providers and communities seemingly require education in the area of trauma-informed care. Not only that 91.89% do not believe that spiritual communities are adequately prepared, additionally, those who noted current practices for intentional engagement with TP identified actions that are either not related to trauma or inadequate for the level of care and purpose of providing care. While neurodivergent persons and/or those utilizing services of food pantries or grief groups may have experienced trauma, those are not examples of traumatized persons. Moreover, acceptance of, and providing information to LGBTQ persons does not address trauma nor provide trauma-informed care.

Despite the information collected, further research is needed. While a majority of traumatized persons noted that there is a part of them that is/was protected, the question of how that impacts (if at all) their feelings regarding worth was not investigated. Furthermore, with 80.95% identifying that spiritual support or connection is meaningful for their trauma recovery and only 48.65% of spiritual care providers identified having training in the same, the question could (and should) be asked where the spiritual care providers were provided that training, when, and do they maintain any continuing education to ensure they are up to date on current understanding and new research. Great harm could be done to traumatized persons in receiving care from those who do not have the education to adequately provide care. An essential question arises, do spiritual care providers have relationships with those in the mental health profession with whom they could refer persons needing trained trauma therapists? Finally, as mental health providers were open to conversation with clients on sacred/spiritual issues, questions arose as to their training and if they have relationships with those in the spiritual community with whom they could refer clients.

Acknowledgments

Many people deserve my deepest appreciation for their support, guidance, wisdom, and love which led and allowed me to write this book. Angela Yarber, Meredith Hoxie Scholl, and Alice Kim were on my doctoral committee. Their guidance and challenges made me stronger and encouraged my growth. Though they did tell me to stop researching and write, I still love them. The church I pastored from 2016 to 2023, First Presbyterian Church, loved me and supported my continued education with their patience with my schedule and their persistence in my wellbeing. In 1994, Jim Litwin gave me my first job in social justice, and I am ever grateful for the lessons I learned and the path on which my feet have found their home.

Emily Hedrick, Paige Rawson, Andrea Miller, Danae Ashley, Sara Webb, Janene Putnam, and Sandy Bean were an amazing group of people who helped me to be a subversive scribe, who brought out my snark and humor and gave me a safe place to land when wounded and exhausted.

On a particularly difficult day, Al McDowell brought me lunch and sat with me. I will never forget that moment of exceptional grace and love.

Karen Harrington, Carol Beechy, and Emily Hedrick read the manuscript and provided invaluable feedback. I could not have continued editing without them. Their grammar, keen questions, and encouragement were sustenance in the desert of writing.

Mary Howell, David Houghton, Tim Iversen, Chris and Bill

Reynolds, Ann and Richard Blabey, Jessica Kelly, and Faith Gay are good friends who never stopped believing in me.

The Nolan Family embraced me and have provided much love, light, and laughter. Especially Natalie, Olivia, and my best friend Scot - for walks and 'pie' and without whom I am sure I would have utilized the paper shredder many times.

Finally, my phenomenal wife Dana, and generous children Robert and Mia. You never doubted me and always provided unconditional love. Moreover, you always knew that I had worth and were determined that I learned to embrace that – even when teaching me wasn't easy. You have my gratitude and my heart.

And to my mom – you have attempted and achieved the impossible, you have gone back in time with me into every dark space and pulled me out, bandaged me up, and held me until it stopped hurting. Thank you for grafting me onto your tree.

Bibliography

"About IFS," June 5, 2023. https://www.foundationifs.org/about/about-ifs.

"About the CDC-Kaiser ACE Study |Violence Prevention|Injury Center|CDC," March 17, 2022. https://www.cdc.gov/violenceprevention/aces/about.html.

"Adverse Childhood Experiences (ACEs)," September 5, 2023. https://www.cdc.gov/violenceprevention/aces/index.html.

"Adverse Childhood Experiences Resources |Violence Prevention|Injury Center|CDC," September 5, 2023. https://www.cdc.gov/violenceprevention/aces/resources.html.

Advisen Ltd. "Insurance Data, Media, and Technology." Accessed January 22, 2024. https://www.advisenltd.com/.

AdvocateWeb. "Sexual Misconduct in the Church When Mentor Becomes Molester Ministers Are Often Granted Immediate Trust . . . but Some Betray It." Accessed November 13, 2023. https://www.advocateweb.org/publications/articles-2/clergy/sexual-misconduct-church-mentor-becomes-molester-ministers-often-granted-immediate-trust-betray/.

Aeon. "How Patience Can Be a Better Balm for Trauma than Resilience | Aeon Essays." Accessed January 5, 2024. https://aeon.co/essays/how-patience-can-be-a-better-balm-for-trauma-than-resilience.

Akram, F. "Moral Injury and the COVID-19 Pandemic: A Philosophical Viewpoint." *Ethics, Medicine, and Public Health* 18 (September 2021): 100661. https://doi.org/10.1016/j.jemep.2021.100661.

All Wales Traumatic Stress Quality Improvement Inc. "Trauma and the Brain." Accessed October 23, 2023. https://traumaticstress.nhs.wales/children-and-young-people/trauma-and-the-brain/.

Alshak, Mark N., and Joe M Das. "Neuroanatomy, Sympathetic Nervous System." In *StatPearls*. Treasure Island (FL): StatPearls Publishing, 2023. http://www.ncbi.nlm.nih.gov/books/NBK542195/.

American Indian Law Alliance. "Doctrine of Discovery." Accessed February 12, 2024. https://aila.ngo/issues/doctrine-of-discovery/.

American Medical Association. "Lack of Access to Evidence-Based Mental Health Care Poses Grave Threat," November 3, 2022. https://www.ama-assn.org/about/leadership/lack-access-evidence-based-mental-health-care-poses-grave-threat.

187

Bibliography

Anda, Dr. Robert. "Why Prevention Matters." Chicago IL: Doris Duke Charitable Foundation, n.d.

Anda, MD, MS, Robert. "The Health and Social Impact of Growing Up with Adverse Childhood Experiences: The Human and Economic Costs of the Status Quo." Trauma Informed Oregon, n.d.

Andrews, Krysta, Sophia L. Roth, Chantelle Lloyd, Alina Protopopescu, Charlene O'Connor, Ruth A. Lanius, and Margaret C. McKinnon. "Development and Preliminary Evaluation of the Moral Injury Assessment for Survivors of Abuse." *Traumatology*, August 31, 2023. https://doi.org/10.1037/trm0000475.

Antal, Chris J., Peter D. Yeomans, Rotunda East, Douglas W. Hickey, Solomon Kalkstein, Kimberly M. Brown, and Dana S. Kaminstein. "Transforming Veteran Identity through Community Engagement: A Chaplain–Psychologist Collaboration to Address Moral Injury." *Journal of Humanistic Psychology* 63, no. 6 (November 2023): 801–26. https://doi.org/10.1177/0022167819844071.

Anzaldúa, Gloria. *Light in the Dark*. Durham, North Carolina: Duke University Press, 2015.

Arel, Stephanie N., and Shelly Rambo, eds. *Post-Traumatic Public Theology*. Cham, Switzerland: Palgrave Macmillan, 2016.

Atri, Ashutosh, and Manoj Sharma. "Psychoeducation: Implications for the Profession of Health Education." *California Journal of Health Promotion* 5, no. 4 (2007): 32–39.

Bailey, Sarah Pulliam. "Southern Baptist Leaders Covered up Sex Abuse, Kept Secret Database, Report Says." *Washington Post*, May 26, 2022. https://www.washingtonpost.com/religion/2022/05/22/southern-baptist-sex-abuse-report/.

Baldwin, Jennifer. *Trauma-Sensitive Theology: Thinking Theologically in the Era of Trauma*. Eugene, Oregon: Cascade Books, 2018.

Barbash, Ph.D., Elyssa. "Different Types of Trauma: Small 't' versus Large 'T' | Psychology Today," July 4, 2023. https://www.psychologytoday.com/us/blog/trauma-and-hope/201703/different-types-trauma-small-t-versus-large-t.

Barnes Ph.D., Haleigh A., Robin A. Hurley, M.D., and Katherine H. Taber, Ph.D. "Moral Injury and PTSD: Often Co-Occurring Yet Mechanistically Different | The Journal of Neuropsychiatry and Clinical Neurosciences," Spring 2019. https://neuro.psychiatryonline.org/doi/full/10.1176/appi.neuropsych.19020036.

BBC News. "Methodist Church Apologises for Abuse Spanning Decades." May 28, 2015, sec. The UK. https://www.bbc.com/news/uk-32909444.

Benjet, C., E. Bromet, E. G. Karam, R. C. Kessler, K. A. McLaughlin, A. M. Ruscio, V. Shahly, et al. "The Epidemiology of Traumatic Event Exposure

Worldwide: Results from the World Mental Health Survey Consortium." *Psychological Medicine* 46, no. 2 (January 2016): 327–43. https://doi.org/10.1017/S0033291715001981.

Benner, David. *Soulful Spirituality: Becoming Fully Alive and Deeply Human.* Grand Rapids, Michigan: Brazos Press, 2011. https://valsec.barnesandnoble.com/w/soulful-spirituality-david-g-benner/1100377796.

Bernardi, Luciano, Peter Sleight, Gabriele Bandinelli, Simone Cencetti, Lamberto Fattorini, Johanna Wdowczyc-Szulc, and Alfonso Lagi. "Effect of Rosary Prayer and Yoga Mantras on Autonomic Cardiovascular Rhythms: Comparative Study." *BMJ : British Medical Journal* 323, no. 7327 (December 22, 2001): 1446–49.

Beste, Jennifer. "Envisioning a Just Response to the Catholic Clergy Sexual Abuse Crisis." *Theological Studies* 82, no. 1 (March 1, 2021): 29–54. https://doi.org/10.1177/0040563921996044.

Big Think. "The Neuroscience of Spiritual Experiences," May 24, 2023. https://bigthink.com/the-well/neuroscience-of-spirituality/.

Bisson, Jonathan I., Lucy Berliner, Marylene Cloitre, David Forbes, Tine K. Jensen, Catrin Lewis, Candice M. Monson, et al. "The International Society for Traumatic Stress Studies New Guidelines for the Prevention and Treatment of Posttraumatic Stress Disorder: Methodology and Development Process." *Journal of Traumatic Stress* 32, no. 4 (August 2019): 475–83. https://doi.org/10.1002/jts.22421.

Boase, Elizabeth, and Christopher G Frechette, eds. *Bible Through the Lens of Trauma.* Atlanta. SBL Press, 2016.

Boccia, Maddalena, Simonetta D'Amico, Filippo Bianchini, Assunta Marano, Anna Maria Giannini, and Laura Piccardi. "Different Neural Modifications Underpin PTSD after Different Traumatic Events: An fMRI Meta-Analytic Study." *Brain Imaging and Behavior* 10, no. 1 (March 1, 2016): 226–37. https://doi.org/10.1007/s11682-015-9387-3.

Borges, Lauren M., Alisha Desai, Sean M. Barnes, and Jacob P. S. Johnson. "The Role of Social Determinants of Health in Moral Injury: Implications and Future Directions." *Current Treatment Options in Psychiatry* 9, no. 3 (September 1, 2022): 202–14. https://doi.org/10.1007/s40501-022-00272-4.

Boston Globe (Online). "Church Allowed Abuse by Priest for Years." January 6, 2002, sec. Special Reports. https://www.proquest.com/usnews/docview/2729068742/citation/AF4F886291DE4B01PQ/2.

Bowler, Kate. *Everything Happens for a Reason.* New York: Random House, 2018

Bremner, J. Douglas. "Traumatic Stress: Effects on the Brain." *Dialogues in Clinical Neuroscience* 8, no. 4 (December 2006): 445–61.

189

Brittain, Christopher Craig. *Religion at Ground Zero*. New York, NY: Continuum International Publishing Group, 2011.

Brock, Rita Nakashima, and Gabriel Lettini. *Soul Repair: Recovering from Moral Injury after War*. Boston, MA: Beacon Press, 2012.

Bureau, US Census. "Census Bureau Releases New Educational Attainment Data." Census.gov. Accessed February 22, 2024. https://www.census.gov/newsroom/press-releases/2022/educational-attainment.html.

Byrne, Libby. "Learning to Breathe." *In God's Image* 40 (June 2021).

"Call The Midwife." BBC, February 8, 2015.

Caminero, Francheska, and Marco Cascella. "Neuroanatomy, Mesencephalon Midbrain." In *StatPearls*. Treasure Island (FL): StatPearls Publishing, 2023. http://www.ncbi.nlm.nih.gov/books/NBK551509/.

Campbell, Denis, and Denis Campbell Health policy editor. "Childhood Abuse Increases Risk of Adult Suicide, Finds Research." *The Guardian*, January 9, 2019, sec. Society. https://www.theguardian.com/society/2019/jan/09/childhood-abuse-increases-risk-of-adult-suicide-finds-research.

Campbell, Stephen M., Connie M. Ulrich, and Christine Grady. "A Broader Understanding of Moral Distress." *The American Journal of Bioethics: AJOB* 16, no. 12 (2016): 2–9.

Carey, Lindsay B., Timothy J. Hodgson, Lillian Krikheli, Rachel Y. Soh, Annie-Rose Armour, Taranjeet K. Singh, and Cassandra G. Impiombato. "Moral Injury, Spiritual Care and the Role of Chaplains: An Exploratory Scoping Review of Literature and Resources." *Journal of Religion and Health* 55, no. 4 (August 1, 2016): 1218–45.

"Carl Jung: The Dynamic Principle Of Fantasy Is Play...Quotations - Carl Jung Depth Psychology." Accessed March 5, 2024. https://carljungdepthpsychologysite.blog/2020/11/09/carl-jung-the-dynamic-principle-of-fantasy-is-play-2/.

Caruth, Cathy, ed. *Trauma: Explorations in Memory*. Baltimore: John Hopkins University Press, 1995.

CDC. "Social Determinants of Health." Centers for Disease Control and Prevention, December 8, 2022. https://www.cdc.gov/about/sdoh/index.html.

"Cerebral Cortex: What It Is, Function & Location." Accessed October 23, 2023. https://my.clevelandclinic.org/health/articles/23073-cerebral-cortex.

Chapin, Theodore J., and Lori A. Russell-Chapin. *Neurotherapy and Neurofeedback: Brain-Based Treatment for Psychological and Behavioral Problems*. Routledge, 2013.

Chappell, Bill. "The Vatican Repudiates 'Doctrine of Discovery,' Which Was Used to Justify Colonialism." *NPR*, March 30, 2023, sec. Religion. https://www.npr.org/2023/03/30/1167056438/vatican-doctrine-of-discovery-colonialism-indigenous.

Charles, Mark, and Soong-Chan Rah. *Unsettling Truths: The Ongoing, Dehumanizing Legacy of the Doctrine of Discovery*. Downers Grove, Illinois: InterVarsity Press, 2019.

"Child Sexual Abuse Statistics – The National Center for Victims of Crime," July 10, 2023. https://victimsofcrime.org/child-sexual-abuse-statistics/.

"Christianity - Soul, Immortality, Moral Perfection, and Theistic Belief | Britannica," May 15, 2023. https://www.britannica.com/topic/Christianity/The-immortality-of-the-soul.

Chwi-Woon Kim. "Psalms of Communal Lament as a Relic of Transgenerational Trauma." *Journal of Biblical Literature* 140, no. 3 (2021): 531–56. https://doi.org/10.15699/jbl.1403.2021.5.

———. "Reading the Book of Habakkuk through a Lens of Cultural Trauma." *Journal for the Study of the Old Testament* 45, no. 2 (December 2020): 217–35. https://doi.org/10.1177/0309089220903347.

"Clergy Sexual Abuse as Moral Injury: Confronting a Wounded and Wounding Church | Published in Journal of Moral Theology." Accessed November 13, 2023. https://jmt.scholasticahq.com/article/72061-clergy-sexual-abuse-as-moral-injury-confronting-a-wounded-and-wounding-church.

Cleveland, Christena. *God Is a Black Woman*. HarperOne, 2022.

Cleveland Clinic. "Emotional Dysregulation: How to Feel about Managing Feelings." Accessed January 9, 2024. https://my.clevelandclinic.org/health/symptoms/25065-emotional-dysregulation.

"Clinical Practice Guideline for the Treatment of Posttraumatic Stress Disorder (PTSD) in Adults. (501872017 001)," 2017. https://doi.org/10.1037/e501872017-001.

Cloitre, Marylene, Christine A. Courtois, Anthony Charuvastra, Richard Carapezza, Bradley C. Stolbach, and Bonnie L. Green. "Treatment of Complex PTSD: Results of the ISTSS Expert Clinician Survey on Best Practices: Treatment of Complex PTSD." *Journal of Traumatic Stress* 24, no. 6 (December 2011): 615–27. https://doi.org/10.1002/jts.20697.

"Collective Trauma: Meaning & Implications | Meridian University," July 13, 2023. https://meridianuniversity.edu/content/collective-trauma-meaning-and-implications.

Comella, Patricia A., Joyce Bader, Judith S. Ball, Kathleen K. Wiseman, and Ruth Riley Sagar, eds. *The Emotional Side of Organizations: Applications of Bowen Theory*. Washington, D.C.: Georgetown Family Center, 1996.

Cullinane, Daniel Burke, Susannah. "Report Details Sexual Abuse by More than 300 Priests in Pennsylvania's Catholic Church." CNN, August 14, 2018. https://www.cnn.com/2018/08/14/us/pennsylvania-catholic-church-grand-jury/index.html.

Cunningham, Katherine C., Joanne L. Davis, Sarah M. Wilson, and Patricia A. Resick. "A Relative Weights Comparison of Trauma-related Shame and Guilt as Predictors of DSM-5 Posttraumatic Stress Disorder Symptom Severity among US Veterans and Military Members." *British Journal of Clinical Psychology* 57, no. 2 (June 2018): 163–76. https://doi.org/10.1111/bjc.12163.

David M. Diamond and Phillip R. Zoladz. "Dysfunctional or Hyperfunctional? The Amygdala in Posttraumatic Stress Disorder Is the Bull in the Evolutionary China Shop." *Journal of Neuroscience Research* 94 (October 29, 2015): 437–44.

"Definition of ADDICTION," December 8, 2023. https://www.merriam-webster.com/dictionary/addiction.

"Definition of RITUAL," March 4, 2024. https://www.merriam-webster.com/dictionary/ritual.

"Definition of THEOLOGY," February 15, 2024. https://www.merriam-webster.com/dictionary/theology.

Denney, Andrew S., and Loyola University New Orleans. "Child Sex Abusers in Protestant Christian Churches: An Offender Typology." *Journal of Qualitative Criminal Justice & Criminology*, January 2, 2023. https://doi.org/10.21428/88de04a1.000ff84d.

Dhaliwal, Kanwarpal. "Racing ACEs Gathering and Reflection: If It's Not Racially Just, It's Not Trauma-Informed." *ACEs Too High* (blog), October 24, 2016. https://acestoohigh.com/2016/10/24/racing-aces-gathering-and-reflection-if-its-not-racially-just-its-not-trauma-informed/.

Dickie, June Frances. "The Intersection of Biblical Lament and Psychotherapy in the Healing of Trauma Memories." *Old Testament Essays* 32, no. 3 (2019): 885–907. https://doi.org/10.17159/2312-3621/2019/v32n3a7.

Downen, Robert. "Southern Baptist Convention Settles High-Profile Lawsuit That Accused Former Leader of Sexual Abuse." The Texas Tribune, December 29, 2023. https://www.texastribune.org/2023/12/29/southern-baptist-convention-sexual-abuse-lawsuit-settlement/.

Downie, Alison. "Christian Shame and Religious Trauma." *Religions* 13, no. 10 (October 2022): 925. https://doi.org/10.3390/rel13100925.

Dutes, Keisha "TK," Connie Hanzhang Jin, Audrey Nguyen, and Vanessa Handy. "Why You Should Stop Complimenting People for Being 'Resilient.'" *NPR*, August 25, 2022. https://www.npr.org/2022/08/16/1117725653/why-being-resilient-might-matter-less-than-you-think.

El-Baba, Rami M., and Mark P. Schury. "Neuroanatomy, Frontal Cortex." In *StatPearls*. Treasure Island (FL): StatPearls Publishing, 2023. http://www.ncbi.nlm.nih.gov/books/NBK554483/.

Elbl, Ivana. "The Bull Romanus Pontifex (1455) and the early European trading in sub-Saharan Atlantic Africa." *Portuguese Studies Review* 17, no. 1 (January 1, 2009): 59–82.

Ellis, Heidi M., Joshua N. Hook, Caleb Freund, Jacob Kranendonk, Sabrina Zuniga, Don E. Davis, and Daryl R. Van Tongeren. "Religious/Spiritual Abuse and Psychological and Spiritual Functioning." *Spirituality in Clinical Practice*, October 12, 2023. https://doi.org/10.1037/scp0000346.

Evinger, James, Carolyn Whitfield, and Judith Wiley. "Final Report of the Independent Abuse Review Panel Presbyterian Church (U.S.A.)." Louisville, KY: Presbyterian Church (U.S.A.), October 2010.

"Executive Summary," November 11, 2021. https://socialwork.web.baylor.edu/executive-summary.

Farley, Wendy. *Tragic Vision and Divine Compassion : A Contemporary Theodicy.* First edition. Westminster/John Knox Press, 1990.

Farnsworth, Jacob K. "Is and Ought: Descriptive and Prescriptive Cognitions in Military-Related Moral Injury." *Journal of Traumatic Stress* 32, no. 3 (June 2019): 373–81. https://doi.org/10.1002/jts.22356.

Farnsworth, Jacob K., Kent D. Drescher, Jason A. Nieuwsma, Robyn B. Walser, and Joseph M. Currier. "The Role of Moral Emotions in Military Trauma: Implications for the Study and Treatment of Moral Injury." *Review of General Psychology* 18, no. 4 (December 2014): 249–62. https://doi.org/10.1037/gpr0000018.

Farside, Charlene. "Insurance Program Benchmarking Methodology." Advisen Ltd., July 6, 2015. https://www.advisenltd.com/data/insurance-program-benchmarking-methodology/.

"Fast Facts: Preventing Child Sexual Abuse |Violence Prevention|Injury Center|CDC," June 9, 2022. https://www.cdc.gov/violenceprevention/child sexualabuse/fastfact.html.

Felitti, Vincent J, Robert F Anda, Dale Nordenberg, David F Williamson, Alison M Spitz, Valerie Edwards, Mary P Koss, and James S Marks. "Relationship of Childhood Abuse and Household Dysfunction to Many of the Leading Causes of Death in Adults: The Adverse Childhood Experiences (ACE) Study." *American Journal of Preventive Medicine* 14, no. 4 (May 1, 1998): 245–58. https://doi.org/10.1016/S0749-3797(98)00017-8.

Feriante, Joshua, and Naveen P. Sharma. "Acute and Chronic Mental Health Trauma." In *StatPearls*. Treasure Island (FL): StatPearls Publishing, 2024. http://www.ncbi.nlm.nih.gov/books/NBK594231/.

Figley, Charles, and Maryann Abendroth. "Vicarious Trauma and the Therapeutic Relationship." Researchgate, 2013. https://www.researchgate.net/publication/259609739.

Focht, Caralie. "'The Joseph Story: A Trauma-Informed Biblical Hermeneutic for

Pastoral Care Providers.'" *Pastoral Psychology* 69, no. 3 (June 2020): 209–23. https://doi.org/10.1007/s11089-020-00901-w.

Forbes Health. "PTSD Statistics And Facts: How Common Is It?," September 14, 2023. https://www.forbes.com/health/mind/ptsd-statistics/.

Fox, Verity, Christina Dalman, Henrik Dal, Anna-Clara Hollander, James B. Kirkbride, and Alexandra Pitman. "Suicide Risk in People with Post-Traumatic Stress Disorder: A Cohort Study of 3.1 Million People in Sweden." *Journal of Affective Disorders* 279 (January 15, 2021): 609–16. https://doi.org/10.1016/j.jad.2020.10.009.

Frechette, Christopher G. "The Old Testament as Controlled Substance." *Interpretation: A Journal of Bible and Theology* 69 (2015): 20–34.

———. "Two Biblical Motifs of Divine Violence as Resources for Meaning-Making in Engaging Self-Blame and Rage after Traumatization." *Pastoral Psychology* 66, no. 2 (April 2017): 239–49. https://doi.org/10.1007/s11089-016-0745-x.

Freedman, Alfred M., Harold I. Kaplan, and Benjamin J. Sadock, eds. *Comprehensive Textbook of Psychiatry, II*. Second Edition. Baltimore: Williams & Wilkins, n.d.

Furman, Refael. "Trauma and Post-Trauma in the Book of Ezekiel." *Old Testament Essays* 33, no. 1 (2020): 32–59.

Gafney, Dr. Wilda. *Womanist Midrash*. Louisville, KY: Westminster John Knox Press, 2017.

Ganzevoort, Reinder Ruard, and Srdan Sremac. *Trauma and Lived Religion : Transcending the Ordinary*. Palgrave Studies in Lived Religion and Societal Challenges. Palgrave Macmillan, 2019.

GARY. "The Psychological Trauma of Leaving Fundamentalist/Conservative Christianity." *Escaping Christian Fundamentalism* (blog), March 19, 2015. https://lutherwasnotbornagaincom.wordpress.com/2015/03/18/the-psychological-trauma-of-leaving-fundamentalistconservative-christianity/.

Gilbert M.D., Roberta M. *The Eight Concepts of Bowen Theory*. Lake Frederick, Virginia: Leading Systems Press, 2004.

Giotakos, O. "Neurobiology of Emotional Trauma." *Psychiatrike = Psychiatriki* 31, no. 2 (2020): 162–71. https://doi.org/10.22365/jpsych.2020.312.162.

"Glossary Definition: Imago Dei ('image of God')," July 14, 2023. https://www.pbs.org/faithandreason/theogloss/imago-body.html.

Graham, Ruth. "Southern Baptists Release List of Alleged Sex Abusers." *The New York Times*, May 27, 2022, sec. U.S. https://www.nytimes.com/2022/05/26/us/southern-baptist-sex-abusers.html.

———. "Why Southern Baptists Are Furious Over a Sex Abuse Case in Kentucky." *The New York Times*, November 7, 2023, sec. U.S. https://www.nytimes.com/2023/11/07/us/baptists-abuse-kentucky.html.

Greenberg, Joy Horner. "The Doctrine of Discovery as a Doctrine of Domination." *Journal for the Study of Religion, Nature and Culture* 10, no. 2 (2016): 236–44.

Grossman, Lt. Col. Dave. "Hope on the Battlefield." Greater Good, n.d. https://greatergood.berkeley.edu/article/item/hope_on_the_battlefield.

Haines, Staci K. *The Politics of Trauma*. Berkeley, California: North Atlantic Books, 2019.

Hankle, Dominick D. "The Therapeutic Implications of the Imprecatory Psalms in the Christian Counseling Setting: Journal of Psychology & Theology." *Journal of Psychology & Theology* 38, no. 4 (2010): 275–80.

"Hans Jonas's Reflections on the Human Soul and the Notion of Imago Dei: An Explanation of Their Role in Ethics and Some Possible Historical Influences on Their Development," August 9, 2023. https://www.tandfonline.com/doi/epdf/10.1080/01916599.2022.2164600?needAccess=true&role=button.

Hardy, Kenneth V. "Healing the Hidden Wounds of Racial Trauma." *Reclaiming Children and Youth* 22, no. 1 (2013): 24–28.

Harnett, Nathaniel G., Adam M. Goodman, and David C. Knight. "PTSD-Related Neuroimaging Abnormalities in Brain Function, Structure, and Biochemistry." *Experimental Neurology* 330 (August 2020): 113331. https://doi.org/10.1016/j.expneurol.2020.113331.

Harris, J. Irene, Christopher R. Erbes, Brian E. Engdahl, Paul Thuras, Nichole Murray-Swank, Dixie Grace, Henry Ogden, et al. "The Effectiveness of a Trauma Focused Spiritually Integrated Intervention for Veterans Exposed to Trauma." *Journal of Clinical Psychology* 67, no. 4 (April 2011): 425–38. https://doi.org/10.1002/jclp.20777.

Harris, J. Irene, Timothy Usset, Cory Voecks, Paul Thuras, Joseph Currier, and Christopher Erbes. "Spiritually Integrated Care for PTSD: A Randomized Controlled Trial of 'Building Spiritual Strength.'" *Psychiatry Research* 267 (September 1, 2018): 420–28. https://doi.org/10.1016/j.psychres.2018.06.045.

Health (OASH), Office of the Assistant Secretary for. "New Surgeon General Advisory Raises Alarm about the Devastating Impact of the Epidemic of Loneliness and Isolation in the United States." Text, May 3, 2023. https://www.hhs.gov/about/news/2023/05/03/new-surgeon-general-advisory-raises-alarm-about-devastating-impact-epidemic-loneliness-isolation-united-states.html.

Heath, Esq., Joseph J. "Statement on the Historic Use of the Doctrine of Christian Discovery by the United States." Onondaga Nation General Counsel, May 24, 2014.

Heather A. King, Keith G. Meador, George L. Jackson, Balmatee Bidassie, Mark J. Bates, Brandolyn S. White, Jason A. Nieuwsma, et al. "Implementing Integrated Mental Health and Chaplain Care in a National Quality Improvement Initiative." *Psychiatric Services* 68 (December 1, 2017): 1213–15.

Hennes, Rebecca. "What We Know about the Southern Baptist Convention's Bombshell Sexual Abuse Report." Houston Chronicle, May 23, 2022. https://www.houstonchronicle.com/news/houston-texas/religion/article/southern-baptist-convention-sex-abuse-report-17192138.php.

Henry, Bitner. "Child Sexual Abuse Is the Second Most Frequent Loss at Religious Institutions." *Bitner Henry Insurance Group* (blog), October 19, 2022. https://bitnerhenry.com/child-sexual-abuse-is-the-second-most-frequent-loss-at-religious-institutions/.

Herman, Judith L. "Recovery from Psychological Trauma." *Psychiatry and Clinical Neurosciences* 52, no. S1 (1998): S98–103. https://doi.org/10.1046/j.1440-1819.1998.0520s5S145.x.

Herman, M. D., Judith. *Trauma and Recovery*. New York, New York: Basic Books, 1997.

Herman, M. D., Judith L. *Truth and Repair: How Trauma Survivors Envision Justice*. New York: Basic Books, 2023.

Hewitt, Simon Thomas. "Aquinas on the Immortality of the Soul." *The Heythrop Journal* LXIV (2023): 30–45.

Hirschberger, Gilad. "Collective Trauma and the Social Construction of Meaning." *Frontiers in Psychology* 9 (August 10, 2018): 1441. https://doi.org/10.3389/fpsyg.2018.01441.

Hodgdon, Hilary B., Frank G. Anderson, Elizabeth Southwell, Wendy Hrubec, and Richard Schwartz. "Internal Family Systems (Ifs) Therapy for Posttraumatic Stress Disorder (Ptsd) among Survivors of Multiple Childhood Trauma: A Pilot Effectiveness Study." *Journal of Aggression, Maltreatment & Trauma*, December 26, 2021. https://doi.org/10.1080/10926771.2021.2013375.

Hodgson, Timothy J., and Lindsay B. Carey. "Moral Injury and Definitional Clarity: Betrayal, Spirituality and the Role of Chaplains." *Journal of Religion and Health* 56, no. 4 (August 1, 2017): 1212–28.

"Home - BishopAccountability.Org," January 1, 2023. https://www.bishop-accountability.org/.

"How Common Is PTSD?" General Information. Accessed October 3, 2023. https://www.ptsd.va.gov/understand/common/common_adults.asp.

"How Much of Communication Is Nonverbal? | UT Permian Basin Online," November 3, 2020. https://online.utpb.edu/about-us/articles/communication/how-much-of-communication-is-nonverbal.

https://www.apa.org. "Treatments for PTSD." Accessed January 3, 2024. https://www.apa.org/ptsd-guideline/treatments.

Hübl, Thomas, and Julie Jordan Avritt. *Healing Collective Trauma: A Process for*

Integrating Our Intergenerational and Cultural Wounds. First Edition. Boulder, Colorado: Sounds True, 2020.

Hughes, Katherine C, and Lisa M Shin. "Functional Neuroimaging Studies of Post-Traumatic Stress Disorder." *Expert Review of Neurotherapeutics* 11, no. 2 (February 2011): 275–85. https://doi.org/10.1586/ern.10.198.

Hunsinger, Deborah van Deusen. *Bearing the Unbearable: Trauma, Gospel, and Pastoral Care*. Grand Rapids, Michigan: William B. Eerdmans Pub. Company, 2015.

———. "Trauma-Informed Spiritual Care: Lifelines for a Healing Journey." *Theology Today* 77, no. 4 (January 2021): 359–71. https://doi.org/10.1177/0040573620961145.

Hurston, Zora Neale. *Dust Tracks on a Road: An Autobiography*. New York: Arno Press, 1969.

indigenous-values-initiative. "Dum Diversas." Doctrine of Discovery, July 23, 2018. https://doctrineofdiscovery.org/dum-diversas/.

Initiative, Indigenous Values. "Doctrine of Discovery." Doctrine of Discovery. Accessed November 7, 2023. https://doctrineofdiscovery.org/.

Jacobsen, David Schnasa. "Preaching as the Unfinished Task of Theology: Grief, Trauma, and Early Christian Texts in Homiletical Interpretation." *Theology Today* 70, no. 4 (January 2014): 407–16. https://doi.org/10.1177/0040573613506732.

Janci, Peter. "Church Sexual Abuse Statistics: Understanding the Prevalence Abuse." *Crew Janci LLP: Sexual Abuse Attorneys* (blog), May 24, 2023. https://www.crewjanci.com/church-sexual-abuse-statistics/.

Jinkerson, Jeremy D. "Defining and Assessing Moral Injury: A Syndrome Perspective." *Traumatology* 22, no. 2 (June 2016): 122–30. https://doi.org/10.1037/trm0000069.

Joelsson, Linda. "Exorcisms as Liberation: Trauma, Differentiation, and Social Systems in Luke." *Studia Theologica* 74, no. 2 (2020): 159–96. https://doi.org/10.1080/0039338x.2020.1785934.

Jones, Ethan Ryan, Danielle Lauricella, Carissa D'Aniello, Maggie Smith, and Justin Romney. "Integrating Internal Family Systems and Solutions Focused Brief Therapy to Treat Survivors of Sexual Trauma." *Contemporary Family Therapy: An International Journal* 44, no. 2 (June 1, 2022): 167–75. https://doi.org/10.1007/s10591-021-09571-z.

Jones, Serene. *Call It Grace: Finding Meaning in a Fractured World*. Penguin Books, 2019.

———. *Trauma and Grace: Theology in a Ruptured World*. 3rd Printing edition. Louisville, Ky: Westminster John Knox Press, 2009.

Kalsched, Donald. *Trauma and the Soul*. London and New York: Routledge, 2013.

Kays, Jill L., Robin A. Hurley, and Katherine H. Taber. "The Dynamic Brain: Neuroplasticity and Mental Health." *The Journal of Neuropsychiatry and Clinical Neurosciences* 24, no. 2 (April 2012): 118–24. https://doi.org/10.1176/appi.neuropsych.12050109.

Kenhub. "Frontal Lobe." Accessed October 23, 2023. https://www.kenhub.com/en/library/anatomy/frontal-lobe.

Kennel, Maxwell. "Religious Studies and Internal Family Systems Therapy." *Implicit Religion* 23, no. 3 (2020): 293–304. https://doi.org/10.1558/imre.41249.

Kent D. Drescher, Todd M. Bishop, Marek S. Kopacz, Craig J. Bryan, Joseph M. Currier, Wilfred R. Pigeon, and April L. Connery. "Moral Injury: A New Challenge for Complementary and Alternative Medicine." *Complementary Therapies in Medicine* 24 (February 1, 2016): 29–33.

Kerr, M.D., Michael E. *One Family's Story: A Primer on Bowen Theory*. Washington, D.C.: Center for the Study of Family, 2013.

Kessler, Ronald C., Wai Tat Chiu, Olga Demler, and Ellen E. Walters. "Prevalence, Severity, and Comorbidity of Twelve-Month DSM-IV Disorders in the National Comorbidity Survey Replication (NCS-R)." *Archives of General Psychiatry* 62, no. 6 (June 2005): 617–27. https://doi.org/10.1001/archpsyc.62.6.617.

Koenig, Harold G., and Faten Al Zaben. "Moral Injury: An Increasingly Recognized and Widespread Syndrome." *Journal of Religion and Health* 60, no. 5 (October 1, 2021): 2989–3011. https://doi.org/10.1007/s10943-021-01328-0.

Koenig, Harold G., Nathan A. Boucher, Rev. John P. Oliver, Nagy Youssef, Scott R. Mooney, Joseph M. Currier, and Michelle Pearce. "Rationale for Spiritually Oriented Cognitive Processing Therapy for Moral Injury in Active Duty Military and Veterans with Posttraumatic Stress Disorder." *Journal of Nervous and Mental Disease* 205, no. 2 (February 2017): 147–53.

Kolk, Bessel van der. "In Terror's Grip: Healing the Ravages of Trauma." *Cerebrum* 4 (January 1, 2002).

Kristof, Nicholas. "Opinion | Pull Yourself Up by Bootstraps? Go Ahead, Try It." *The New York Times*, February 20, 2020, sec. Opinion. https://www.nytimes.com/2020/02/19/opinion/economic-mobility.html.

Kumar, David R., Florence Aslinia, Steven H. Yale, and Joseph J. Mazza. "Jean-Martin Charcot: The Father of Neurology." *Clinical Medicine & Research* 9, no. 1 (March 2011): 46–49. https://doi.org/10.3121/cmr.2009.883.

Kunimatsu, Akira, Koichiro Yasaka, Hiroyuki Akai, Natsuko Kunimatsu, and Osamu Abe. "MRI Findings in Posttraumatic Stress Disorder." *Journal of Magnetic Resonance Imaging: JMRI* 52, no. 2 (August 2020): 380–96. https://doi.org/10.1002/jmri.26929.

Kvitsiani, Mariam, Maia Mestvirishvili, Khatuna Martskvishvili, and Mariam Odilavadze. "Dynamic Model of Moral Injury." *European Journal of Trauma & Dissociation* 7, no. 1 (2023). https://doi.org/10.1016/j.ejtd.2023.100313.

Lawrence, Ryan E, Maria A. Oquendo, and Barbara Stanley. "Religion and Suicide Risk: A Systematic Review." *Archives of Suicide Research : Official Journal of the International Academy for Suicide Research* 20, no. 1 (2016): 1–21. https://doi.org/10.1080/13811118.2015.1004494.

Lee, Young-Joo. "Women in the Pulpit: Characteristics of Protestant Churches Led by a Female Pastor." *Nonprofit Management and Leadership* n/a, no. n/a. Accessed February 24, 2024. https://doi.org/10.1002/nml.21612.

Levine Ph.D., Peter A. *Trauma and Memory*. Berkeley, California: North Atlantic Books, 2015.

LII / Legal Information Institute. "Doctrine of Discovery." Accessed November 8, 2023. https://www.law.cornell.edu/wex/doctrine_of_discovery.

"Limbic System | Description, Components, Function, History of Study, & Facts | Britannica," December 15, 2023. https://www.britannica.com/science/limbic-system.

Litz, Brett T., Ateka A. Contractor, Charla Rhodes, Katherine A. Dondanville, Alexander H. Jordan, Patricia A. Resick, Edna B. Foa, et al. "Distinct Trauma Types in Military Service Members Seeking Treatment for Posttraumatic Stress Disorder." *Journal of Traumatic Stress* 31, no. 2 (April 2018): 286–95. https://doi.org/10.1002/jts.22276.

Litz, Brett T., Rachel A. Plouffe, Anthony Nazarov, Dominic Murphy, Andrea Phelps, Alanna Coady, Stephanie A. Houle, et al. "Defining and Assessing the Syndrome of Moral Injury: Initial Findings of the Moral Injury Outcome Scale Consortium." *Frontiers in Psychiatry* 13 (2022). https://www.frontiersin.org/articles/10.3389/fpsyt.2022.923928.

Litz, Brett T., Nathan Stein, Eileen Delaney, Leslie Lebowitz, William P. Nash, Caroline Silva, and Shira Maguen. "Moral Injury and Moral Repair in War Veterans: A Preliminary Model and Intervention Strategy." *Clinical Psychology Review* 29, no. 8 (January 1, 2009): 695–706. https://doi.org/10.1016/j.cpr.2009.07.003.

Loewenthal, Kate Miriam. "Religious Change and Post-Traumatic Growth Following EMDR Trauma Therapy." *Mental Health, Religion & Culture* 25, no. 3 (2022): 380–87. https://doi.org/10.1080/13674676.2021.2016668.

Logue, Mark W., Sanne J.H. van Rooij, Emily L. Dennis, Sarah L. Davis, Jasmeet P. Hayes, Jennifer S. Stevens, Maria Densmore, et al. "Smaller Hippocampal Volume in Posttraumatic Stress Disorder: A Multisite ENIGMA-PGC Study: Subcortical Volumetry Results From Posttraumatic Stress Disorder Consortia."

Biological Psychiatry 83, no. 3 (February 1, 2018): 244–53. https://doi.org/10. 1016/j.biopsych.2017.09.006.

"Long Working Hours and Health." *The Lancet Regional Health – Western Pacific* 11 (June 1, 2021). https://doi.org/10.1016/j.lanwpc.2021.100199.

Lorenz, Hendrik. "Ancient Theories of Soul." In *The Stanford Encyclopedia of Philosophy*, edited by Edward N. Zalta, Summer 2009. Metaphysics Research Lab, Stanford University, 2009. https://plato.stanford.edu/archives/sum2009/ entries/ancient-soul/.

Lorraine A. Smith-MacDonald, Jean-Sébastien Morin, and Suzette Brémault-Phillips. "Spiritual Dimensions of Moral Injury: Contributions of Mental Health Chaplains in the Canadian Armed Forces." *Frontiers in Psychiatry* 9 (November 1, 2018). https://doi.org/10.3389/fpsyt.2018.00592.

Love, Psychotherapist, Jenny. PTSD Support and Care, February 28, 2024.

Lu, Jing, Hua Yang, Xingxing Zhang, Hui He, Cheng Luo, and Dezhong Yao. "The Brain Functional State of Music Creation: An fMRI Study of Composers." *Scientific Reports* 5 (July 23, 2015): 12277. https://doi.org/10.1038/ srep12277.

Lufkin, Bryan. "Why Do We Buy into the 'cult' of Overwork?" Accessed October 23, 2023. https://www.bbc.com/worklife/article/20210507-why-we-glorify-the-cult-of-burnout-and-overwork.

Lunkenheimer, Erika, Alex Busuito, Kayla M. Brown, Carlomagno Panlilio, and Elizabeth A. Skowron. "The Interpersonal Neurobiology of Child Maltreatment: Parasympathetic Substrates of Interactive Repair in Maltreating and Nonmaltreating Mother-Child Dyads." *Child Maltreatment* 24, no. 4 (November 2019): 353–63. https://doi.org/10.1177/1077559518824058.

Maingard, Julian. "Frontal Lobe | Radiology Reference Article | Radiopaedia.Org." Radiopaedia. Accessed October 23, 2023. https://doi.org/10.53347/rID-25358.

Marlowe, W. Creighton. "Soul Survivor." *Currents in Theology and Mission* 48, no. 4 (September 15, 2021). https://currentsjournal.org/index.php/currents/arti cle/view/326.

Marsden, Daphne. "Okay, Now You Can Turn It Off." *Stimulus* 21, no. 3 (November 2014): 4–13.

Maté, Gabor, and Daniel Maté. *The Myth of Normal: Trauma, Illness & Healing in a Toxic Culture.* First Edition. New York, NY: Avery, 2022.

McCann, I. Lisa, and Laurie Anne Pearlman. "Vicarious Traumatization: A Framework for Understanding the Psychological Effects of Working with Victims." *Journal of Traumatic Stress* 3, no. 1 (January 1, 1990): 131–49. https://doi.org/10.1007/bf00975140.

McClintock, Karen A. *Trauma-Informed Pastoral Care: How to Respond When Things Fall Apart*. Fortress Press, 2022. My Book.

McCullough, Psychotherapist, Rebecca. Discussion on Lament and PTSD, February 22, 2024.

McGraw, Danielle, Marjan Ebadi, Constance Dalenberg, Vanessa Wu, Brandi Naish, and Lisa Nunez. "Consequences of Abuse by Religious Authorities: A Review." In *124th APA Convention*. Denver, Colorado: California School of Professional Psychology, 2016.

Mead, Veronique. "Adverse Childhood Experiences Increase Risk for Chronic Diseases - It's Not Psychological." PACEsConnection, July 18, 2019. https://www.pacesconnection.com/blog/adverse-childhood-experiences-increase-risk-for-chronic-diseases-it-s-not-psychological.

Meconi, Federica, Juan Linde-Domingo, Catarina S Ferreira, Sebastian Michelmann, Bernhard Staresina, Ian A. Apperly, and Simon Hanslmayr. "EEG and fMRI Evidence for Autobiographical Memory Reactivation in Empathy." *Human Brain Mapping* 42, no. 14 (October 1, 2021): 4448–64. https://doi.org/10.1002/hbm.25557.

Mental Health Conditions. "PTSD and the Difference Between Big 'T' and Little 't' Traumas," July 4, 2023. https://www.talkspace.com/mental-health/conditions/articles/ptsd-big-t-little-t-trauma/.

Mescher, Marcus. "Clergy Sexual Abuse as Moral Injury: Confronting a Wounded and Wounding Church." *Journal of Moral Theology* 3, no. CTEWC Book Series 3 (March 16, 2023): 122–39. https://doi.org/10.55476/001c.72061.

"MeToo Movement." In *Wikipedia*, October 5, 2023. https://en.wikipedia.org/w/index.php?title=MeToo_movement&oldid=1178664664.

Miller, Lisa. *The Awakened Brain*. New York: Random House, 2021. https://www.penguinrandomhouse.com/books/608347/the-awakened-brain-by-lisa-miller-phd/.

Miller, Robert J. "The Doctrine of Discovery: The International Law of Colonialism." *The Indigenous Peoples' Journal of Law, Culture & Resistance* 5, no. 1 (2019). https://doi.org/10.5070/P651043048.

Milstein, Glen. "Disasters, Psychological Traumas, and Religions: Resiliencies Examined." *Psychological Trauma: Theory, Research, Practice and Policy* 11, no. 6 (September 2019): 559–62. https://doi.org/10.1037/tra0000510.

"Moral Injury, Meaning Making, and Mental Health in Returning Veterans: ScholarSearch: Discovery Service for Drew University Library." Accessed December 5, 2023. https://eds.p.ebscohost.com/eds/detail/detail?vid=18&sid=a159de1f-0fb8-403e-beof-d23e1d09284e%40redis&bdata=JkF1dGhUeXBlPXNzbyZza XRlPWVkcy1saXZlJnNjb3BlPXNpdGU%3d#AN=100952805&db=ehh.

Morriss, Margaux, and David Berle. "Measuring Moral Injury: Further Validation of the Mies-c and Emis-c in a Civilian Population." *Journal of Psychopathology and Behavioral Assessment*, July 19, 2023. https://doi.org/10.1007/s10862-023-10071-7.

National Academies of Sciences, Engineering, Health and Medicine Division, Division of Behavioral and Social Sciences and Education, Youth Board on Children, Roundtable on the Promotion of Health Equity, Affective Forum for Children's Well-Being: Promoting Cognitive, Wendy Keenan, Clarissa E. Sanchez, Erin Kellogg, and Sarah M. Tracey. "Addressing Historical, Intergenerational, and Chronic Trauma: Impacts on Children, Families, and Communities." In *Achieving Behavioral Health Equity for Children, Families, and Communities: Proceedings of a Workshop*. National Academies Press (US), 2019. https://www.ncbi.nlm.nih.gov/books/NBK540764/.

National Council for Mental Wellbeing. "Study Reveals Lack of Access as Root Cause for Mental Health Crisis in America." Accessed January 19, 2024. https://www.thenationalcouncil.org/news/lack-of-access-root-cause-mental-health-crisis-in-america/.

National Institute of Mental Health (NIMH). "Post-Traumatic Stress Disorder (PTSD)," June 16, 2022. https://www.nimh.nih.gov/health/statistics/post-traumatic-stress-disorder-ptsd.

National Institutes of Health. "Post-Traumatic Stress Disorder (PTSD) 2023." Text, June 2, 2021. https://hr.nih.gov/working-nih/civil/post-traumatic-stress-disorder-ptsd-2023.

NBC News. "Almost 1,700 Priests and Clergy Accused of Sex Abuse Are Unsupervised," October 4, 2019. https://www.nbcnews.com/news/religion/nearly-1-700-priests-clergy-accused-sex-abuse-are-unsupervised-n1062396.

NBC News. "Catholic Clergy Sexually Abused Nearly 2,000 Kids in Illinois, State Finds," May 23, 2023. https://www.nbcnews.com/news/us-news/catholic-clergy-sexually-abused-nearly-2000-kids-illinois-state-finds-rcna85856.

Neria, Yuval. "Functional Neuroimaging in PTSD: From Discovery of Underlying Mechanisms to Addressing Diagnostic Heterogeneity." *American Journal of Psychiatry* 178, no. 2 (February 2021): 128–35. https://doi.org/10.1176/appi.ajp.2020.20121727.

Niemiec, Ryan M., Pninit Russo-Netzer, and Kenneth I. Pargament. "The Decoding of the Human Spirit: A Synergy of Spirituality and Character Strengths Toward Wholeness." *Frontiers in Psychology* 11 (2020). https://www.frontiersin.org/articles/10.3389/fpsyg.2020.02040.

Nietlong, Joseph, and Gideon Kato. "Aquinas on the Soul." *Pinisi Journal of Art, Humanity and Social Studies* 1, no. 3 (2021): 6–10.

"No One Can Make You Feel Inferior... Eleanor Roosevelt - Forbes Quotes." Accessed February 29, 2024. https://www.forbes.com/quotes/2610/.

Not In Our Church. "Church Abuse Statistics." Accessed January 22, 2024. https://www.notinourchurch.com/statistics.html.

O'Donnell, Karen, and Katie Cross, eds. *Bearing Witness: Intersectional Perspectives on Trauma Theology*. London, UK: SCM Press, 2022.

———, eds. *Feminist Trauma Theologies*. London, UK: SCM Press, 2020.

O'Garo, Keisha-Gaye N., and Harold G. Koenig. "Spiritually Integrated Cognitive Processing Therapy for Moral Injury in the Setting of PTSD: Initial Evidence of Therapeutic Efficacy." *Journal of Nervous and Mental Disease* 211, no. 9 (September 2023): 656–63. https://doi.org/10.1097/NMD.0000000000001686.

Ogden, Pat, and Janina Fisher. *Sensorimotor Psychotherapy: Interventions for Trauma and Attachment*. New York and London: W. W. Norton & Company, 2015.

O'Shea Brown, Gillian. "Internal Family Systems Informed Eye Movement Desensitization and Reprocessing: An Integrative Technique for Treatment of Complex Posttraumatic Stress Disorder." *International Body Psychotherapy Journal*, 20th Anniversary Edition, 19, no. 2 (Fal-Win 2020): 112–22.

O'Tuama, Padraig. *In the Shelter: Finding a Home in the World*. Broadleaf Books, 2021.

"Overview of Psychotherapy for PTSD - PTSD: National Center for PTSD." Accessed January 3, 2024. https://www.ptsd.va.gov/professional/treat/txessentials/overview_therapy.asp.

Ozawa, Sachiyo, Hironori Nakatani, Carlos Makoto Miyauchi, Kazuo Hiraki, and Kazuo Okanoya. "Synergistic Effects of Disgust and Anger on Amygdala Activation While Recalling Memories of Interpersonal Stress: An fMRI Study." *International Journal of Psychophysiology: Official Journal of the International Organization of Psychophysiology* 182 (December 2022): 39–46. https://doi.org/10.1016/j.ijpsycho.2022.09.008.

Pafumi, G. R. "VictimsSpeakDB.Org Data Infers Suicide Rates Among Victims of Clergy Sex Abuse Exceed 50 Times the General Population." EIN Presswire, November 13, 2018. https://www.einpresswire.com/article/467186245/victimsspeakdb-org-data-infers-suicide-rates-among-victims-of-clergy-sex-abuse-exceed-50-times-the-general-population.

Pangowish, Stephanie. "Kanoronhkwá: A Haudenosaunee Anishnawbe Woman's View on the Impact of the Doctrine of Discovery on Haudenosaunee Women," January 1, 2023.

Paperny, Tanya. "Do Some Trauma Survivors Cope by Overworking?" *The*

Atlantic (blog), February 16, 2017. https://www.theatlantic.com/health/archive/2017/02/do-some-trauma-survivors-cope-by-overworking/516540/.

Parker, Eve Rebecca. "The Virgin and the Whore - An Interreligious Challenge for Our Times: Exploring the Politics of Religious Belonging with Tamar." *The Ecumenical Review* 71, no. 5 (December 2019): 693–705. https://doi.org/10.1111/erev.12473.

Pasnau, Robert. "Thomas Aquinas." In *The Stanford Encyclopedia of Philosophy*, edited by Edward N. Zalta and Uri Nodelman, Spring 2023. Metaphysics Research Lab, Stanford University, 2023. https://plato.stanford.edu/archives/spr2023/entries/aquinas/.

Ping Zheng, M. D., and M. D. Andreas Maercker. "Resiliency and Posttraumatic Growth: Cultural Implications for Psychiatrists," Vol 38, Issue 7, July 23, 2021. https://www.psychiatrictimes.com/view/resiliency-and-posttraumatic-growth-cultural-implications-for-psychiatrists.

Pleijel, Richard. "Translating the Biblical Hebrew Word Nephesh in Light of New Research." *United Bible Societies* 70, no. 2 (2019): 154–66.

Poe Hays, Rebecca W. "Trauma, Remembrance, and Healing: The Meeting of Wisdom and History in Psalm 78." *Journal for the Study of the Old Testament* 41, no. 2 (2016): 183–204.

Porges, Stephen W. *The Polyvagal Theory: Neurophysiological Foundations of Emotions Attachment Communication Self-Regulation*. New York: W. W. Norton & Company, 2011.

"Post-Traumatic Stress Disorder (PTSD) 2023." Text, June 2, 2021. https://hr.nih.gov/working-nih/civil/post-traumatic-stress-disorder-ptsd-2023.

"Preaching In/and the Borderlands," August 9, 2023. My Book.

Pressley Psy.D., Jana. "The Complexity of Adaptation to Trauma." Presented at the Traumatic Stress Certification, Brookline, MA, 2022.

———. "Trauma-Informed, Spiritually Aware." February 2019.

Rabin, Sarah, Natalia Kika, Danielle Lamb, Dominic Murphy, Sharon Am Stevelink, Victoria Williamson, Simon Wessely, and Neil Greenberg. "Moral Injuries in Healthcare Workers: What Causes Them and What to Do About Them?" *Journal of Healthcare Leadership* 15 (2023): 153–60. https://doi.org/10.2147/JHL.S396659.

Rah, Soong-Chan. *Prophetic Lament: A Call for Justice in Troubled Times*. Downers Grove, Illinois: InterVarsity Press, 2015.

Raise-Abdullahi, Payman, Morvarid Meamar, Abbas Ali Vafaei, Maryam Alizadeh, Masoomeh Dadkhah, Sakineh Shafia, Mohadeseh Ghalandari-Shamami, Ramtin Naderian, Seyed Afshin Samaei, and Ali Rashidy-Pour. "Hypothalamus and Post-Traumatic Stress Disorder: A Review." *Brain*

Sciences 13, no. 7 (June 29, 2023): 1010. https://doi.org/10.3390/brain sci13071010.

Rajmohan, V., and E. Mohandas. "The Limbic System." *Indian Journal of Psychiatry* 49, no. 2 (2007): 132–39. https://doi.org/10.4103/0019-5545.33264.

Rambo, Shelly. *Resurrecting Wounds: Living in the Afterlife of Trauma.* Illustrated edition. Baylor University Press, 2018.

———. *Spirit and Trauma: A Theology of Remaining.* First edition. Westminster John Knox Press, 2010.

———. "Trauma and Faith: Reading the Narrative of the Hemorrhaging Woman." *International Journal of Practical Theology* 13, no. 2 (2009): 233–57. https://doi.org/10.1515/IJPT.2009.15.

Rao, Uma. "DSM-5: Disruptive Mood Dysregulation Disorder." *Asian Journal of Psychiatry* 0 (October 2014): 119–23. https://doi.org/10.1016/j.ajp.2014.03.002.

"Resilience." In *Oxford Languages.* Oxford University Press, 2024.

Richards-Ward, Llewelyn. "The Impact of Trauma on Faith." *Stimulus* 4, no. 2 (May 1996).

Riedel, Priya-Lena, Alexander Kreh, Vanessa Kulcar, Angela Lieber, and Barbara Juen. "A Scoping Review of Moral Stressors, Moral Distress and Moral Injury in Healthcare Workers during COVID-19." *International Journal of Environmental Research and Public Health* 19, no. 3 (February 1, 2022): 1666. https://doi.org/10.3390/ijerph19031666.

Roberts, A. L., S. E. Gilman, J. Breslau, N. Breslau, and K. C. Koenen. "Race/Ethnic Differences in Exposure to Traumatic Events, Development of Post-Traumatic Stress Disorder, and Treatment Seeking for Post-Traumatic Stress Disorder in the United States." *Psychological Medicine* 41, no. 1 (January 2011): 71–83. https://doi.org/10.1017/S0033291710000401.

Roberts, Matthias. "Healing from Religious Trauma." *Sojourners Magazine*, Washington, United States: Sojourners, October 2023.

Robinson, Ph.D, Bryan. "Why The Word For 2021 Is 'Resilience' And How It Affects Mental Health." Forbes. Accessed January 6, 2024. https://www.forbes.com/sites/bryanrobinson/2020/12/06/why-the-word-for-2021-is-resilience-and-how-it-affects-mental-health/.

Rochester, Kathleen. "Reading the Exodus Story Alongside Case Studies of Abuse and Betrayal in Family Relationships." *The Expository Times* 129, no. 4 (2018): 158–64. https://doi.org/10.1177/0014524617731664.

Rolls, Edmund T. "Limbic Systems for Emotion and for Memory, but No Single Limbic System." *Cortex*, Special issue: The clinical anatomy of the limbic lobe and connected structures, 62 (January 1, 2015): 119–57. https://doi.org/10.1016/j.cortex.2013.12.005.

Romm, Tony. "FEMA Delays $2.8 Billion in Disaster Aid to Keep from Running out of Money." *Washington Post*, September 28, 2023. https://www.washing tonpost.com/business/2023/09/27/government-shutdown-fema-disaster-aid-delays/.

Roxo, Marcelo R., Paulo R. Franceschini, Carlos Zubaran, Fabrício D. Kleber, and Josemir W. Sander. "The Limbic System Conception and Its Historical Evolution." *The Scientific World Journal* 11 (December 8, 2011): 2428–41. https://doi.org/10.1100/2011/157150.

Rugenstein Ph.D., Kellyanne. "Dissertation," n.d.

———. Relationship Dynamics, January 31, 2024.

RYSE Center. "Field Building." Accessed January 19, 2024. https://rysecenter.org/field-building.

RYSE Center. "Trauma and Social Location." RYSE Center, 2015. rysecenter.org/field-building.

Sandage, S. J., D. Rupert, G. S. Stavros, and N. G. Devor. *Relational Spirituality in Psychotherapy: Healing Suffering and Promoting Growth.* American Psychological Association, 2020.

Sandage, Steven J., David Rupert, George Stavros, and Nancy G. Devor. "Anxiety, Relational Trauma, and Suffering." In *Relational Spirituality in Psychotherapy: Healing Suffering and Promoting Growth*, 81–105. Washington, DC, US: American Psychological Association, 2020. https://doi.org/10.1037/0000174-005.

Sarah Clark Miller. "Moral Injury and Relational Harm: Analyzing Rape in Darfur." *Journal of Social Philosophy* 40 (December 1, 2009): 504–23.

Sarkhel, Sujit, O. P. Singh, and Manu Arora. "Clinical Practice Guidelines for Psychoeducation in Psychiatric Disorders General Principles of Psychoeducation." *Indian Journal of Psychiatry* 62, no. Suppl 2 (January 2020): S319–23. https://doi.org/10.4103/psychiatry.IndianJPsychiatry_780_19.

Sartor, Dan. "Attachment Theory and the Cry of Dereliction." *Theologica*, 2022, 150–77.

Satterfield, Jamie, Tennessee Lookout June 7, and 2022. "Court Allows John Does to Sue Presbyterian Church over Decades-Old Sexual Abuse." *Tennessee Lookout* (blog), June 7, 2022. https://tennesseelookout.com/2022/06/07/court-allows-john-does-to-sue-presbyterian-church-over-decades-old-sexual-abuse/.

Schrader, Christian, and Abigail Ross. "A Review of PTSD and Current Treatment Strategies." *Missouri Medicine* 118, no. 6 (2021): 546–51.

Schwartz, Richard C., and Robert R. Falconer. *Many Minds, One Self: Evidence for a Radical Shift in Paradigm.* Oak Park, Illinois: Trailheads Publications, 2017.

Schwartz, Richard C., and Martha Sweezy. *Internal Family Systems Therapy.* Second edition. New York: The Guilford Press, 2019.

Serfioti, Danai, Dominic Murphy, Neil Greenberg, and Victoria Williamson. "Professionals' Perspectives on Relevant Approaches to Psychological Care in Moral Injury: A Qualitative Study." *Journal of Clinical Psychology* 79, no. 10 (October 2023): 2404–21. https://doi.org/10.1002/jclp.23556.

"Sexual Abuse Scandal in the Roman Catholic Archdiocese of Boston." In *Wikipedia*, January 28, 2024. https://en.wikipedia.org/w/index.php?title=Sexual_abuse_scandal_in_the_Roman_Catholic_Archdiocese_of_Boston&oldid=1200177852#cite_note-Bruni336-5.

Seymour Epstein. *Cognitive-Experiential Theory: An Integrative Theory of Personality.* Oxford, England: Oxford University Press, 2014. https://search.ebscohost.com/login.aspx?direct=true&AuthType=sso&db=nlebk&AN=751872&site=eds-live&scope=site&custid=s8998431.

Shay, Jonathan. *Achilles in Vietnam: Combat Trauma and the Undoing of Character.* Atheneum, 1994.

———. "Moral Injury." *Psychoanalytic Psychology* 31, no. 2 (April 2014): 182–91. https://doi.org/10.1037/a0036090.

Sherin, Jonathan E., and Charles B. Nemeroff. "Post-Traumatic Stress Disorder: The Neurobiological Impact of Psychological Trauma." *Dialogues in Clinical Neuroscience* 13, no. 3 (September 2011): 263. https://doi.org/10.31887/DCNS.2011.13.2/jsherin.

Shin, Lisa M., Scott L. Rauch, and Roger K. Pitman. "Amygdala, Medial Prefrontal Cortex, and Hippocampal Function in PTSD." *Annals of the New York Academy of Sciences* 1071 (July 2006): 67–79. https://doi.org/10.1196/annals.1364.007.

Simango, Daniel, and P. Paul Krüger. "An Overview of the Study of Imprecatory Psalms: Reformed and Evangelical Approaches to the Interpretation of Imprecatory Psalms." *Old Testament Essays* 29, no. 3 (2016): 581–600. https://doi.org/10.17159/2312-3621/2016/v29n3a13.

Singh, Narendra Kumar, Pradeep Kumar, Sanjay K. Munda, and Basudeb Das. "Psychoeducation: A Measure to Strengthen Psychiatric Treatment." *Delhi Psychiatry Journal* 14, no. 1 (April 2011): 33–39.

Smardon, Andrea. "For Mormon Women, Saying #MeToo Presents a Particular Challenge." *The Guardian*, November 29, 2017, sec. World news. https://www.theguardian.com/world/2017/nov/29/mormon-women-metoo-particular-challenge-sexual-abuse.

"Soul | Religion, Philosophy & Nature of Being | Britannica." Accessed November 20, 2023. https://www.britannica.com/topic/soul-religion-and-philosophy.

"Southern Baptist Convention." In *Wikipedia*, February 23, 2024. https://en.wiki

pedia.org/w/index.php?title=Southern_Baptist_Convention&oldid= 1209798707.

"Southern Baptist Convention Membership Declines in 2022." Accessed February 24, 2024. https://www.tennessean.com/story/news/religion/2023/05/09/ southern-baptist-convention-membership-declines-in-2022/70199505007/.

"Speaking of God in a Time of Terror," April 25, 2023. http://www.theologyan dreligiononline.com/tarocol/encyclopedia-chapter.

Spreier, Scott, Mary H. Fontaine, and Ruth Malloy. "Leadership Run Amok: The Destructive Potential of Overachievers." *Harvard Business Review*, June 1, 2006. https://hbr.org/2006/06/leadership-run-amok-the-destructive-potential-of-overachievers.

Steffen, Patrick R., Dawson Hedges, and Rebekka Matheson. "The Brain Is Adaptive Not Triune: How the Brain Responds to Threat, Challenge, and Change." *Frontiers in Psychiatry* 13 (April 1, 2022). https://doi.org/10.3389/fpsyt.2022. 802606.

Stephens, Darryl W. "A Deacon's Eye for Healing Congregations." *Currents in Theology and Mission* 42, no. 3 (July 2015): 213–19.

———. "What Is Trauma?: What Is a Trauma-Informed Approach?" *Spotlight on Teaching*, March 2021, 9–18.

Stevens, Francis L., Robin A. Hurley, Katherine H. Taber, Robin A. Hurley, L. Anne Hayman, and Katherine H. Taber. "Anterior Cingulate Cortex: Unique Role in Cognition and Emotion." *The Journal of Neuropsychiatry and Clinical Neurosciences* 23, no. 2 (April 2011): 121–25. https://doi.org/10.1176/jnp.23. 2.jnp121.

Streets, Frederick J. "Social Work and a Trauma-Informed Ministry and Pastoral Care: A Collaborative Agenda." *Social Work & Christianity* 42, no. 4 (2015): 470–87.

"Strong's Greek: 2309. Θέλω (Theló) -- to Will, Wish." Accessed February 22, 2024. https://biblehub.com/greek/2309.htm.

Suarez-Jimenez, Benjamin. "Researchers Reveal How Trauma Changes the Brain." URMC Newsroom, June 19, 2023. https://www.urmc.rochester.edu/news/ publications/neuroscience/researchers-reveal-how-trauma-changes-the-brain.

Terrizzi Jr., John A., and Natalie J. Shook. "On the Origin of Shame: Does Shame Emerge From an Evolved Disease-Avoidance Architecture?" *Frontiers in Behavioral Neuroscience* 14 (2020). https://www.frontiersin.org/articles/10. 3389/fnbeh.2020.00019.

The Association of Theological Schools. "Annual Data Tables: 2022-2023." Pittsburgh, PA: The Commission on Accrediting, 2023.

"The Doctrine of Discovery, 1493 | Gilder Lehrman Institute of American History." Accessed November 7, 2023. https://www.gilderlehrman.org/history-resources/spotlight-primary-source/doctrine-discovery-1493.

"The Galileo Project | Christianity | The Inquisition." Accessed November 7, 2023. http://galileo.rice.edu/chr/inquisition.html.

"The Impact of Racism on Child and Adolescent Health | Pediatrics | American Academy of Pediatrics." Accessed January 19, 2024. https://publications.aap.org/pediatrics/article/144/2/e20191765/38466/The-Impact-of-Racism-on-Child-and-Adolescent?autologincheck=redirected.

"The Neurophysiology Behind Trauma-Focused Therapy Modalities Used to Treat Post-Traumatic Stress Disorder Across the Life Course: A Systematic Review." Accessed January 6, 2024. https://doi.org/10.1177/15248380211048446.

The On Being Project. "Janine Benyus — Biomimicry, an Operating Manual for Earthlings." Accessed October 30, 2023. https://onbeing.org/programs/janine-benyus-biomimicry-an-operating-manual-for-earthlings/.

The On Being Project. "Vivek Murthy — To Be a Healer." Accessed January 9, 2024. https://onbeing.org/programs/vivek-murthy-to-be-a-healer/.

"The Presbyterian Church in America Has an Abuse Crisis Too......| News & Reporting | Christianity Today." Accessed February 24, 2024. https://www.christianitytoday.com/news/2023/june/presbyterian-church-in-america-abuse-response.html.

Thomas, Gabrielle. "The Human Icon: Gregory of Nazianzus on Being an Imago Dei." *Cambridge University Press*, 2019.

Thomas, Victoria, Boris Bizumic, Tegan Cruwys, and Erin Walsh. "Measuring Civilian Moral Injury: Adaptation and Validation of the Moral Injury Events Scale (Civilian) and Expressions of Moral Injury Scale (Civilian)." *Psychological Trauma: Theory, Research, Practice, and Policy*, May 11, 2023. https://doi.org/10.1037/tra0001490.supp.

Thurman, Howard, and Vincent Harding. *Jesus and the Disinherited*. Reprint edition. Boston, MA: Beacon Press, 1996.

Tierney, Adrienne L., and Charles A. Nelson. "Brain Development and the Role of Experience in the Early Years." *Zero to Three* 30, no. 2 (November 1, 2009): 9–13.

"Timeline: The History of Post-Traumatic Stress Disorder and How We Treat It," July 10, 2023. https://www.newsweek.com/post-traumatic-stress-disorder-timeline-571664.

Tindle, Jacob, and Prasanna Tadi. "Neuroanatomy, Parasympathetic Nervous System." In *StatPearls*. Treasure Island (FL): StatPearls Publishing, 2023. http://www.ncbi.nlm.nih.gov/books/NBK553141/.

Torrico, Tyler J., and Sara Abdijadid. "Neuroanatomy, Limbic System." In *Stat-*

Pearls. Treasure Island (FL): StatPearls Publishing, 2023. http://www.ncbi. nlm.nih.gov/books/NBK538491/.

Torrico, Tyler J., and Sunil Munakomi. "Neuroanatomy, Thalamus." In *StatPearls.* Treasure Island (FL): StatPearls Publishing, 2023. http://www.ncbi.nlm.nih. gov/books/NBK542184/.

"Trauma & PTSD: What You Need To Know | McLean Hospital," June 16, 2022. https://www.mcleanhospital.org/essential/trauma-ptsd.

Trauma-Informed Care Implementation Resource Center. "What Is Trauma?," March 20, 2018. https://www.traumainformedcare.chcs.org/what-is-trauma/.

"Traumatic Experiences Change the Brain Even in Those without PTSD | University of Oxford." Accessed December 16, 2023. https://www.ox.ac.uk/news/ 2015-08-04-traumatic-experiences-change-brain-even-those-without-ptsd.

Travis, Sarah. *Unspeakable: Preaching and Trauma-Informed Theology.* Eugene, Oregon: Cascade Books, 2021.

Treatment (US), Center for Substance Abuse. "Exhibit 1.3-4, DSM-5 Diagnostic Criteria for PTSD." Text. Substance Abuse and Mental Health Services Administration (US), 2014. https://www.ncbi.nlm.nih.gov/books/NBK207191/.

———. "Historical Account of Trauma." In *Trauma-Informed Care in Behavioral Health Services.* Substance Abuse and Mental Health Services Administration (US), 2014. https://www.ncbi.nlm.nih.gov/books/NBK207202/.

———. *Trauma Awareness. Trauma-Informed Care in Behavioral Health Services.* Substance Abuse and Mental Health Services Administration (US), 2014. https://www.ncbi.nlm.nih.gov/books/NBK207203/.

———. *Understanding the Impact of Trauma. Trauma-Informed Care in Behavioral Health Services.* Substance Abuse and Mental Health Services Administration (US), 2014. https://www.ncbi.nlm.nih.gov/books/NBK207191/.

"Trust and Trauma : An Interdisciplinary Study in Human Nature: ScholarSearch: Discovery Service for Drew University Library," September 14, 2022. https:// eds.s.ebscohost.com/eds/detail/detail?vid=3&sid=1cee82cc-f9cf-414d-8d4b-51b3c52dbb1c%40redis&bdata=JnNpdGU9ZWRzLWxpdmUmc2Nvc GU9c2loZZQ%3d%3d#AN=2680797&db=nlebk.

Tumminio, Danielle Elizabeth. "We're All Traumatized Now: Four Ways to Shift to Trauma-Informed Ministry." *The Christian Century* 137, no. 21 (October 7, 2020): 10–11.

United Methodist News Service. "Clergyman Accused of Sexual Misconduct, Abuse." Accessed February 24, 2024. https://www.umnews.org/en/news/cler gyman-accused-of-sexual-misconduct-abuse.

Upenieks, Laura. "Unpacking the Relationship Between Prayer and Anxiety: A Consideration of Prayer Types and Expectations in the United States." *Journal of Religion and Health* 62, no. 3 (2023): 1810–31. https://doi.org/10.1007/s10943-022-01708-0.

Uytun, Merve Cikili. "Development Period of Prefrontal Cortex." In *Prefrontal Cortex*. IntechOpen, 2018. https://doi.org/10.5772/intechopen.78697.

"VA.Gov | Veterans Affairs." General Information. Accessed January 15, 2024. https://www.ptsd.va.gov/understand/common/common_adults.asp.

Van Der Kolk, M.D., Bessell. *The Body Keeps the Score: Brain, Mind, and Body in the Healing of Trauma*. Reprint edition. New York, NY: Penguin Publishing Group, 2015.

———. "Trauma, Body, and the Brain." Kripalu, August 1, 2023.

Van Der Kolk, M.D., Bessell, Alexander C. McFarlane, and Lars Weisaeth, eds. *Traumatic Stress: The Effects of Overwhelming Experience on Mind, Body, and Society*. Paperback Edition 2007. New York: The Guilford Press, 2007.

Vanden Heuvel, Emily. "'WHY, GOD?': A Trauma-Informed Worship Service." *Reformed Worship* 128 (June 2018): 22–23.

"Vatican Rejects Doctrine That Fueled Centuries of Colonialism | AP News." Accessed November 7, 2023. https://apnews.com/article/vatican-indigenous-papal-bulls-pope-francis-062e39ce5f7594a81bb80d0417b3f902.

Vitz, Paul C., and Craig Steven Titus. "Psychology and the Soul: A New Perspective on an Old Interpretation." *Journal of Psychology and Christianity* 41, no. 2 (Summer 2022): 130–39.

Wade, Natalia R. "Integrating Cognitive Processing Therapy and Spirituality for the Treatment of Post-Traumatic Stress Disorder in the Military." *Social Work & Christianity*, Religious and spiritually-oriented Interventions with veteran and military populations, 43, no. 3 (Fal 2016): 59–72.

Waraich, Manni, and Shailesh Shah. "The Life and Work of Jean-Martin Charcot (1825–1893): 'The Napoleon of Neuroses.'" *Journal of the Intensive Care Society* 19, no. 1 (February 2018): 48–49. https://doi.org/10.1177/1751143717709420.

Wasson, Winn. "Research Guides: The Land You're On: Acknowledging the Haudenosaunee: Episode 2: The Doctrine of Discovery." Accessed November 7, 2023. https://researchguides.library.syr.edu/theLand/episode2.

Waxenbaum, Joshua A., Vamsi Reddy, and Matthew Varacallo. "Anatomy, Autonomic Nervous System." In *StatPearls*. Treasure Island (FL): StatPearls Publishing, 2023. http://www.ncbi.nlm.nih.gov/books/NBK539845/.

webfeller. "Romanus Pontifex." *Papal Encyclicals* (blog), June 16, 2017. https://www.papalencyclicals.net/nicholo5/romanus-pontifex.htm.

Webster, Erica M. "The Impact of Adverse Childhood Experiences on Health and Development in Young Children." *Global Pediatric Health* 9 (February 26,

2022): 2333794X221078708. https://doi.org/10.1177/2333794X221078708.

Weinberg, Michael, Michal Soffer, and Ohad Gilbar. "PTSD and Public Stigma: Examining the Relationship between Public Stigmas Attached to PTSD and Self-Esteem, Spirituality, and Well-Being." *Psychological Trauma: Theory, Research, Practice, and Policy* 16, no. 1 (January 2024): 116–24. https://doi.org/10.1037/tra0001501.supp.

"What Is Emotional Dysregulation? | Psychology Today." Accessed January 9, 2024. https://www.psychologytoday.com/us/blog/click-here-happiness/202108/what-is-emotional-dysregulation.

"What Is Moral Injury - The Moral Injury Project – Syracuse University." Accessed December 4, 2023. https://moralinjuryproject.syr.edu/about-moral-injury/.

"What Is Posttraumatic Stress Disorder (PTSD)?" Accessed January 15, 2024. https://www.psychiatry.org:443/patients-families/ptsd/what-is-ptsd.

Winterhalter, Elizabeth. "The Tragedy at Buffalo Creek." JSTOR Daily, February 3, 2021. https://daily.jstor.org/the-tragedy-at-buffalo-creek/.

"Witness, n. Meanings, Etymology and More | Oxford English Dictionary." Accessed October 20, 2023. https://www.oed.com/dictionary/witness_n?tab=meaning_and_use#14197730.

Wong, Kapo, Alan H. S. Chan, and S. C. Ngan. "The Effect of Long Working Hours and Overtime on Occupational Health: A Meta-Analysis of Evidence from 1998 to 2018." *International Journal of Environmental Research and Public Health* 16, no. 12 (June 2019): 2102. https://doi.org/10.3390/ijerph16122102.

Xue, Man, Wan-Tong Shi, Si-Bo Zhou, Ya-Nan Li, Feng-Yi Wu, Qi-Yu Chen, Ren-Hao Liu, et al. "Mapping Thalamic-Anterior Cingulate Monosynaptic Inputs in Adult Mice." *Molecular Pain* 18 (April 12, 2022): 17448069221087034. https://doi.org/10.1177/17448069221087034.

Yardley, Jim. "Abuse by Clergy Is Not Just a Catholic Problem." *The New York Times*, April 13, 2002, sec. U.S. https://www.nytimes.com/2002/04/13/us/abuse-by-clergy-is-not-just-a-catholic-problem.html.

www.ingramcontent.com/pod-product-compliance
Lightning Source LLC
Chambersburg PA
CBHW062129020426
42335CB00013B/1153

9 781966 655091